D1374565

Archaeological Theory

For Jo,
who learnt to love theory

Archaeological Theory

An Introduction

Matthew Johnson

First published 1999

2 4 6 8 10 9 7 5 3 1

Blackwell Publishers Ltd
108 Cowley Road
Oxford OX4 1JF
UK

Blackwell Publishers Inc.
350 Main Street
Malden, Massachusetts 02148
USA

British Library Cataloguing in Publication Data

A CIP catalogue record for this book is available from the British Library.

Library of Congress Cataloging-in-Publication Data

Johnson, Matthew.
Archaeological theory: an introduction / Matthew Johnson.
p. cm.
Includes bibliographical references and index.
ISBN 0-631-20295-1 (acid-free paper). — ISBN 0-631-20296-X
(pbk.: acid-free paper)
1. Archaeology—Philosophy. I. Title.
CC72.J65. 1999
930.1′01—dc21 98-56262
CIP

Typeset in 10.5pt on 12pt Sabon
by Kolam Information Services Pvt Ltd, Pondicherry, India
Printed in Great Britain by MPG Books Ltd, Bodmin, Cornwall

This book is printed on acid-free paper

Contents

List of Figures

Acknowledgements

The author and publishers gratefully acknowledge the following for permission to reproduce copyright material:

Preface cartoon © Anthony Hadon-Guest; figure 2.2 from Childe, V. G., *The Danube in Prehistory* (Oxford University Press, 1929); figure 2.3 from Piggott, S., *Ancient Europe* (Edinburgh University Press, 1968); figure 2.4 from Clarke, D., *Analytical Archaeology* (second revised edition) (Routledge, London, 1976); figure 2.5 from Daniel, G. E., 'The dual nature of the megalithic colonisation of prehistoric Europe', *Proceedings of the Prehistoric Society* 7, 1941, courtesy of The Prehistoric Society, Salisbury; figure 2.6 from Renfrew, A. C., *Before Civilisation: The Radiocarbon Revolution and Prehistoric Europe* (Penguin Books, Harmondsworth, 1973); figure 3.1 © The Kobal Collection; figure 4.3 from Hillman, G., 'Interpretation of archaeological plant remains', reprinted from Lone, F. A., Khan, M. and Buth, G. M., *Palaeoethnobotany – Plants and Ancient Man in Kashmir* (A A Balkema, Rotterdam, 1993); figure 5.1 from Clarke, D., *Analytical Archaeology* (second revised edition) (Routledge, London, 1976); figure 5.3 from Gary Larson, *Prehistory of the Far Side*, © Universal Press Syndicate Inc.; figure 7.1 from Hodder, I. and Orton, C., *Spatial Analysis in Archaeology* (Cambridge University Press, 1976); figure 7.3 from Tilley, C., *Material Culture and Text: The Art of Ambiguity* (Routledge, London, 1991, © Dr Christopher Tilley); figure 7.4 OXBOW *IS* ORIGINAL PUBLICATION; figure 8.1 from Unstead, R. J., *Looking at History 1: From Cavemen to Vikings* (Black, London, 1953); figure 8.2 © Klammers and the University of Minnesota Collections; figure 8.3 © Minnesota Historical Society; figure 9.2 © The British Museum, London; figure 9.3 © The British Museum, London; figure 9.4 from Clarke, D., *Analytical*

Archaeology (Routledge, London, 1976); figure 10.2 © Crown Copyright, RCHME.

The publishers apologize for any errors or omissions in the above list and would be grateful to be notified of any corrections that should be incorporated in the next edition or reprint of this book.

Preface

The Contradictions of Theory

This book is an introductory essay on archaeological theory. It tries to explain something of what 'theory' is, its relationship to archaeological practice, how it has developed within archaeology over the last few decades, and how archaeological thought relates to theory in the human sciences and the intellectual world generally.

To many, 'theory' is a dirty word both within and outside archaeology. Prince Charles earned almost universal approbation when he condemned 'trendy theorists' in education; nobody however, including the Prince himself, seemed to be very clear precisely who he meant. When visiting an archaeological site a few years ago a suggestion of mine met with laughter and the response 'that's a typical suggestion of a theorist'. I don't recall anyone telling me exactly why my suggestion was so absurd, and when I visited the site the following year the strategy had been adopted. For the meat-and-potatoes Anglo-Saxon world in particular, theory is an object of profound suspicion. It is a popular saying that for the English, to be called an intellectual is to be suspected of wanting to steal someone's wife (sexism in the original). Theory, 'political correctness' and being 'foreign' stand together in the dock as traits to be regarded with hostility in the English-speaking world at least. I shall look at some of the reasons why this is so in chapter 1.

At the same time, however, theory is increasingly popular, and seen as increasingly important, both within and outside archaeology. Valentine Cunningham recently commented in *The Times Higher Education Supplement* that theorists in academia are 'a surging band, cocky, confident in academic credentials, job security and intellectual prestige', inspiring the columnist Laurie Taylor to write a memorable account of a bunch of theorists intellectually roughing up a more empirical colleague at a seminar before departing to the local bar for some brand-name lagers and a few

'You're a terrorist? Thank God. I understood Meg to say you were a *theorist*.' From Culler (1997: 16).

ironic choruses of 'Ere We Go'. His account was fictitious but contained much truth.

There are various indices of the 'success' of archaeological theory; one might cite the frequency of 'theoretical' symposia at major conferences such as the Society for American Archaeology, or the success of Michael Schiffer's series *Advances in Archaeological Method and Theory.* One particularly telling index is the rise and rise of the British Theoretical Archaeology Group conference (TAG). This was formed as a small talking-shop for British archaeological theorists in the late 1970s, but since then has become the largest annual archaeological conference in Britain with substantial participation from North America and Europe. The conferences at Durham and Bradford held in 1993 and 1994 respectively both counted over 650 participants.

It is true that a lot of papers delivered at TAG scarcely merit the term 'theoretical', and even more true that many of the 650 only come for the infamous TAG party in any case. It must also be conceded that the degree of impact of TAG's and 'theory's' influence on the 'real world' of archaeological practice is debatable. In concluding this book, for example, I shall put forward my personal view that the whole thrust of recent theory has made a division of archaeological activity into 'science-based archaeology' and 'everybody else' increasingly artificial. This view was also put forward 15 years ago by Lewis Binford in his comments on British archaeology in his *In Pursuit of the Past* (1983a: 15–16). Despite such critique, however, the environmental and dating laboratories still remain funded by NERC (Natural Environment Research Council) and self-styled 'humanistic' or 'cultural' archaeology by the British Academy and Arts and Humanities Research Board. The theorist often feels like Cassandra, constantly giving what he or she sees as profound predictions and insight and constantly being ignored by the decision makers.

This book is written to give the student an introduction to some of the strands of current thinking in archaeological theory. It is deliberately written as an introduction, in as clear and jargon-free a fashion as the author can manage (though as we shall see, criteria of clarity and of what constitutes jargon are riddled with problems).

It is intended as a 'route map' for the student. That is, it seeks to point out prominent landmarks on the terrain of theory, comment on relationships between different bodies of thought, and to clarify the intellectual underpinnings of certain views. As such, it is anything but an encyclopaedia; it is hardly one-tenth of a comprehensive guide to the field, if such a guide could be written. For example, Binford's middle-range theory is emphasized at the expense of Schiffer's behavioural archaeology in chapter 4, and linguistic models of meaning are emphasized over the current fashion for phenomenology in chapter 7. The text should be read with reference to the Further Reading and Glossary sections, and over-generalization, oversimplification and caricatures of viewpoints are necessary evils.

To pursue the route map analogy, the route followed here is one of several that could be taken through the terrain of archaeological theory. I could have devoted a chapter each to different thematic areas: Space, Trade and Exchange, Cultures and Style, State Formation, and so on. In each case, a variety of approaches to that theme could be given to show how different theories contradict or complement each other and produce different sorts of explanation of the archaeological record. Alternatively, a tour could be taken through different 'isms': positivism, functionalism, Marxism, structuralism, poststructuralism, feminism. These would be reasonable paths, and ones moreover that have been taken by other authors.

This book, however, tries above all to bring out the relationship between archaeological thought and wider strands of theory in intellectual life as a whole. It seeks to show how specific theoretical positions taken by individual archaeologists 'make sense' within a wider context, cultural, social and political as well as academic. This book also seeks to bring out the relationship between archaeological theory and practice more clearly than has been done in the past. The structure adopted here, of an historical approach focusing initially on the New Archaeology and reactions to it before moving on to current debates, fitted this purpose best.

Many areas are left out of such a route map. Its coverage is almost exclusively Anglo-American in scope; major traditions of archaeological thought in Latin America, Asia, Africa and continental Europe are not addressed. Again, suggestions for further reading on these themes have been given in the Further Reading section.

I have written above that this book is a guide for 'the student'; I mean the student in the broadest sense. Many practising archaeologists employed outside the academic world in both North America and Britain have told me that they are interested in current theoretical debates, and see such debates as of potential relevance to their work. Nevertheless many feel alienated by what they see as the unnecessary obscurity and pretentiousness that is central to the theoretical scene. I don't subscribe to such an analysis, but I have to acknowledge that it is widespread. Right or wrong, I hope that they may find that what follows is of some help.

In trying to survey many different theoretical strands, I have been torn between trying to write a 'neutral', 'objective' survey of different currents of thought on the one hand, and a committed polemic advancing my own views on the other. The end product lies, perhaps a little unhappily, somewhere between these extremes. On the one hand, the construction of a completely objective survey simply isn't intellectually possible; the most biased and partial views on any academic subject consistently come from those who overtly proclaim that their own position is neutral, detached and value-free. In addition, it would be disingenuous to claim that the book is written from a disinterested viewpoint – that it is a guide pure and simple. Obviously an interest in theory goes hand-in-hand with a passionate belief in its importance, and an attachment to certain more or less controversial views within the field.

On the other hand, if we want to understand why theory is where it is today, any account of a wide diversity of intellectual positions must endeavour to be reasonably sympathetic to all parties. As R. G. Collingwood pointed out in relation to the history of philosophy, most theoretical positions arise out of the perceived importance of certain contexts or issues; that is, philosophical beliefs are in part responses to particular sets of problems, and have to be understood as such rather than given an intellectual mugging. One's intellectual opponents are never all morons or charlatans to the last man and woman and one's bedfellows are rarely all exciting, first-rate scholars. Before we get carried away with such piety it must be remembered that this does not mean that certain positions are not therefore immune from criticism. For example, the aims and approaches of the New Archaeology are made much clearer when understood in terms of the intellectual and practical environment of the time – in particular the sort of archaeology that preceded it. Its stress on 'science' in particular is intelligible in this context (see chapter 2). Such an observation helps the student to understand the origins and impetus behind the New Archaeology. This does not mean however that the programme of the New Archaeology was entirely free of intellectual and practical problems.

The adoption of an informal tone and omission of detailed referencing from the text is deliberate. It is to help, I hope, the clarity of its arguments and the ease with which it can be read. Many 'academic' writers have often been taught to forsake the use of the 'I' word, to attempt to render our writing neutral and distant, to avoid a conversational or informal tone, all in the name of scientific or scholarly detachment. This may or may not be a valid project. The aim here however is educational rather than scholarly in the narrow sense.

One of my central points, particularly in the first chapter, is that all practising archaeologists use theory whether they like it or not. To make this point clear and to furnish examples I have often quoted passages from avowedly 'atheoretical' writers and commented upon them, to draw out the theories and assumptions that lie implicit within those passages. In most cases the passages come from the first suitable book to hand. I want to stress that critiques of these examples are not personal attacks on the writers concerned. Here, the need to use practical examples to make a theoretical point clear clashes with the desire to avoid a perception of unfair, personalized criticism.

The text is based in part on lecture notes for various undergraduate courses I have taught at Sheffield, Lampeter and Durham. The students at all three institutions are thanked for their constructive and helpful responses. Some Durham students may recognize themselves in the dialogues in some of the chapters, and I ask their forgiveness for this.

The book was partly conceived while a Research Fellow at the University of California at Berkeley in the spring of 1995. I would like to thank Meg Conkey, Christine Hastorf, Marcia-Ann Dobres, Margot Winer and many others too numerous to mention for their hospitality during that time, and for making my stay so enjoyable and profitable. I also thank the University of Durham for giving me study leave for that term, and more generally for its support of my changing vision of archaeology over the last seven years.

A number of reviewers, some anonymous, made a string of invaluable comments without which the book would have been much more opinionated and parochial and much less comprehensible. These include especially Randy McGuire, Jim Hill, Chris Tilley and Elizabeth Brumfiel. Robert Preucel and Ian Hodder reviewed the final draft extensively. Dominic McNamara drew my attention to the Foucault quotation in chapter 6.

Within the Department of Archaeology at Durham, Helena Hamerow, Colin Haselgrove, Anthony Harding, Simon James, Sam Lucy and Martin Millett read and made invaluable comments on the first draft. Conversations on the philosophy of science with my father C. David Johnson clarified many points. Conversations with Chris Taylor, Paul Everson and David Stocker informed the discussion of Bodiam in chapter 10, though errors and misconceptions in this discussion remain my responsibility. John Davey and Tessa Harvey at Blackwell were always patient, encouraging and ready with practical help when needed. My wife Becky made comments on successive drafts; proof-read the final manuscript; and most importantly, provided emotional and intellectual support without which this book would never have been written. In return, I hope this book explains to her why archaeologists are such a peculiar bunch of human beings, though I know she has her own theories in this respect. My thanks to everybody.

1

Common Sense is Not Enough

Archaeology can be very boring, distressing and physically uncomfortable. Every year we excavate thousands of sites, some with painstaking and mind-numbing patience, some in a great and undignified hurry. Every year we get chilled to the marrow or bitten half to death by mosquitoes while visiting some unprepossessing, grassy mound in the middle of nowhere. Miles from a decent restaurant or even a warm bath, we try to look interested while the rain comes down in sheets and some great professor whose best work was 20 years ago witters on in a monotone about what was found in Trench 4B. Every year we churn out thousands of interminable, stultifyingly dull site reports, fretting over the accuracy of plans and diagrams, collating lists of grubby artefacts to go on microfiche that few will ever consult or use again.

Why?

We could spend the money on hospitals. Alternatively we could quietly pocket the cash and write a much more entertaining, fictitious version of what the past was like while we sat on a sun-kissed terrace somewhere in southern California. If we were feeling ideologically sound we could raise an International Brigade for a liberation struggle somewhere. Each of these alternatives has its attractions, but we don't do any of these things. We go on as we have done before.

One reason we don't do these things is because *archaeology is very important*. The past is dead and gone, but it is also very powerful. It is so powerful that an entire nation (Zimbabwe) can name itself after an archaeological site. It is so powerful that archaeological sites are surrounded by police and are the subject of attempted occupations by New Age travellers. It is so powerful that even individual groups of artefacts like the Parthenon frieze are the subject of major international disputes.

The question 'why do we do archaeology?' is therefore bound up with the question 'why is archaeology – the study of the past through its material remains – so important to us?' And this again leads on to the question of 'us', of our identity – *who are we?* And these are all theoretical questions.

Definitions of Theory

'Theory' is a very difficult word to define. Indeed, I shall return to this topic in the final chapter, since different theoretical views define 'theory' in different ways. Different definitions cannot therefore be fully explored without prior explanation of those views.

So instead of including a complete definition of theory here, I will try to leave any attempt to define theory till the last chapter. For the time being, we can note that most archaeologists would include within the purview of theory *why we do archaeology* and the social and cultural context of archaeology. They would also refer to *issues of interpretation*. Most archaeologists would agree that the way we interpret the past has 'theoretical' aspects in the broad sense. For example, we could cite general theories such as social and biological evolution, issues of how we go about testing our ideas, debates over how we should think about stylistic or decorative change in artefacts.

There is disagreement over whether many concepts can be considered 'theoretical' or whether they are merely neutral techniques or methods outside the purview of theory. Stratigraphy, excavation and recording techniques, and the use of statistical methods are for example considered 'theoretical' by some but 'just practical' or 'simply techniques' by others. Theory and method are often confused by archaeologists. In the strict sense, if theory covers the 'why' questions, method or methodology covers the 'how' questions. So theory covers *why* we selected this site to dig, method *how* we dig it. However, theory and method are obviously closely related, and many archaeologists including myself regard such a straightforward division as too simple.

To give an example of the relationship between theory and method, we might consider different methods of investigating social ranking in the archaeological record. Thus the method we might use would be to compare graves 'richly' endowed with lots of grave goods with poorer, unadorned graves. It is evident in this exercise that certain ideas or theories about the nature of social ranking are being assumed (that social ranking will be reflected in treatment of the body at death, that material goods are unequally distributed through society and that this has a direct relationship to social inequality, and so on). These ideas are themselves theoretical in nature.

Perhaps theory and method are one and the same thing and cannot be separated; perhaps they have to be separated if archaeology is to be a rigorous discipline that is capable of testing its theories against its data. This is a debate we shall return to in chapter 4.

I'm sorry to butt in, but all this discussion of theory and method clearly demonstrates just how sterile and boring theory really is. You're already lost in definitions and semantics, you haven't mentioned a single fact about the past, and I'm beginning to wish I hadn't bothered to start reading this and had turned my attention to that new book about the Hopewell culture instead. Theory is irrelevant to the practice of archaeology; we can just use our common sense.

Ah, Roger, the eternal empiricist. (Roger Beefy is an undergraduate student at Northern University, England, though women and men like Roger can be found in any archaeological institution. Roger fell in love with archaeology when he was a child, scrambling up and down the ruins of local castles, burial mounds and other sites. Roger spent a year after school before coming to Northern University digging and working in museums. Roger loves handling archaeological material, and is happiest when drawing a section or talking about seriation techniques over a beer. Now, in his second year at Northern University, Roger has found himself in the middle of a compulsory 'theory course'. Full of twaddle about middle-range theory, hermeneutics and poststructuralism, it seems to have nothing to do with the subject he loves.)

So, you want to know why theory is 'relevant' to archaeological practice. Perhaps you will bear with me while I discuss four possible reasons.

1 *We need to justify what we do*

Our audience (other archaeologists, people in other disciplines, the 'general public' however defined) needs to have a clear idea from us of why our research is important, why it is worth paying for, why we are worth listening to. There are a thousand possible answers to this *challenge of justification*, for example:

- The past is intrinsically important, and we need to find out about it for its own sake.

- We need to know where we came from to know where we're going next. Knowledge of the past leads to better judgements about the future.
- Only archaeology has the time depth of many thousands of years needed to generate cross-cultural generalizations about long-term culture processes.
- Archaeology is one medium of cultural revolution that will emancipate ordinary people from repressive ideologies.

The chances are that you disagree with at least one of these statements, and agree with at least one other. That doesn't change the fact that *each statement is a theoretical proposition* that needs justifying, arguing through, and debating before it can be accepted or rejected. None of the statements given above is obvious, self-evident or common-sensical when examined closely. Indeed, very little in the world is obvious or self-evident when examined closely, though our political leaders would have us think otherwise.

2 *We need to evaluate one interpretation of the past against another, to decide which is the stronger*

Archaeology relies in part for its intellectual credibility on being able to distinguish 'good' from 'bad' interpretations of the past. Were the people who lived on this site hunter-gatherers, or were they aliens from the planet Zog? Which is the stronger interpretation?

It's impossible to decide what is a strong archaeological interpretation on the basis of 'common sense' alone. Common sense might suggest, for example, that we accept the explanation that covers the greatest number of facts. There may be thousands of sherds of pottery dating from the first millennium BC on a site, all factual in their own way, but one other fact – a tree-ring date of AD 750, for example – may suggest that they might be all 'residual' or left over from an earlier period. In practice, every day of our working lives as archaeologists, *we decide on which order to put our facts in*, what degree of importance to place on different pieces of evidence. When we do this, we use theoretical criteria to decide which facts are important and which are not worth bothering with.

A good example of the inadequacy of common sense in deciding what is a strong or weak archaeological explanation is that of ley lines. Ley lines were 'discovered' by Alfred Watkins in the 1920s, when he noticed that many ancient archaeological sites in Britain could be linked up by straight lines. The idea that ancient sites lay on straight lines could be 'proved' easily by taking a map upon which such ancient monuments were marked and drawing such lines through them. Watkins suggested these lines represented prehistoric trackways. Nonsense, said the professional archaeological community. It was common sense that prehistoric peoples living thousands of years before literacy or formal geometry were far too primitive to lay out such geometrically sophisticated lines. Watkins had intended his book as a genuine contribution to archaeology, but his research, sincerely carried out, was laughed out of court and consigned to the ranks of lunatic 'fringe archaeology'. Other writers took his thesis up in succeeding decades but extended it by suggesting that the lines were of sacred significance or mystical power.

Now it is quite clear today that prehistoric peoples would have been quite capable of laying out such lines. The original, commonsensical criteria used by archaeologists for rejecting Watkins's thesis were completely invalid.

Ley lines do not exist. This was shown by Tom Williamson and Liz Bellamy in *Ley Lines in Question*, which analysed such lines statistically and showed that the density of archaeological sites in the British landscape is so great that a line drawn through virtually anywhere will 'clip' a number of sites. It took Williamson and Bellamy a book's worth of effort and statistical sophistication to prove this, however.

The moral of the debate over ley lines is that what is considered to constitute a strong or a weak explanation is not simply a matter of 'common sense'. I would argue that if we really want to understand what drove and continues to drive the ley line debate, we have to look at class divides in British archaeology. In his time Watkins was derided as a vulgar amateur, while today the tradition of ley line searchers continues strongly in 'alternative' or New Age circles. New Age travellers and others in their turn view middle-class professional archaeologists with suspicion. Others might dispute this social interpretation and suggest alternative reasons for the intellectual development of the issue. I might reply: we would then be having a theoretical debate.

3 We must be explicit in what we do as archaeologists

In other words, we must be as open as possible about our reasons, approaches and biases, rather than trying to conceal them or pretend that they do not exist. This is a basic rule of academic discourse, though it is not always followed. Lewis Binford, a character we shall meet properly in the next chapter, made the point that all scientists of all disciplines need to be aware of the assumptions they are making if they wish to be productive.

It goes without saying that we can never be completely explicit about our biases and preconceptions. This should not stop us trying.

4 *We don't 'need' theory, we all use theory whether we like it or not*

Put another way, *we are all theorists*. This is the most important point of all. The most lowly troweller, the most bored washer of ceramics, the most alienated finds assistant or lab technician, are all theoreticians in the sense that they all use theories, concepts, ideas, assumptions in their work. (The theory may have been imposed on them by the project director or funding body, but it is theory nevertheless.) Put another way, the driest, most descriptive text or site report is already theoretical. Somebody wielding a WHS or Marshalltown trowel relies on theories of soil colour change and stratigraphy in his or her work; editorial judgements about the relative weighting and order given to pottery and artefact reports in a site monograph depend on a judgement on what is 'significant' about that particular site which in turn rests on theoretical criteria.

Any archaeologist who therefore tells you that their work is 'atheoretical', that they are 'not interested in theory', or that they are doing 'real archaeology' as opposed to those 'trendy theorists' is not telling the whole truth. They are as much theorists as anyone else, though they might choose to mask their theoretical preconceptions by labelling them 'pragmatism' or 'common sense'. In doing so, I would argue that they are by passing their responsibility to make clear the intellectual basis of their work, trying to hide the theoretical assumptions and approaches that they are in fact using from critical scrutiny. They are indulging in an intellectual sleight of hand.

I would go further: pretending to be atheoretical is an attempt to impose a kind of *machismo* on to archaeological practice. As we shall see in chapter 8, archaeological practice is bound up with gendered notions of what is or is not valuable. There is, at least in the Anglo-American world, always something vaguely effeminate (and therefore, it is implied, somehow secondary) about talking, reasoning, discussing, trying to think clearly and explicitly. It is difficult to see Kurt Russell at a philosophy discussion group. 'Real men' don't do isms and ologies; they just dig – preferably with a really large, heavy pickaxe.

I've listened long enough to this; you're descending into abuse now. I'm willing to concede that we all use theory in some sense, but at the end of the day it's the facts, the raw data, that count.

I'm not going to argue now about whether 'raw data' really exist independently of theory – that will come later. Let's suppose for now that raw data really do exist. Where does that get us? There is an infinity of archaeological facts. They are piled in their millions in museum and laboratory storerooms, in microfiche lists and in tables of data. Here are some pretty undeniable 'facts':

The pot I am holding is 600 years old.
Colono Ware pottery has been found in Virginia.
A skeleton was excavated at Maiden Castle, Dorset, England, with an iron projectile lodged in its spine.
Great Basin projectile points come in different sizes.
The Bronze Age preceded the Iron Age.
Tikal was a major ceremonial centre for the Ancient Maya.
There are usually lots of clay pipe fragments on post-1500 sites.
The Dordogne area of France is full of cave art.
This photograph is of Monks Mound at Cahokia.
In Chaco Canyon the ancient pueblos are built of stone.

Do the sentences above add up to a meaningful account of the past, a coherent archaeological narrative? No. Simply dredging up facts and waiting for them to cohere into an orderly account of the past is like putting a number of monkeys in front of typewriters and waiting for them to come up with the complete works of Shakespeare.

What makes us archaeologists as opposed to mindless collectors of old junk is *the set of rules we use to translate those facts into meaningful accounts of the past*, accounts that 'make sense' to us as archaeologists and (it is hoped) to our general audience. And those rules, whether they are implicit or explicit, are theoretical in nature. Facts are important, but without theory they remain utterly silent.

Let's take the example of a distinguished Professor of Archaeology who claims to be writing in an atheoretical, factual manner using 'common sense', and see what he is really doing. I have selected this text more or less at random:

> It is worth stressing that Romano-British culture was based on a money economy. In south-eastern Britain coins were indeed in use before the conquest, but the Romans were responsible for spreading their circulation throughout the island. The extent to which currency permeated

> the whole commercial life of the country, down to the smallest transactions, may be gauged from the occurrence of coins on the humblest Romano-British sites and in the remotest part of the province.
> (Alcock 1976: 174)

One theoretical assumption being made here is that ideas like 'transaction' and 'commercial life', which only gain their modern meaning in the later eighteenth century and only arguably so even then, can easily be applied to Roman Britain without further explication. It follows that the writer must expect the reader to use his or her modern experience of transactions and commercial life – market oriented, largely unconnected with social relations, mediated by a common means of monetary exchange – to understand the meaning of the sentence. This and other assumptions may or may not be true, but they are theoretical in nature.

A second is a 'middle-range' assumption: that is, it connects particular facts on the one hand to general theories on the other (see chapter 4). Alcock assumes that the relative numbers of coins on different site types (note the use of an implicit site hierarchy that equates with a social hierarchy, assumed rather than demonstrated: 'the humblest sites') will accurately reflect the level of what Alcock has termed 'commercial activity'. Of course, we have already acknowledged that commercial activity is a much more theoretically complex beast. Again, this is a theoretical proposition.

Alcock's account may or may not be 'true', a 'fair picture' or 'valid'; that is a matter for debate among those specializing in this period. It is certainly deeply theoretical.

I could go on analysing the passage for several more pages, but the point has been made that even the most apparently straightforward, transparent prose conceals theoretical depths.

All this is very plausible and convincing, but I still dislike theory intensely. Theorists seem constantly to use incomprehensible jargon, write in an impenetrable style, and never to get anywhere tangible. You might persuade me there is a point to theory, but you can't stop me being irritated and alienated by what theorists write.

No, I can't. I get irritated by a lot of theoretical writing, just as I get irritated by all sorts of archaeological writing. But you've raised a lot of points here that are worth taking in turn.

First, why the 'jargon'? Long words with specialized meanings are not confined to archaeological theory. Every area within archaeology has its own specialist terms of reference; in this sense jargon is in the eye of the beholder. My familiar terms as a theorist or as a specialist in vernacular architecture may seem jargon to the environmental specialist, and those of the environmental specialist may equally seem jargon to me.

There is a deeper problem with the accusation of jargon, however. There seems to be an assumption behind such an accusation that we can always express what we want to say in 'clear, simple and easy' language. If only archaeology were so straightforward! If it were, we might have concluded the archaeological project with a perfect understanding of the past hundreds of years ago. Archaeology is, if nothing else, about new ideas about the past. We express ideas in words, and it may be appropriate to use new words to lead the reader to think in new ways.

Human societies were and are very complex things. As part of the natural world they share its complexity, and also have a social and cultural complexity all of their own. We don't complain when the chemist or biologist uses technical language incomprehensible to the lay person, so why should we when the archaeologist does so?

The point I am making here is that we expect the finer techniques of archaeological practice to be difficult to comprehend and master; that is the nature of our discipline. We are prepared to put effort into mastering the language and practice of stratigraphy, Harris matrices, seriation, scientific dating techniques, even the half-intuitive practical skill of differentiating between layers by the feel of the soil under the trowel. But the 'theory' side of what we do – using the tiny scraps of information thus gained to tell us about the human past in all its richness and complexity – must be at least equally difficult as these 'practical' tasks. It fact, it must be one of the most intellectually demanding tasks we as a species have ever set ourselves.

I think you're missing the point. The suspicion is that jargon is being used to mystify, to create a language of exclusion where the outsider is made to feel small.

There is some justice in this charge. Certain forms of academic rhetoric are used, intentionally or unintentionally, to set up in-groups and out-groups. I do not defend such a practice. But again, one hears the vague murmur of pots calling kettles black; all sectional interests within and outside archaeology do this. Read any article in *Vernacular Architecture* on the classification of scarf-joints with squinted and pegged abutments, or a medieval historian on enfeoffments and sub-infeudation.

Finally, 'writing clearly' assumes that one is *writing about something else*. In other words, that there is a real, external world out there with certain essential, concrete features, features that language can describe in a more or less clear and neutral manner. Now whether one is describing the decoration on pots or suggesting what it might have been like to live in the Bronze Age, this is a highly debatable assumption. Certainly the past doesn't exist anywhere outside our own heads. I have never touched, kicked or felt the past.

Theory is difficult. If one accepts that we are all theorists, then logically it is no more or less difficult than any other branch of archaeology. But archaeology itself is difficult. We have set ourselves an incredibly daunting task. We want to understand human societies that have been dead and gone for thousands of years, whose customs, values and attitudes were almost certainly utterly different from our own. We have to do this without talking to the people themselves. What is more, we want to understand how and why they changed in the way they did. And the only materials we have to achieve this immense task are a few paltry scraps of rubbish they left behind on the way, most of which have long since decayed into dust. Such a task is not a simple one; the wish that it be an intellectually easy one is quite understandable, but very naive.

Theory is also difficult for reasons that have less to do with jargon as such and more to do with academic practice. Practitioners in theory will often say one thing and do quite another. A theoretical article will proclaim that it is tackling a problem from a new, exciting perspective and just churn out the same old approach thinly disguised. Another article will accuse a rival of a string of theoretical iniquities and then do exactly the same things itself using different language.

Which leads to my final point: theory is difficult, in the last analysis, because it requires one to think for oneself. When a student writes a term paper or essay on southwestern Native American pottery, he or she can churn out a series of 'facts' gleaned from the standard textbooks. Such a list of facts, or more accurately a repetition of the textbooks' narratives, may not get a particularly good mark in the absence of any critical analysis or independent thinking whatsoever, but the student will get by. Such an approach comes unstuck, however, in writing a theory essay. It's more difficult to regurgitate things copied out of books and not really deeply understood when one is dealing with abstract ideas, particularly when one writer disagrees so clearly and fundamentally with another. Though any crop of undergraduate essays will demonstrate that it is not impossible.

Thinking for oneself, however, is something every student of archaeology (or any other critical discipline for that matter) is (or should be) in the business of doing. Ultimately it is the only justification of a liberal education. In an age when education is increasingly seen as a commodity, in which knowledge can, it is implied, be bought and sold in the marketplace, the idea of an education as learning the abstract skills of thinking critically is more and more under attack. Perhaps it is this cultural context that has led to some of the sharpness of the recent backlash against theory.

Understanding Theory

Well, I still feel pretty dubious about theory, but I'm prepared to go along with you for a bit. Where do we go from here?

The rest of this book will try to illuminate some of the major trends in archaeological theory, starting with the 1960s and moving on from there. To try to make this book as clear as possible, I am going to adopt two strategies.

First, from time to time I shall talk at length about developments in associated disciplines and in intellectual thought as a whole. As a result, long passages and even sub-sections of chapters may seem utterly irrelevant to the practising archaeologist. The reason I do this is because archaeology has had a habit of picking up ideas second-hand from other disciplines. Ideas have been changed, even confused and distorted in the process. As a result, it is necessary to go back 'to source' to explain them clearly and to understand precisely how they have been used and abused by archaeologists. So please bear with the text, plod through the 'irrelevant' material, and I will then try to explain its relevance to archaeological thought.

Second, I shall look at the development of theory historically, looking first at the origins of the New Archaeology, then at reactions to it. I suggest that by understanding the historical context of a set of ideas such as 'New Archaeology' or 'postprocessual archaeology', one may more easily sympathize with its aims and grasp some of its underlying principles and concerns. By understanding this context we can also put many of the features of contemporary archaeology in their historical surroundings rather than place them in a vacuum.

The next chapter will discuss the New Archaeology; the following three will look at the questions of 'science' and 'anthropology' that it raised. The intellectual questions raised by the New Archaeology are, I will suggest, absolutely central to contemporary archaeological theory and practice.

2

The 'New Archaeology'

Most archaeologists fall in love with the subject by getting 'hooked' on things. The things vary from case to case – castles, Roman baths, Native American arrowheads, Neolithic pots, Maya temples – but in most cases the immediate appeal is of mystery and romance, of the past calling to us through its remains. This romantic appeal is often aesthetic and sensual as well as intellectual. We all love clambering round medieval ruins or handling pottery sherds. We try to persuade ourselves, however, that these ruins or sherds are mere 'data'. (One colleague told me that as a result of the acute boredom of his researches he now loathes Neolithic pottery to the depths of his soul, but I interpret this as another, rather twisted form of love.) Artefacts, whether as small as an arrowhead or as large as a royal palace, fascinate us.

This love of artefacts, in itself, has nothing to do with archaeology in the strict sense as the study of the past. Artefacts *tell us nothing about the past* in themselves. I have stood in the middle of countless ruins of castles and ancient palaces and listened very carefully, and not heard a single syllable. Colleagues tell me that they have had similar distressing experiences with pottery, bones, bags of seeds. They love handling and experiencing their material, but it remains silent. In and of itself, it tells them precisely nothing.

Artefacts can't tell us anything about the past because the past does not exist. We cannot touch the past, see it or feel it; it is utterly dead and gone. *Our beloved artefacts actually belong to the present.* They exist in the here and now. They may or may not have been made and used by real people thousands of years ago, but our assessment of the date of their manufacture and use is itself an assessment that we make, that is made in the present.

Until we invent a time machine, *the past exists only in the things we say about it.* We choose to ask certain questions of our material: 'How many beads were found in this grave?' 'Do we see a shift to intensive exploitation of llamas in the Formative Period?' 'What was it like to live in the Bronze Age?' 'What degree of social inequality do we see in this period?' We make general or particular statements about the past: 'There was increased use of obsidian in Phase 3B of this site'; 'There were more elements of cultural continuity between Mesolithic and Neolithic populations than have hitherto been assumed'; 'Gender relations became less equal through time'; 'The Romans were a cruel and vicious people'. These are all statements made here, now, in the present, as I write and you read. They do not belong to the past.

It is only in works of fiction, or if you believe in ghosts, that past and present can really be made to collide and merge into each other. It is striking that many writers have used this collision with great effect to disturb and horrify the 'rational' Western mind (the novels of Peter Ackroyd are excellent examples of this). This collision of past and present is also possible within 'non-Western' schemes of thought; hence in part the conflicts between different cultures over, for example, excavation and reburial of Native American human remains, where the belief that time moves in a cycle rather than in a line makes archaeological excavation a threat to the present through its desecration of the past.

Now it is the task of archaeologists to find out about the past. We want to know what really happened back then. Our source materials – stones, bones, pots – are in the present, and the past that we create is also in the present. We will never 'know' what the past was 'really like', but we all can and do try to write the 'best' account we can, an account that is informed by the evidence that we have and that tries to be coherent and satisfying to us.

One of the basic problems of archaeology, then, is summarized in figure 2.1. Somehow we have to take the archaeological materials that we have and through our questioning get them to give us information about the past. There is a gulf between past and present, a gulf that the archaeologist has to bridge somehow even if it can never be bridged securely or definitively. Otherwise we risk a descent into mere *antiquarianism*: that is, of simply assembling and collating old objects for their own sake, rather than as evidence for the past.

I am labouring this point because it is easy to fall into the trap of believing that the very physicality of archaeological material will in itself tell us what the past was like. It will not. Kick a megalith and it hurts; stand in a castle chamber and see nothing but medieval fabric. But kicking the megalith or standing in that cold chamber will tell you nothing about what the Neolithic or the Middle Ages were 'really like', or what processes led to the construction and use of the megalith

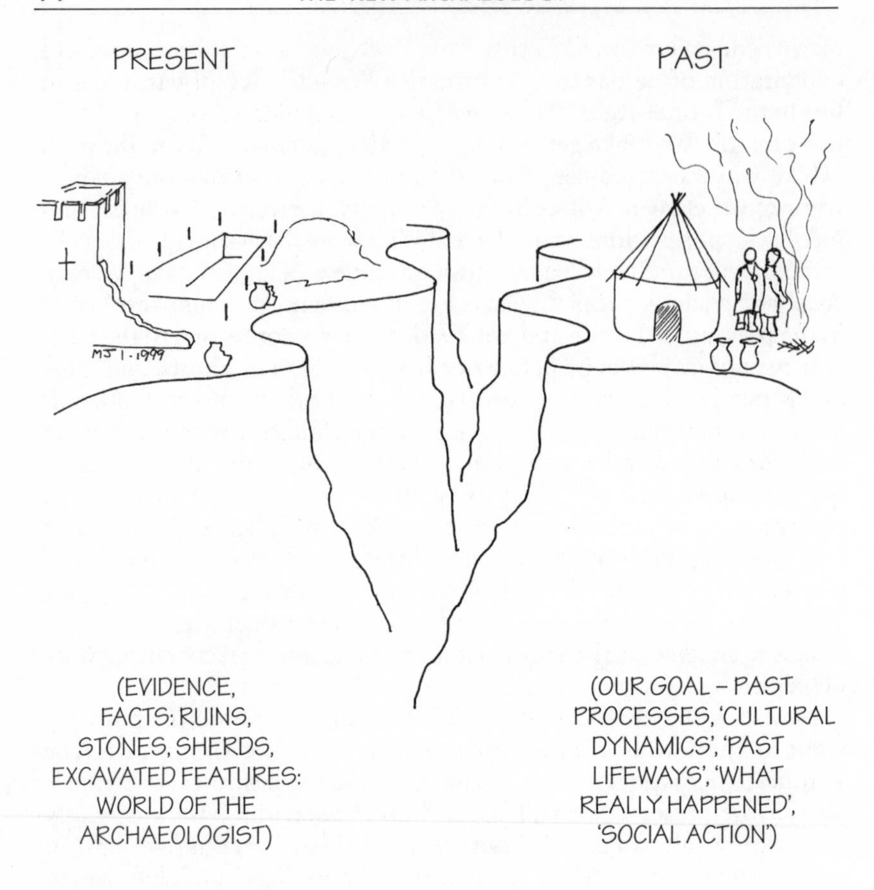

Figure 2.1 The gulf between present and past.

or castle. We only see megalith and castle in the present, the here and now. This is a present that is framed by our ideas, attitudes and assumptions. We see megalith and castle through our eyes, not the eyes of the prehistoric or medieval observer.

I am also labouring this point because it can be seen as *the point of departure for very different views of archaeological theory.* One of the few areas of common ground for most archaeological theorists is that we all want to talk about the past, and we all use archaeological material in the present to do so. But how do we do this? One possible suggestion is that we should use the methods of the natural sciences on our material, to try to test alternative hypotheses about past events and processes against that material and so expand and develop our understanding. Another possibility is to view artefacts like literary texts, to 'read' them as we would a piece of writing, and so begin to uncover the rich complexity of past cultural meanings.

There are a multiplicity of other views; and the problem has been perceived for some centuries. The English humanist Sir Thomas Browne centred his wonderful mid-seventeenth century essay *Hydrotaphia* around the discovery of cremation urns that we now believe to be of Anglo-Saxon origin, fifth to seventh century AD in date. Browne contrasted the physical solidity of the urns with the impossibility of understanding the religious beliefs that they expressed, or even the impossibility of assigning a date to them (he speculated that they might be Roman).

The question of how to link present and past, however, surfaced in its most explicit form with the New Archaeology of the 1960s and 1970s.

Before the New Archaeology

There is an ongoing debate about the nature of archaeological theory before the New Archaeology. There is not space here to do this debate justice.

Some historians of archaeology maintain that the century before 1960 was the 'long sleep' of archaeological theory, in which very little explicit discussion of theory took place. They argue that archaeologists concentrated on collecting masses of archaeological material within an unquestioned, generally assumed framework. Others deny this, maintaining that this period did see lively theoretical debates of various kinds. They further maintain that the importance of the New Archaeology for the development of archaeological thought has been grossly overestimated.

What I do want to stress is that one of the starting points of the so-called 'New Archaeology' lay in what I have discussed above, that is in the notion that mere data collection – the acquisition of more stuff – did not in itself lead to a better understanding of the past. David Clarke, one of the principal proponents of the New Archaeology, started his classic book *Analytical Archaeology* with a telling quote from Lewis Carroll:

> Now here, you see, it takes all the running you can do, to keep in the same place.
>
> The Queen to Alice, *Through the Looking-Glass*, Chapter 2, Lewis Carroll, 1832–98.

> Every year produces a fresh crop of archaeological excavations, a new harvest of prehistoric artefacts.... The archaeologists come and go, new names and sites outshine the old, while hundreds of years of collected material overflows and submerges our museum storerooms. At the same time a relentless current of articles and books describe and label the new material so that the intrepid archaeologist, by dint of furious activity, can just maintain his [*sic*] status quo against the constant stream of data. However, the nebulous doubt arises in our minds that a modern empirical discipline ought to be able to aim at more rewarding results than the maintenance of a relative status quo and a steady flow of counterfeit history books. (Clarke 1972:3)

Clarke, then, was not at all sure that the methods of archaeologists actually gave us better and more reliable versions of the past: we seemed to dig up more and more things but stay in the same place in terms of our ideas. Our knowledge of artefacts in the present grew better and better, but because we did not bridge the gulf with the past very well, progress in understanding that past did not follow.

What were the theories Clarke was dissatisfied with? In other words, how did archaeologists before the 1960s translate archaeological material into statements about the past? It is easy to over-generalize here, and exceptions can always be found. One of the basic building-blocks, however, was the idea of an archaeological culture and what it meant in terms of past human populations. In the words of Gordon Childe:

> We find certain types of remains – pots, implements, ornaments, burial rites, and house forms – constantly recurring together. Such a complex of associated traits we shall term a 'cultural group' or just a 'culture'. We assume that such a complex is the material expression of what today would be called a 'people'. (Childe 1929: v–vi)

Such an idea of culture has been called *normative*. That is, it depends on two assumptions: first, that *artefacts are expressions of cultural norms*, ideas in people's heads, and second, that *those norms define what 'culture' is*. I will give two examples, one from the present and one from the past.

1 The English are the English because they drink tea, speak English, don't eat horse, and queue in an orderly fashion, often for hours without complaint. This distinguishes them from the French who drink coffee, speak French, eat horse and do not queue with such equanimity. (These are, of course, all cultural norms, ideas about what is the right way to behave, and one can easily see that they

are in fact ideals (in this case crude stereotypes) that don't necessarily correspond to reality in every case.)

2 The *Linearbandkeramik* archaeological culture differs from the *Trichterbandkeramik* in Neolithic Europe: in LBK areas we find rectangular house forms, pottery decorated with linear designs, a certain form of arable economy. In TRB areas house form, pottery decoration and economy are all different. (Again, this is an ideal: not every TRB or LBK site will share all the features of all the others.)

Such a concept of culture is also *polythetic*: that is, it depends on a number of different traits occurring together rather than on one trait alone. Drinking coffee does not make an English person French; a single rectangular house does not turn an TRB settlement into an LBK village. It is a number of traits occurring together, as Childe stressed, that defines culture. In North America, lists of traits were tabulated and added up from site to site.

So to summarize, in the traditional view we translate present into past by collecting artefacts into groups, and naming those groups as archaeological cultures. We then make the equation between an archaeological culture and a human culture by making the assumption that artefacts are expressions of cultural ideas or norms.

This approach has several consequences. In the first place, it leads to a tendency to *particularize* what archaeologists say about the past rather than generalize. What this means is that instead of stressing the similarities between things, one stressed the differences and particularities between them.

One might, for example, want to generalize between the LBK and TRB, to stress that these different groups were at the same 'level' of social or economic development. They might both be classified as societies with a certain level of social ranking, for example, or with certain similar modes of subsistence economy, or exchange and trade. The culture-oriented approach, however, tends to direct attention away from such general features towards what makes the TRB and LBK distinctive, both from each other and from other cultures. It encourages us to stress their differences, their diagnostic and peculiar features, their particular forms of house type and burial rite, the contrast between the zigging of one form of pottery decoration and the zagging of another form, rather than those they have in common.

The second consequence of a normative view of culture is that cultures tend to be viewed as *unchanging*. To repeat, the normative approach sees artefacts as expressions of shared ideas. If people in the LBK all shared the same ideas on how to build houses, make pots and bury their dead, where did change come from? The easiest way to explain change is to suggest that it was brought in from outside, from another human group. Such outside 'influence' can be of one of two forms: migration of peoples, or of *diffusion* – the spread of ideas through contact between groups.

Accounts of prehistory before the New Archaeology, then, tended to consist of two elements. The first was a chronological sequence of cultures, a sort of timetable with culture groups listed instead of trains. The second was a map full of arrows to indicate the migration and diffusion of ideas that marked change between cultures (for example figures 2.2 and 2.3).

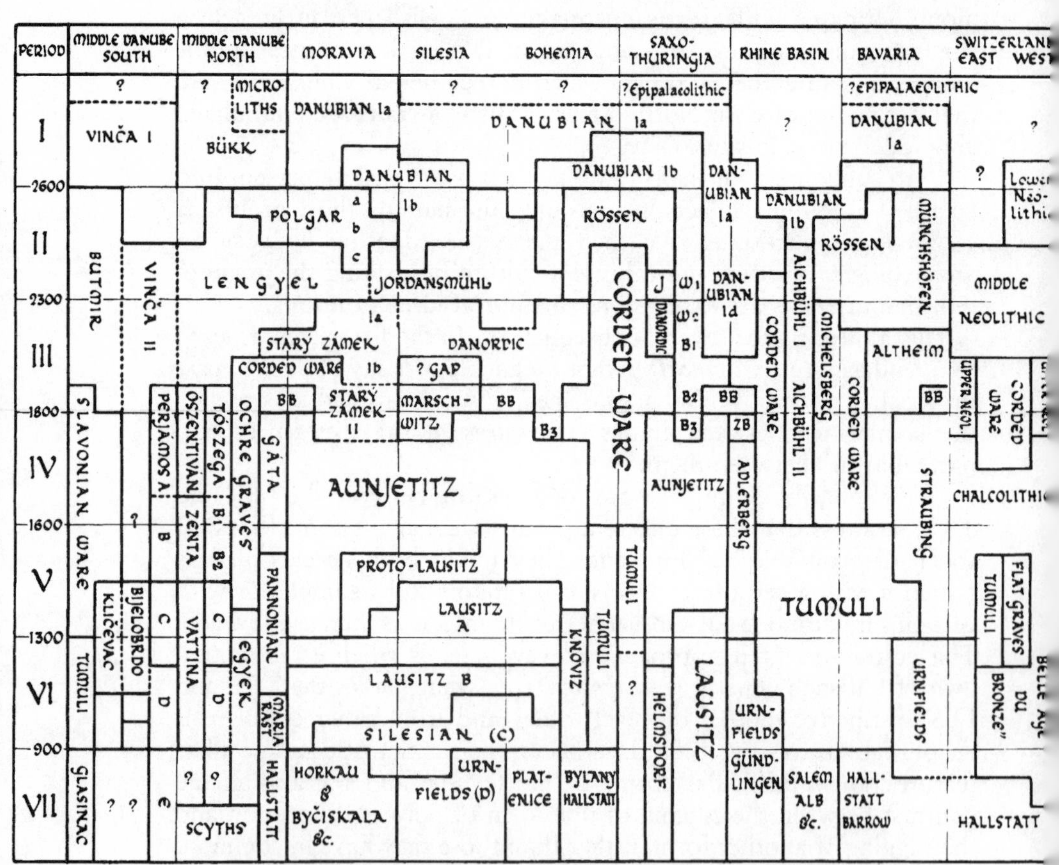

Figure 2.2 'Cultures' in space and time, from Childe (1929).

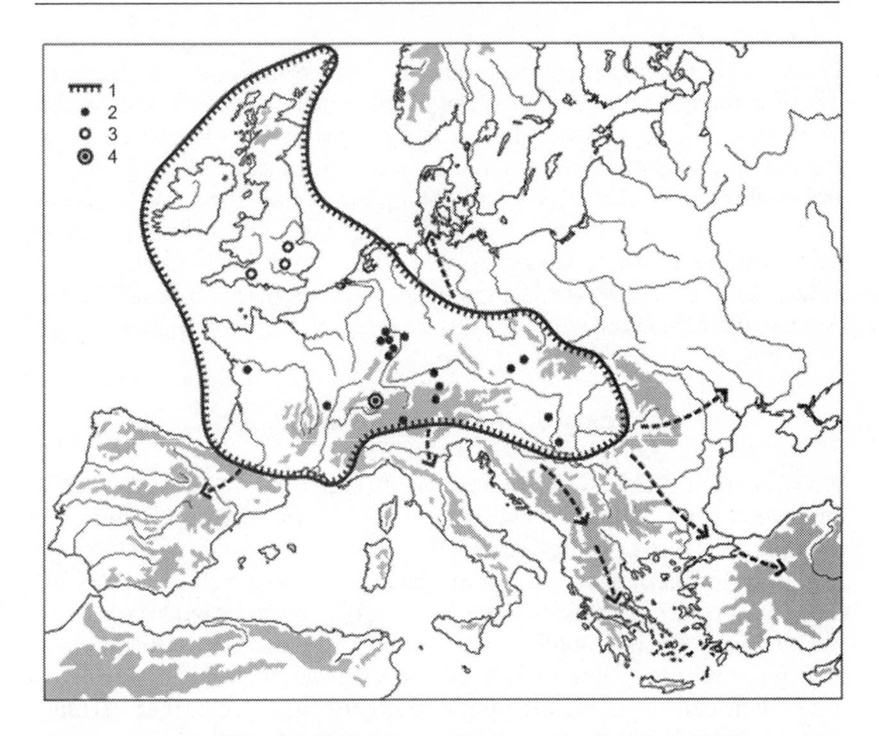

Figure 2.3 Piggott's (1968) view of culture. Piggott's caption reads: 'Distribution of mature La Tène culture and influences; 2, Sword scabbards in Swiss style; 3, British derivatives; 4, Many scabbards'.

The whole synthesis thus produced tended to be *descriptive*. That is, it described phases and areas of cultural change: this culture followed that culture, this innovation spread or diffused at that rate. Much traditional prehistory read like much traditional history, that is like a chronicle of events held together by a narrative. There was little explicit explanation of why this or that pottery style changed, why this or that culture spread or changed.

Lewis Binford called this view of change 'an aquatic view of culture' (Binford 1964). Binford's image was a caricature, but like all good caricatures it contained an essence of truth. What Binford meant was that traditional archaeologists saw the map of the prehistoric world as being a little like a large pool of water. When an innovation was made for whatever reason in a given place, it would tend to spread through the process of 'influence' or diffusion in all directions, like the ripples from a stone dropped in the pool. In any given location, then, one would see cross-cutting 'ripples' of influence.

I want to repeat that this characterization of archaeology before the 1960s is far too brief, over-simplified and over-generalized. Suggestions for further accounts are given in the Further Reading section. In particular, it leans too heavily on what New Archaeologists such as David Clarke, Colin Renfrew and Lewis Binford said that traditional archaeology was like. Many have complained that the New Archaeology set up a distorted image of traditional thought for its own polemical purposes, a 'straw person' that could easily be knocked down. But if this is what New Archaeology thought traditional thinking was like, this was what New Archaeology was reacting against.

Origins of the New Archaeology

What, then, was the 'New Archaeology'? One thing is certain: it is no longer new. The term 'New Archaeology' is applied to a school of thought that swept through Anglo-American archaeology in the 1960s and early 1970s. It must be seen in the contexts of similar currents of thought in other disciplines – the New Geography in particular.

The 'New Archaeology' was also not a single set of beliefs or theories. One does not expect all members of a political party to have identical views on all policy matters; there are rather certain core ideas and values that inform the approach of any one party. Similarly, under the banner of the New Archaeology was a very diverse set of archaeologists with different approaches and beliefs. What united them all was a sense of dissatisfaction with the way archaeology was going, a sense that things had to change and that they, as a thrusting new generation of 'young Turks', were going to change it.

This dissatisfaction with traditional archaeology was crystallized in the phrase: 'we must be more *scientific* and more *anthropological*'. In this one phrase can be seen New Archaeology's source of disaffection with what went before, the foundations of its rise, and in my view the seeds of subsequent developments.

Why was culture history seen as unscientific? We must go back to David Clarke's comments on running harder and harder to stay in the same place. Traditional archaeologists accumulated more and more information, but this did not automatically mean a better and better idea of what the past was like, for all the reasons discussed above. We simply fitted more and more archaeological material into the same endless sequence of cultures. 'Science', argued the New Archaeologists, used its data to test hypotheses about the way the world worked, and generalized from these conclusions. 'Science' progressed; it did not simply collate its facts into orderly patterns, rather it made larger and larger and deeper and deeper its understanding of the world. The natural sciences were developing better and better understandings of the world around us.

Why was culture history seen as not anthropological? Traditional archaeologists, in sorting artefacts into cultures, often seemed to ignore human beings: pottery styles seemed to get up and march around with no reference to the humans that produced them. In this sense it was *fetishistic*. A fetish is a thing that comes to stand for something else such as a human or a human group: traditional archaeologists often seemed to spend their time describing the movement of these things without thinking about the human beings, the cultural systems, behind them. Pottery styles and house types seemed to develop little legs and run around without any help from human beings.

At a deeper level, traditional archaeology was not anthropological in the sense that there seemed to be no guarantee that the archaeological 'cultures' so lovingly produced by culture historians had any relationship to real human communities. Many New Archaeologists questioned the link between archaeological cultures – Childe's recurring assemblages of traits – and past peoples. Childe himself had come to doubt whether we really could equate archaeological cultures and past peoples:

> It would be rash to define precisely what sort of social group corresponds to the archaeologist's 'culture'.... Culture and language need not coincide. (Childe 1942: 26–7)

This is why many New Archaeologists moved away from the normative conception of culture and looked for other ways to explain the things we dug up. In Clarke's phrase, archaeology experienced a 'loss of innocence'. The innocent equations archaeology had made between artefacts, cultures and peoples, or between data and interpretation more generally, had to be questioned.

To repeat, the New Archaeology must be understood as a movement or mood of dissatisfaction rather than as a specific set of beliefs. David Clarke called it 'a set of questions rather than a set of answers'. It was certainly marked with revolutionary fervour. Lewis Binford, its most famous figure, tells a story that sums up both this fervour and its irritation with the particularism of traditional methods:

> I remember one day when one of the traditional Griffin students had returned from a field trip to the Upper Illinois valley. He had burst into the museum with the announcement that he had found a 'unique' item, a negative-painted sherd from the——site. Griffin was obviously stimulated, and Papworth said, 'Let me see'. He took the sherd, looked

> at it and then threw it on the floor and ground it to pieces with the heel of his shoe. 'That's what I think of your "unique" sherd'. Griffin was in total shock, the student was practically in tears, and I was laughing inside. (Binford 1972: 130–1)

New Archaeology: Key Points

As the New Archaeology developed, certain key themes came to be repeated in the writings of its proponents. I will try to summarize these under seven points. If the descriptions seem brief and oversimplified, many of these themes will be discussed further in future chapters. The important thing here is to get an overall sense of the spirit of the movement.

First, an emphasis on *cultural evolution*. The word 'evolution' has a series of different though related meanings stretching back to the work of Darwin in the nineteenth century (see chapter 9). For some within New Archaeology, it meant in part that societies could be classified on a scale from simple to complex. Cultures in this view evolved from one state to another, for example from 'band' societies to 'tribal' networks to 'chiefdoms'.

This stress was in part a rejection of the aquatic view of culture, with its random ripples spreading across the map. Instead New Archaeologists wanted to look at the internal dynamics of a society, what was driving its general direction of social development (the phrase often used was 'cultural trajectory').

Evolution was also part of a conscious stress on generalities rather than particularities. Cultures might differ in their specific forms of jewellery and house type, one pottery style might zig and the other zag. But both societies might be comparable on the same level on an evolutionary scale. So we could generalize about, say, the evolution of state level societies from chiefdom level societies, without worrying too much about the different art styles or pottery decoration in each case.

Second, an emphasis on *systems thinking* (see figure 2.4 and chapter 5). Culture wasn't just a mixed bag of different randomly acquired norms, as culture history had implied; rather it was a system. Lewis Binford (1964) defined culture as 'man's extrasomatic means of adaptation'.

To clarify Binford's point, other animals are adapted to their environment through their bodies – the giraffe has a long neck to reach to the tops of trees in the savannah, polar bears have lots of fur to deal with the Arctic winter. Humans adapt through culture – the Inuit

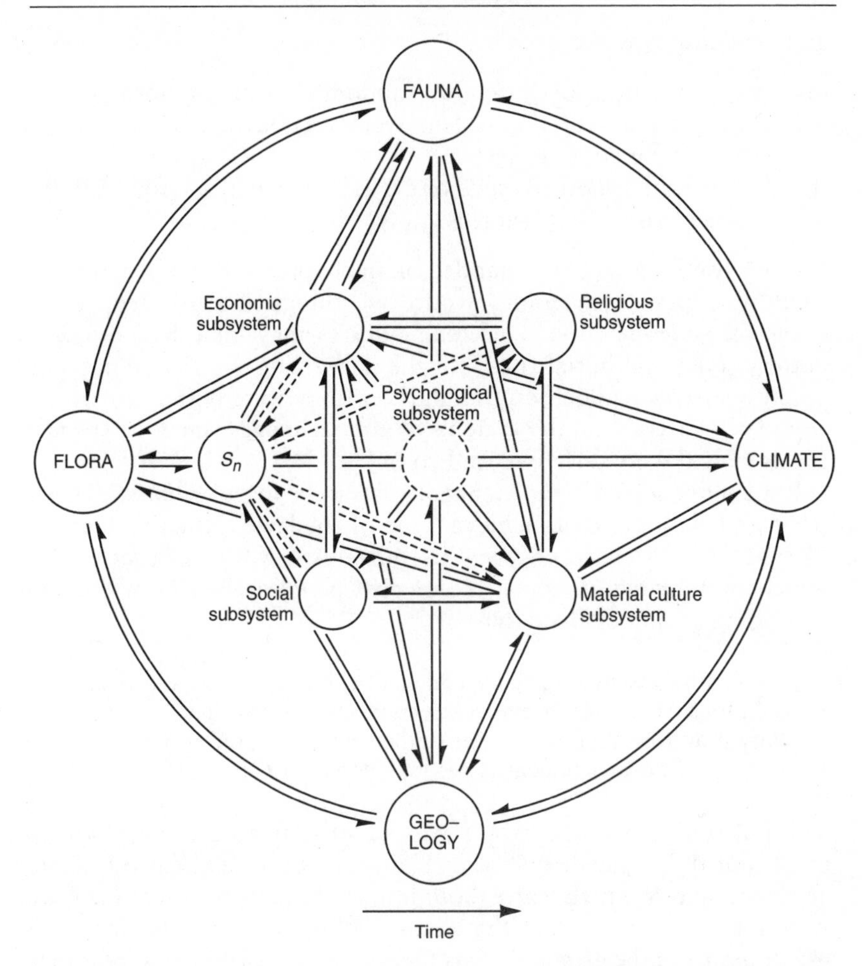

Figure 2.4 David Clarke's (1976) systemic view of culture. In language characteristic of the New Archaeology, Clark's caption reads: 'A static and schematic model of the dynamic equilibrium between the subsystem networks of a single sociocultural system and its total environmental system. S_n represents the summation of the effects of alien sociocultural systems connected to S by cultural 'coactions' (dashed lines) and to the environment by 'interactions' (solid lines). To set the model in motion all the components must oscillate randomly along intercorrelated trending trajectories'.

wear furs and live in igloos, the !Kung San have an extensive range of specialized hunting equipment. These cultural adaptations are all outside (*extra*) the body (*soma*), hence 'extrasomatic'.

So past cultures were:

(a) not just a bag of different, randomly acquired norms – the different parts of the system were related one to another as part of a functioning system;
(b) comparable to other kinds of system such as those found in the physical and animal worlds.

Systems thinking will be expanded on in chapter 5. But note here that it allowed New Archaeology to do two things. It firstly helped the stress on *generalization*. Different cultures may have had different pottery styles and burial rites, but the underlying social system could be shown to have underlying similarities (they were both more or less complex, practised similar systems of gift exchange even if the specific goods traded were different, and so on).

It secondly helped New Archaeologists to be more *optimistic* about what archaeology could achieve. One of the least attractive features of traditional archaeology was its pessimism: we can never reconstruct the religious or social life of past peoples, we can only build chronologies. James Deetz wrote:

> Stress on the essential interrelatedness of cultural systems allows us to reach understandings of many aspects from a relative few...this certainty is at least a partial answer to the problems posed by the incompleteness of the archaeological record. (Deetz 1972: 112)

Third, if culture was adaptive, it was adaptive to an external environment. For the archaeologist Kent Flannery, we were not just looking at objects and trying to learn about human cultures through them; we were trying to reconstruct the whole ecological system behind both 'the Indian and the artefact'. This theoretical stress on the importance of the external environment led to interest in cultural materialism (in which the material world is seen as more important than the mental world), cultural ecology, modelling of the subsistence economy. Here, new theoretical attitudes went hand-in-hand with the new *scientific techniques* that were developed in the postwar period: faunal analysis, palaeoethnobotany, carbon-14 dating, dendrochronology, and so on.

Fourth, there was stress on a *scientific approach*. New Archaeologists saw traditional archaeology as modelling itself on the techniques of traditional history, with cultures taking the place of historical actors and the aim being the reconstruction of individual events in time. This may not have been a fair characterization, either of what archaeologists actually did or what traditional historians actually did, but it led New Archaeologists in part to embrace Science as the way forward. According to Watson, Redman and LeBlanc in their *Explanation in Archaeology: An Explicitly Scientific Approach* (1972), one index of the progress of archaeology is the extent to which hypotheses are scientifically tested.

Fifth, there was stress on the idea of *culture process*. The idea of 'process' was central to New Archaeology, but it is a difficult idea to grasp. It involves several related themes that have already been touched on:

(a) We want to explain rather than be merely descriptive – to ask 'why?' rather than merely 'when?' A traditional culture sequence such as that of Childe's (figure 2.2) may be valuable in describing a sequence, but it tells us nothing about why one culture succeeded another, or why, for example, innovations like agriculture or metallurgy spread quickly or slowly. You can see that the 'why?' questions link with the New Archaeology's first point, looking at cultural evolution.

(b) We want to look at the underlying process rather than the 'noise' on top. Why pottery decoration zigs or zags is unimportant in this view; instead, what is important is to look at pottery as one artefact of trade or of craft specialization, and to chart the process by which, for example, the long-term development of market networks relates to such specialization. Particular phenomena will always vary: as with economics or sociology, what may be important is the underlying trend.

(c) We want to look at change in the long term. Many New Archaeologists argued that if you wanted to do anthropology, the obvious place to start was in the present. Archaeology's great, possibly its only, contribution to the wider study of human beings had to be through its long-term perspective which cultural anthropologists, working only in the present or recent past, did not have.

In this sense, the New Archaeology shared many of the concerns with the rhythms of long-term history as discussed by *Annales* historians such as Fernand Braudel, though at the time these parallels in thinking were little noted and it fell to a later generation of theorists writing in the 1980s to point out the similarities (see chapter 10).

Many New Archaeologists contrasted culture process to culture history. In this view, traditional history simply described a set of more or less random political events such as battles and births and deaths of monarchs without ever really explaining anything. By substituting process for history, the long-term trends or processes beneath the surface of such events became the important objects of study.

Sixth and more generally, there was a trend to attempt to become more explicit about one's biases. A good scientist, argued New Archaeologists, did not use intuition and implicit assumptions; he or she made clear their aims and interests. Much of the New Archaeology was concerned with making what had been unspoken formally outlined. A good example is the technique of typology, or the classification of objects according to their changing form. It had long been accepted that one could classify objects, and that this classification had something to do with chronological order: archaeologists made statements like 'pottery vessels get baggier through time', or 'this jewellery style goes out of fashion in this period'. But the criteria by which a typologist suggested one piece of jewellery or architectural style was 'early' and another one was 'late' was rarely clearly spelt out.

In his book *Analytical Archaeology*, David Clarke used many of the concepts of traditional archaeology – typology, assemblage and culture for example – but discussed openly, explicitly and at length how they should be defined. For Clarke, the need to be explicit and precise in one's terms to replace 'the murky exhalation that passes for "interpretative thinking" in archaeology' was one of the main thrusts of the New Archaeology.

A related aspect of making one's biases explicit was *problem orientation*, or the belief that one should survey and dig sites, or do research more generally, with clear research questions in mind. Again, this linked in with being scientific – the scientist tested specific hypotheses, he or she brought specific questions to the data. In chapter 3, we will see how asking specific questions or testing specific hypotheses was central to the idea of archaeology as a science.

A seventh and final concern of New Archaeology was the understanding of *variability*. What this meant was a basic understanding of our material in statistical terms. Previous archaeologists had often concentrated on the biggest and best sites, or the most beautiful artefacts. New Archaeologists pointed out that we couldn't understand, say, a major urban civilization without looking at its rural infrastructure (the importance of looking at the whole system again), and we couldn't understand the rural infrastructure without knowing just how many rural sites there were on the ground. So to really get to grips with understanding that civilization, the archaeologist might want to forgo digging yet another élite site with lots of pretty, exotic artefacts and instead concentrate on systematic survey of ordinary farmsteads. The finds might be less spectacular, but the understanding of the settlement system would be much greater.

To understand variability, New Archaeologists looked much more critically at sampling theory and techniques. To be sure of variability, at the very least we had to be sure we were looking at a representative sample of sites. Kent Flannery told a memorable parable of a Mesoamerican archaeologist who only stopped to record archaeological sites if he was forced to put his Jeep into first gear to get over the top of them. In response, New Archaeologists explored methods of sampling randomly or at least systematically.

Many of the worst aspects of the traditional attitudes the New Archaeology castigated still survive today. A few years ago I remember asking a prominent, senior scholar who had written several influential books on traditional architecture how many houses of a certain date and type there were in a certain county of England. 'Oh', he said, 'an awful lot'. Yes, but how many? Tens, hundreds, thousands? 'Well, a lot, but I really couldn't put a figure to it' came the reply. And how many were there in an adjacent area? 'Oh, not many at all . . .'. And what, statistically, was the proportion of Type A houses to Type B houses in the two areas? 'Ah . . .'. And yet you are quite confident in saying that Type A houses are more frequently found than Type B houses in this area but not that, and we can indeed go on from this observation to draw conclusions about relative levels of wealth in the two areas? 'Oh yes, that's quite clear . . .'. One does not have to be a paid-up New Archaeologist to see that such reasoning is an insecure foundation for any understanding of the archaeological record.

I'm a bit sceptical about all this. In the first place, archaeologists before New Archaeology were not the dry, traditional dullards that New Archaeologists made out. They did many of these things already. Look, for example, at Grahame Clark's work at Star Carr, where environmental analysis was used in the 1950s. Or Alfred Kidder's work in Mesoamerica and the American Southwest. And Gordon Childe can hardly be accused of many of the sins the New Archaeology tried to pin on culture historians. His books Man Makes Himself *and* What Happened in History *are full of dynamic pictures – they try to explain things, they deal with underlying processes . . .*

Your analysis contains a lot of truth. Traditional archaeology was not necessarily the narrowly descriptive, sterile pursuit that New Archaeology painted it. It can be argued, for example, that traditional accounts of migration and diffusion *did* address 'why?' questions rather than simply describe the data. Certainly books like Childe's *The Prehistory of European Society* presented a dynamic model in which indigenous cultures were seen as creative and dynamic and in which modified diffusion played a key role in explanation. Again, in North America the 'culture history' model was in part caricatured by New Archaeology.

Nevertheless New Archaeology's criticisms were pertinent. For our purposes in trying to understand where theory is today, it isn't of primary importance to ascertain whether New Archaeology was *accurate* in its criticisms; we want to understand why New Archaeology developed in the way it did. Our all-too-brief sketch serves for this purpose.

It is equally true that much of New Archaeology was not really new. Like so many theoretical movements in archaeology, it borrowed from other disciplines. The work of the cultural anthropologist Leslie White was especially influential. His book *The Science of Culture* stressed the need for a scientific approach and the idea of culture as a system. Again, another anthropologist, Julian Steward, had stressed cultural ecology and adaptation in his work. Binford's early work makes clear his profound debt to both White and Steward. Finally, stress on systems thinking owed much to Walter Taylor's emphasis on what he called a 'conjunctive approach' in his 1948 *A Study of Archeology.* But don't forget that White, Steward and Taylor were in a minority within their own disciplines. White in particular was writing *against* the orthodox cultural anthropology of his time when his thinking was adopted by archaeologists.

The New Archaeology, particularly in its stress on anthropology, can be particularly associated with the New World. In Britain New Archaeologists such as Clarke and Renfrew had a great impact, but overall the impact of the New Archaeology was not as revolutionary or as hard-hitting as in North America. I suggest there were several reasons for this.

One is the institutional set-up of archaeology. In North America, there are few Departments of Archaeology. Most academic archaeologists have posts within Departments of Anthropology, and form a 'minority' within those departments. Some classical and historical archaeologists are employed elsewhere. By contrast, in Britain Departments of Archaeology are largely separate institutions, or are more closely linked to Departments of History. Hence, an American graduate student in the 1960s and 1970s intending to do their Ph.D. on an archaeological topic and go on to an academic career would be expected to read extensively and take courses in anthropological theory, where she or he would encounter many of the ideas of evolution and systemic analysis discussed above. By contrast, a British graduate student would probably have less theoretical training in general and often very little encounter with anthropological method.

Underlying this institutional difference are different perceptions of the past. American archaeology is split between study of 'native' New World cultures and the Old World and the 'historical archaeology' of its colonies, to the extent that Native American archaeology is often spelt differently – 'archeology'. The anthropologist Franz Boas played a pivotal role in keeping archaeology within the ambit of anthropology in North America in the earlier twentieth century. Now anthropology has traditionally been concerned with 'other cultures' rather than with 'us'. As very few Native Americans are employed within American archaeology, New World cultures were and are perceived very much as 'them'. If you go to the Smithsonian Museum in Washington, the Museum of American History is in one place; Native American exhibits are kept in the Museum of Natural History, alongside the flora and fauna of the New World (though as I write plans are unfolding to change this situation). In the past, archaeological remains such as burial mounds and cliff dwellings had been interpreted as evidence for the Lost Tribes of Israel or analogous groups, it being assumed that Native Americans were too 'primitive' to have produced such cultures; but such theories had been completely abandoned by the archaeological profession by the 1960s.

For British archaeologists the situation is different. The prehistoric site of Stonehenge is used as a symbol of 'English Heritage', though it was built 2–3,000 years before the 'English', according to traditional history, arrived on what is now the English coast. The British, like Europeans generally, perceive prehistoric archaeology as part of 'their' past. Right or wrong, this perception has meant that both past and present archaeological interpretation has been thoroughly permeated with nationalist concerns, often of a politically unpleasant variety. Also, prehistory and history are seen as much more of a continuum: Iron Age studies blend into the Roman and early medieval periods. There is therefore not such a radical divide between prehistoric and historical archaeology.

So British archaeologists tend not to worry so much about the need to make explicitly theoretical generalizations in order to justify their work, and are much more comfortable with the idea of archaeology as the 'handmaiden of history'. New Archaeology had even less impact in continental Europe than it did in Britain, again for complex historical reasons. It also had less influence on the study of later periods: 'New Archaeology' had a major impact on the study of European prehistory, arguably most of all on the Palaeolithic, but less on Roman, medieval and post-medieval archaeology.

I think that there was also a practical element in the differential impact of New Archaeology. Stand in the middle of the Arizona desert and the need for sampling theory, understanding of variability, and so on is all too clear. By contrast, the British landscape is cramped; it has been intensively settled for millennia, and intensively studied for centuries. Most of its basic units (administrative boundaries, patches of woodland) are irregular in shape and are themselves hundreds if not thousands of years old. As a result, many of the techniques of New Archaeology such as sampling theory make clear sense as practical strategy in the Arizona desert, but are counter-intuitive in the densely settled palimpsest that is Wessex.

Anyway, what happened to all this youthful enthusiasm? I bet it didn't get very far.

Many of the ways in which New Archaeology developed will be picked up in later chapters. One thing that inevitably happened is that New Archaeologists got older. From being pushy young research students intent on causing a fuss, they became tenured lecturers and professors with job security, positions on powerful committees and funding bodies and supervising pushy graduate students of their own. Indeed, many of the key youthful figures in early New Archaeology are today's generation of senior academics.

As New Archaeology got older and developed as a body of thought it became known as *processualism*. Processualism is so called because of its stress on culture process (point five above); processualists also like to generalize, and tend to use a systemic or functional model.

Case Study: The Enigma of the Megaliths

An excellent example of the way New Archaeology led to new ways of thinking about the past was that of megalithic tombs in Western Europe. These are burial monuments built with large stones, within which collective burials often took place.

Traditional studies of megaliths had concentrated on dating, typology and diffusion. Scholars such as Glyn Daniel had defined megaliths into sub-groups based on their position around the Western Mediterranean and Atlantic seaboard (figure 2.5). They tried to date these groups in the absence of scientific dating techniques such as carbon-14; the only way of doing this was to look for similarities in the form of the monuments and assume that similarities had been produced through contact. Ultimately, then, megaliths could be dated by reference to their presumed ancestors in the Mediterranean such as the Maltese temples. These could then be cross-dated in turn with

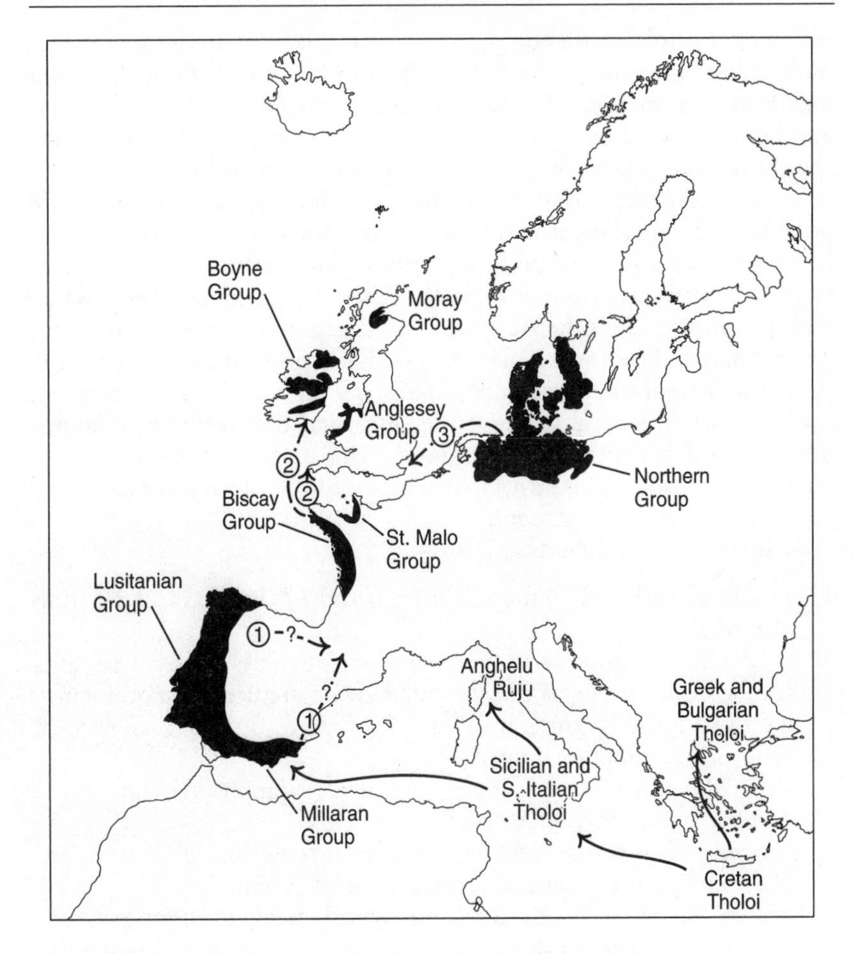

Figure 2.5 Glyn Daniel's (1941) view of megalith origins.

reference to the literate civilizations of the Eastern Mediterranean. There was a clear link here between theory (the importance of typology and the dominant idea of diffusion) and archaeological practice (the need to set up a working chronology, without which we couldn't really say anything at all).

Colin Renfrew questioned this work. He used the tree-ring calibration of radiocarbon dates to show that the megaliths on the Atlantic seaboard were in fact much older than their supposed 'origins' in the Mediterranean. Some scholars responded by simply reversing the arrows so that the 'influence' went in the opposite direction, but Renfrew suggested that instead of trying to prove or disprove diffusionary links, we should instead ask why the monuments were built in the first place. In short, *we should look less at chronology and diffusion and more at the underlying process involved.* Or to put it another way, we should not be content with dating and describing; we should try to explain the phenomenon of the megaliths.

Renfrew suggested that megaliths might be territorial markers. He pointed out that whereas early agricultural communities moving from east to west across Europe had plenty of land, being able to simply expand westwards into new territory when things got cramped, when such peoples reached the Atlantic coast there was nowhere left to go. Additionally, these areas also had a high population level in the preceding Mesolithic period, populations who would also be pressing for territory. In such a situation he suggested that different communities would be competing for land. The megalithic tombs, then, would mark out the land of particular groups, by reference to the ancestors buried within them.

So Renfrew's arguments:

1 explained rather than merely described the existence and distribution of megaliths;
2 used ethnographic analogies from societies assumed to be at a similar level of social development to strengthen his argument – monumental structures in Polynesia, linked to particular descent groups in competition over land;
3 stressed environmental factors and hence adaptation to the environment – the shortage of land;
4 saw megaliths not as one diagnostic trait to define cultures, but as one functional element of a total cultural system;
5 'tested' his model – by drawing hypothetical divisions between megaliths on the Scottish island of Orkney, Renfrew claimed to demonstrate that the megaliths were spaced at the centre of possible territories, each territory being of approximately equal size (figure 2.6).

Conclusion

If the New Archaeology was a revolution, it suffered the same fundamental problems of any revolution. New Archaeology had a double slogan: science and anthropology. But like many revolutionary slogans, discord and disagreement broke out when archaeologists tried to work out in practice what those slogans really meant.

The next two chapters will deal with these questions. Chapter 3 will ask: What do we really mean by the term 'science'? Chapter 4 will

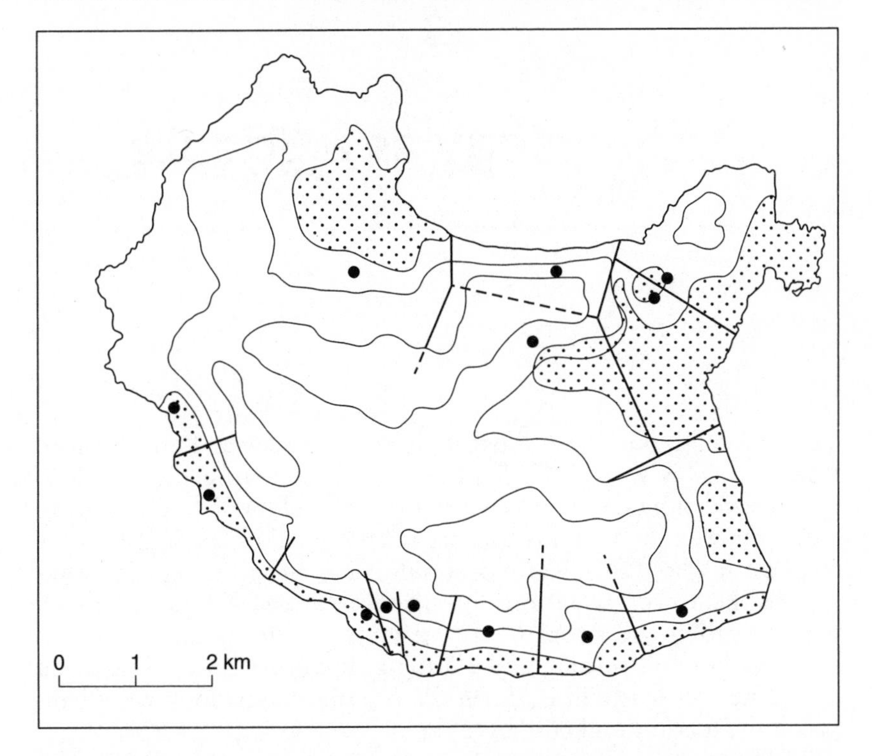

Figure 2.6 Renfrew's megaliths on Rousay, Orkney Islands, showing 'distribution of chambered tombs in relation to modern arable land (stippled), with hypothetical territorial boundaries' (Renfrew 1973).

ask: What do we really mean by the word 'testing'? Chapter 5 will ask: How do societies work, what do we really mean by 'anthropology'?

We shall see in the process that debates within archaeological theory mirror debates in the human sciences such as history, sociology, cultural anthropology, politics and economics very closely. Questions of science, testing and how societies really work are central to the human sciences as a whole.

3

Archaeology as a Science

There are both positive and negative views of science. In the positive view, science is wonderful. It has given us modern medicine, transport, a level of material affluence few of us would wish to give up. We know the way the world is because scientists tell us so. Scientists are so powerful, hold such a grip over our beliefs and sentiments, that we believe them even when our strongest intuitions tell us otherwise, when boarding an aeroplane for example. But in the negative view science can be disturbing and alarming. It can be dangerous, it can offend human sensibilities. Science has moral limits: look what happened to Doctor Frankenstein (figure 3.1).

Both positive and negative views of science are culturally loaded. To clarify, *Science is viewed in a certain way within Western culture.* The sociologist Auguste Comte suggested that science is an institution of authority for us in the same way that the Catholic Church was for the people of medieval Europe.

Modern Western society is partly based on the idea of Science with a capital S. We all use the term 'scientific' as a form of approbation, and that of 'unscientific' as one of abuse. But we are less sure what we actually mean by the term 'Science', which I have dignified here with a capital S to distinguish the image from the reality. What is Science, are there different forms of Science, and which forms (if any) can or should archaeology strive to approximate to?

This was one of the problems that faced the New Archaeology as it matured. As we have seen, 'we must be more scientific' was a good slogan, and concentrated appropriate criticism on the implicit and unsystematic nature of much of the work of a previous generation. But New Archaeology found that deciding what it actually meant by its slogan was more difficult.

One of the ways in which archaeology was certainly becoming more 'scientific' was in its techniques. The period after the Second

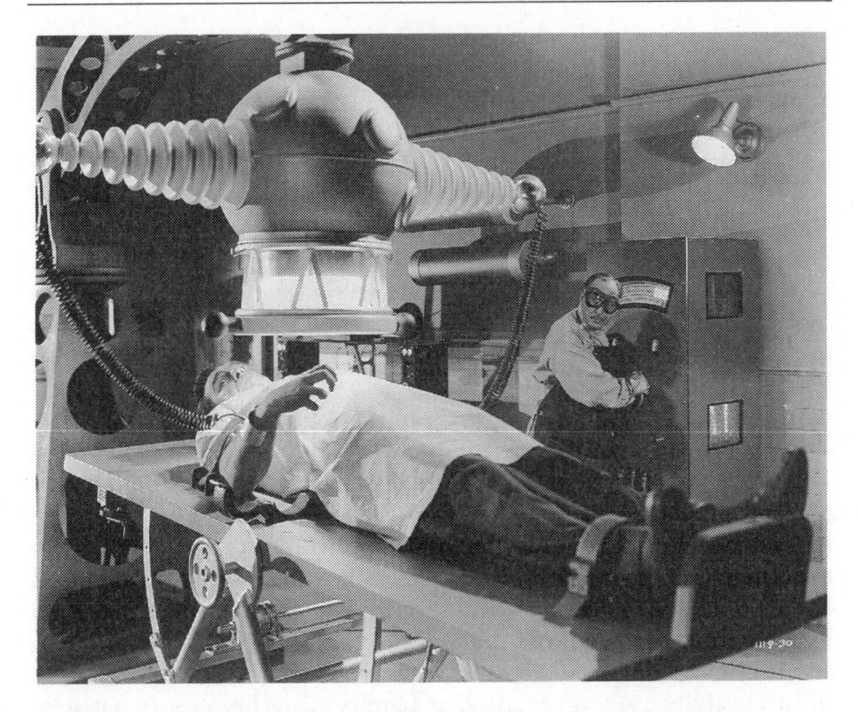

Figure 3.1 Lon Chaney, Jr (left) and Lionel Atwill in *Man Made Monster* (1941, Universal): still from Everson, W. K. 1974 *Classics of the Horror Film* (Secaucus, NJ, The Citadel Press), 152–3.

World War had seen an explosion in the number and range of 'science-based' techniques used in archaeology. These included the use of computers, the study of environmental remains, pollen diagrams, dating techniques such as carbon-14 and dendrochronology, soil geomorphology, paleopathology, and so on. Though I did not discuss these at any length in the last chapter, for many people, such as David Clarke, this development and growth in use of scientific techniques was a central part of the New Archaeology.

This development of scientific techniques led to a problem of technical specialization. An archaeologist in 1945 had to have an understanding of some statistics, and the principles of geology; by 1980 she or he had to know how to use a pollen diagram, how to manipulate statistical packages on computers, and at the very least how to understand and use the findings of a range of other very complex and specialized techniques.

It also led to changes in the pattern of funding of academic archaeology. In the USA, archaeology was increasingly funded under the aegis of the National Science Foundation. In Britain as in much of Europe, funding remained predominantly 'humanistic'. Increasing amounts of money for scientific techniques were made available, however, at first through the Science-Based Archaeology Committee, and later through the Natural Environment Research Council.

In this sense the general atmosphere of the practice of archaeology was becoming more 'scientific'. Where archaeologists used to work in dusty backrooms full of old junk, their offices were often now part of suites of laboratories (often taken over second-hand from other, more 'respectable' physicists, biologists or chemists who had moved into newer, smarter accommodation). In many universities, particularly in North America, smart white labcoats succeeded frayed tweed jackets with elbow-patches as the uniform of the academic archaeologist.

In its essentials, however, *the use of scientific techniques did not imply the use of 'science' as a distinctive approach to finding out about the past.* David Clarke wrote that the use of scientific techniques 'no more make archaeology into a science than a wooden leg turns a man into a tree' (Clarke, 1978: 465). For the traditional archaeologist Jacquetta Hawkes, archaeology remained essentially a humanistic, not a scientific, pursuit: 'however scientific the methods employed, the final aims are historical' (Hawkes, 1968: 257).

To clarify, we use an increasing battery of techniques to assist in dating, the environment, geophysical techniques, and so on. These techniques have given us more and more data of potential use in the study of the past. But we are still left with the gulf between present and past discussed in chapter 2 and presented in figure 2.1. Our 'science-based' techniques accumulate even more data in the present. If that gulf between present and past remains unbridgeable, then the statements we make about the past remain 'unscientific' however clean our white coats are or how much money we spend on the many machines that go ping! in our laboratories. If, on the other hand, the gulf can be bridged securely, using the methods of the natural sciences as New Archaeology argued, then archaeology really can be called scientific, regardless of whether or not we wear white coats and use lots of expensive equipment.

Definitions of Science

New Archaeology suggested the use of 'science' as the solution to the *problem of inference*, then, discussed in the last chapter. If archaeologists had no reliable means of assessing how valid their arguments really were, it was only natural to look at how natural scientists did it.

The natural sciences of physics, chemistry, biology, after all, appeared to have demonstrable and spectacular success in terms of their ability to accurately describe and explain the world when compared with other forms of thought such as religion or mysticism.

Such an argument was reinforced by the disciplinary success of science. Whatever one's views of science as a theory, there was no disputing its success as a discipline. Scientists were well funded, they had the ear of government.

Positivism

In one sense there is no argument about whether archaeologists should be scientific. If science is about the rational accumulation of knowledge, assessed in rigorous, systematic ways, then we are all scientists. (At least, we would all claim to be scientists, though our opponents always seem to be lacking in rigour, system or method.) Science in this broad sense is often referred to by the German term *Wissenschaft*. Even the most fervent opponent of 'archaeology-as-science' would probably consider themselves scientists in this sense.

There are, however, more narrow definitions of what science is (figure 3.2). One of these definitions is called *positivism*, which is another word with several meanings. Theorists confusingly use the word 'positivism' in different senses in different contexts. Here, I shall isolate two.

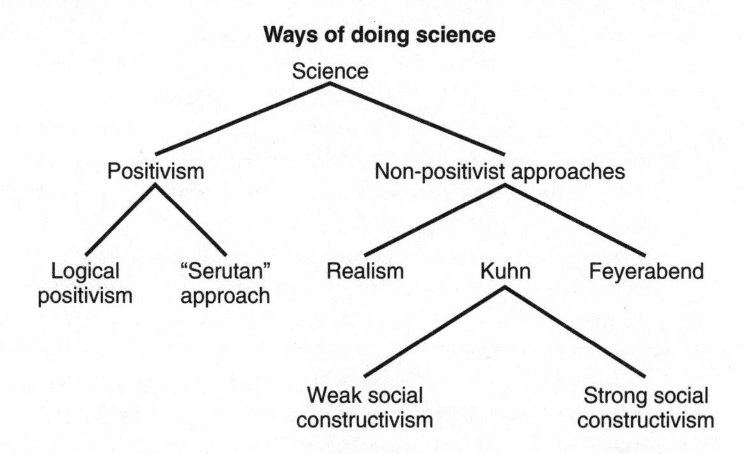

Figure 3.2 A selective diagram showing some schools within the philosophy of science.

1 *A set of beliefs about how we should conduct scientific enquiry*

These beliefs include:

(a) The idea that we should separate theory from method. If we have two or more competing theories to explain a phenomenon, then we have to have some kind of independent and neutral method to judge which theory is the better. It is no good trying to conduct such an independent test if our method is not independent and neutral, but is predicated on one of the theories being true.

(b) The separation of the *context of the discovery of an idea from the context of its evaluation*. It doesn't matter whether the law of gravity came to us sitting under an apple tree or in a book-lined office or in a drug-crazed hallucination; what is important is that the existence of such a law is evaluated scientifically separately from this context. Again, we might get some perfectly good ideas about processes in the prehistoric past from comparative ethnography or from a novel or a dream; what is important, in this view, is that we then test the ideas against the archaeological record to see whether they are valid or not.

Archaeologists will often claim, therefore, that they are using a particular idea or model only for *heuristic* or learning purposes; that is, they find the model of value in throwing up new hypotheses or possible interpretations. They might well insist that such hypotheses or interpretations need then to be formally tested.

(c) *A generalizing explanation is the only valid form*. Here, generality is closely linked to the importance of predictability and testability. Results have to be predictable and repeated for scientific validity. We can test the law of gravity by observing apples dropping from trees again and again and again. The law of gravity is framed as a general proposition that has predictable consequences, all other things being equal.

If an explanation is not generalizing, if it cannot suggest a consistent pattern of results, it will not be predictable and therefore will not be amenable to testing again and again.

(d) *Untestable statements are outside the domain of science*. In less extreme forms of positivism, this does not mean that untestable statements are unimportant. For example, moral and metaphysical questions may be untestable but central to our lives. Whether God exists or whether slavery or child labour are morally wrong are clearly important issues for us to discuss and act upon as human beings; but they are not scientifically testable one way or the other. Science therefore, in this view, has nothing to say about them.

(e) It follows from (d) that *scientific thought should be independent of value judgements* and political action. The threat to use nuclear weapons or investment in countries with repressive regimes may or may not be morally or politically wrong; we all, scientists or non-scientists, make value judgements concerning these matters as human beings living in the world today. But the scientist cannot bring these judgements into his or her work. She or he might comment on them in other spheres, even campaign against nuclear weapons or repressive regimes, but must draw a clear line between (morally neutral) scientific knowledge and moral judgement and action.

Positivism in this sense has tended to be linked with a specific method of testing propositions, called the *Hypothetico-deductive-nomological* model, or HDN for short. The HDN model suggests that one proceeds as a scientist by taking a specific hypothesis and testing it. The deductions one makes from the result of the test should then be used to produce generalizing explanations ('nomothetic' or 'nomological' means generalizing). The need to test specific hypotheses, rather than just dig sites because we might find something interesting, was an issue we saw in the last chapter.

But positivism also, confusingly, has a second set of meanings attached to it:

2 The belief that the social sciences, including archaeology, should try to follow the historical path of development of the natural sciences

This argument was advanced for sociology by Auguste Comte, who was one of the key figures in the development of the human sciences in general. Comte looked to the example of biology. Before the eighteenth century, biology had, in Comte's view, been a speculative and unsystematic pursuit at a time when the scientific techniques and methods of physics and chemistry were already established. By modelling its disciplinary rules on the 'hard sciences' of physics and chemistry, however, biology had freed itself from the shackles of prescientific beliefs and become a rigorous science. Comte suggested that social sciences like sociology could follow a similar route, moving from their present unscientific state to that of a natural science.

New Archaeology can clearly be identified with positivism in both the senses outlined above. New Archaeology tried to generalize; it tried to adopt an HDN model of testing; its whole project was that of Comte's, that of leading archaeology along an analogous path to that of the natural sciences to a mature, rigorous, self-critical discipline. For David Clarke (1973), this was part of archaeology's 'loss of innocence'.

Logical Positivism

This was where confusion started. Some New Archaeologists, searching through the libraries for advice from philosophers on how to do science, came across an extreme version of positivism called *logical-positivism*. For logical-positivists, untestable statements were not only outside the domain of Science; they were utterly valueless. Logical-positivism was in this sense *scientistic*. Scientism is the belief that scientific thought is inherently superior to other modes of thinking. So moral, religious or political judgements were not merely outside the domain of science; they were inferior modes of thought. Explanation did not merely have to be generalizing: it had to be expressed in terms of a tightly worded 'covering law' applicable in all times and places.

Logical-positivism was a dead end. How many covering laws do you know of in archaeology? Watson, Redman and LeBlanc wrote their book *Explanation in Archaeology: An Explicitly Scientific Approach* in 1971. In it, they adopted a logical-positivist framework and spilt much ink discussing precisely what this was. By the second edition of the book in 1984 this position had been considerably 'softened'.

I mention logical-positivism here because it is a cautionary tale. It shows that a little learning in other disciplines can be a dangerous thing in archaeology. Archaeologists read about logical-positivism without understanding that it was very much a minority view within the philosophy of science. We shall see in other chapters how borrowing concepts from other disciplines can be very fruitful, but can also be the source of much confusion.

Examples

For New Archaeology, then, and later for 'processual archaeology', we should adopt a broadly positivist definition of what we do. We should be trying to test hypotheses about the past, and to draw generalizations from those hypotheses.

Such a model might proceed as follows:

1 Hypothesis: early states involve differential access to resources, in other words that élites have greater access to basic goods (a hypothesis suggested maybe by political anthropologists).
2 Test: dig a cemetery from an early state society and chemically analyse the bones.
3 Deduction: the élite ate more meat, so we deduce that they did indeed have greater access to nutrition.
4 Generalization: early states do have such differential access, subject to further testing, other examples from other cultures at the same phase of social development, etc.

Another example might be hunter-gatherers and social complexity:

1 Hypothesis: that hunter-gatherer groups adapt to marginal environments in part through greater economic specialization and social complexity (suggested perhaps by study of modern ethnographies).
2 Test: take a marginal environment such as Upper Palaeolithic Europe in the last Ice Age, and look for different types of site suggesting task differentiation, the presence or absence of trade goods suggesting social alliances, etc.
3 Deduction: that social alliance and logistical hunting strategies are responses to harsher climates.
4 Generalization: there is a positive correlation between increasingly marginal environments and greater social complexity.

Note that in both these examples there is a *tendency to generalize.* General statements tend to emerge from the discussion: for example, that increasing complexity of trading networks tends to be linked to élites and thus to development of social ranking, whether this is in late prehistoric Europe, Mesoamerica or Polynesia. Look at the titles of some typical edited volumes in the processual mould, in which different articles often based on data sets from around the world and different time periods focus on certain processes which are held to be general and cross-cultural: *Ranking, Resource and Exchange... Specialisation, Exchange and Complex Societies... Peer Polity Interaction and Socio-Political Change...*

Such generalizations are what is meant by a 'softer' approach to covering laws than that taken by logical-positivism. Kent Flannery called this the 'Serutan' approach, a phrase that needs explaining to a non-American audience – Serutan is a laxative that promotes 'natural regularities'.

To clarify, New Archaeologists soon found that the development of formal covering laws that were true for human populations in all times and in all places was an impossibility. This did not mean, however, that generalization was not a valid or an unimportant goal – indeed, for the reasons discussed above, for a discipline that saw itself as a science in which propositions were testable, generalization or general theory had to be a central component of archaeology.

Objections to 'Science'

We noted that if part of the appeal of 'Science' comes from its cultural value in modern society, so opposition to 'Science' is similarly culturally loaded. For some, archaeology can never be scientific; rather, it is a noble, aesthetic, romantic pursuit into the essence of humanity and civilization, untainted by the vulgarities of labcoats and test-tubes. In this view, human beings are special because they are unique and unpredictable: they simply can't be generalized about or subsumed in statistics. Further, many of the things that are most 'distinctively human' and therefore most worthy of humanistic study (great art and literature, for example) are precisely those that in this view are least amenable to scientific enquiry. Such a view, though particularly popular among traditional classicists and art historians, is demonstrably untrue (if humans really were unique and unpredictable, opinion polls would produce completely random results and any attempt at social or economic policy by government agencies would start and end in chaos), but is a very popular and emotionally powerful one. We like to think that we are unique, are beyond statistics; but wishing something does not make it true.

A series of more powerful objections to the positivist conception of archaeology-as-science are commonly brought up. I shall deal with them in turn.

1. Science is based on testing and observation of results. The past, however, is dead and gone. We will never be able to directly observe it. *Can we ever test propositions about the past* as we can (it is argued) in science? Possibly not; this is a question I shall address below and more particularly in the next chapter. It is worth noting that archaeology in this respect shares some of the interpretative problems with other sciences that interpret phenomena observed now in terms of processes and events that occurred in the distant past, such as geology and astronomy.
2. Atoms, chemicals and even biological organisms can be seen as insensate things that behave in predictable ways. Human behaviour, however, can be seen as *purposive* or *intentional*. In other

words, human actions can only be explained by reference to the ideas and intentions that humans have. Ideas and intentions do not have any physical existence; they only exist as thoughts, between our ears. They can't be directly observed or 'measured' by the archaeologist. Interpretation in archaeology is therefore, in this view, always *hermeneutic* (about ideas, meanings and symbols) in nature rather than scientific. This argument is one of the central planks of postprocessual archaeology.

Kuhn and Feyerabend

For me, the final and most serious objection to positivism is that it is not a theory but a myth. In other words, positivism is an ideal model of scientific philosophy, but is a bit of a fraud in practice: it gives a false idea of what scientists actually do. To ask archaeology to follow the rules of positivist science is therefore asking them to follow a chimera.

There is much confusion here over whether positivism describes *what scientists actually do*, or whether it is merely an *ideal statement of what they should do*. Some philosophers claim that it is merely an ideal statement.

If positivism is only an ideal account, what do scientists actually get up to in their laboratories? This is a topic that sociologists and ethnographers have recently become interested in. Many have argued that what counts as an 'observation' and 'fact' is decided by social rules, not by purely objective enquiry based on the testing of hypotheses at all. Instead, scientific debates are decided through processes that are thoroughly enmeshed in social relations, not disengaged from society.

Two philosophers of science are often cited in non-positivist accounts of science. The first is Thomas Kuhn. Kuhn argued that the history of science is not just a simple progressively upward success story of hypothesis testing leading to expanded knowledge. Rather, it is one of successive *paradigms*. A paradigm is much deeper than a single theory or proposition: it is a set of beliefs about the way the world works that underlies the whole everyday process of science very deeply, so deeply that it is rarely overtly put into words. During a period of 'normal science' in Kuhn's terms, one paradigm enjoys such undisputed sway over science that its assumptions are rarely even stated explicitly, let alone questioned or debated. Everyone just gets on with scientific labour within the assumptions of the paradigm.

Kuhn suggested that a paradigm will break down eventually. When it does, it is eventually replaced by a new paradigm in a 'paradigm shift'. Such a period of paradigm shift is intense, emotional, revolutionary, rather than cool and detached; a spirit of revolutionary fervour militates against 'rational' argument.

The story of science, then, is one of successive paradigms succeeding one another via revolutionary upheavals rather than of steady accumulation of better and better knowledge of the world around us. Colin Renfrew and others argued in the 1960s and 1970s that the New Archaeology represented a 'paradigm shift' and that we should therefore expect processual archaeology to settle down to a new period of 'normal science' (something that, as we shall see, has arguably not happened). There was an irony here, in that Renfrew was citing with approval a philosopher of science whose work actually tended to undermine the positivist assumptions of New Archaeology.

Kuhn himself repudiated the idea that science didn't progress; his view was that paradigms broke down under the steadily increasing weight of contradictory evidence, and that each paradigm was a successively better and more accurate way of looking at the world. Renfrew and others agree with him in this respect. Other scholars, however, took Kuhn's ideas and extended them in ways that Kuhn himself opposed. They drew different and more wide-ranging morals from his work: in particular, that:

1 What constituted valid 'facts' or 'observations' depended on the prevailing paradigm. In other words, what was relevant evidence, and what was ruled out of court, depended at least in part on one's initial paradigmatic assumptions. *Facts are therefore always theory-dependent.*
2 Social and political forces, not just disinterested scientific enquiry, played a key part in prompting and shaping paradigm shifts.

Kuhn's main influence on the philosophy of science, therefore, has been in a move away from positivist assumptions about the nature of scientific progress and a questioning of the use of a single positivist method in scientific enquiry.

The second key figure is Paul Feyerabend, whose description of the way science works is always popular since it consists of two words: *Anything Goes*. Feyerabend questioned whether science had a single method at all. He suggested that if we looked historically at the development of science, change in scientific beliefs had always been marked by a diversity of methods.

Feyerabend used the example of the astronomer Galileo, who, he argued, moved science forward by breaking all the rules, using political rhetoric and appeals to emotion and working within the social and political context of seventeenth-century Italy: 'Galileo prevails because of his style and his clever techniques of persuasion, because he writes in Italian rather than in Latin, and because he appeals to people who are temperamentally opposed to the old ideas and the standards of learning connected with them' (Feyerabend 1988: 13).

For Feyerabend, the lesson of the history of scientific ideas was that to achieve better results, we should reject the use of a single method. Rather, we should encourage an unlimited diversity of methods and groups within sciences, and to allow and even encourage 'unscientific' strategies such as appeals to emotion. Feyerabend stressed the social and political forces that shape scientific enquiry. He pointed out that the relative merits of scientific ideas are not tested out on a level playing field. He stressed the enormously powerful nature of scientific institutions and argued that they hid their partiality behind their 'objective' façade. Positivism in the form of a single method, in Feyerabend's view, masks 'institutional intimidation' by pretending to be neutral, hinders the development of science, and encourages scientism and the 'cult of the expert'.

Social Constructivism

It is important to stress that Kuhn and Feyerabend saw their work as describing what scientists actually do, rather than as a prescription of what they should do. Recently, such accounts have become more popular, and have coalesced into a school of thought calling itself *social constructivism* or *constructionism*: the belief that scientific knowledge is not purely objective, but is at least partly or entirely socially constructed. ('Weak social constructivism' holds that it is partly socially constructed; 'strong social constructivism' that it is entirely so.)

Examples from the natural sciences include:

1 *Quarks*. Andrew Pickering discussed the 'discovery' of this subatomic particle. He stressed that rather than quarks 'really existing' and waiting to be discovered, a full account of the scientific activity leading to the definition of quarks must look at such things as the decisions of funding bodies, personal and institutional relationships, university and state politics, and so on. Quarks in this view were not 'discovered'; rather, they were actively 'constructed' by the scientists involved. And this construction was a social one; it depended on the interaction of scientists, politicians, funding agencies, universities and the wider public.

2 *Races*. Scientific definitions of different races in physical anthropology are, it can be argued, impositions on a continuum of physical types across the globe. Where, then, do classifications by physical anthropologists into different races come from? It can be argued that scientific classifications of 'types' are not neutral devices for objective classification, but are in fact derived from the end points of trade routes from Europe to and from the 'colonies' in the nineteenth century, that is at precisely that time when the basic classifications of physical anthropology were being formed: Northern Europeans, West Africans, Hong Kong Chinese, American 'Indians' . . .

If social constructivism is a correct analysis of science, then the question 'should archaeology be a science or a humanity?' is rendered meaningless. Constructivism questions the claim of science to be a distinctive form of knowledge in the first place. It therefore denies any basic, *a priori* differences between science and non-science. It suggests that we should look at what human beings do in laboratories in the same way as we look at what they do in other walks of life.

All this is fine, but I find it difficult to understand how this might apply to archaeology. Which version of science do archaeologists currently prefer? Do they come down on one side or the other of the debate?

Different archaeologists advocate different forms of scientific philosophy. For Mike Shanks and Chris Tilley, positivism is dead in archaeology. Shanks and Tilley argue that positivism's stress on separating method from theory is fraudulent, because theory and method can never be separated. Like Feyerabend, they see positivism as a covert, underhand way of controlling what we can and cannot say and do in archaeology. Positivism for them is an archaeology of NO. They write in a spirit of sarcasm:

> It doesn't matter what you say as long as you say it in the right way; as long as you conform to the rules of positivist/empiricist discourse, rational method; as long as what you say is reasonable, not fantasy or extreme, is open to 'testing' against the data, is not overtly political, is not subjective. And if you transgress these laws of discourse, the epistemology . . . police are waiting. (Shanks and Tilley 1992: 23)

For Shanks and Tilley, the way we write about the past is largely about political rules. They want to unmask the political nature of these rules.

Opponents reply: if we abandon positivist criteria, what alternatives are there? If we accept Shanks's and Tilley's views, aren't beliefs in magic or in mystical forces just as 'scientific' as rational debate? Others ask: if we have to abandon positivism, can we nevertheless salvage something from the wreckage – keep hold of some idea of rigour and method? And so debate continues. There is no one answer to your question; you will have to make up your own mind. These issues will come up in later chapters, when we come to discuss 'postprocessual' archaeology.

But if you find the same range of views within archaeology, it's also worth pointing out that the debate over positivism in archaeology is a re-run of a similar debate in virtually every other social science. Behavioural psychologists claim that thoughts are beyond the domain of science, so we should concentrate on people's behaviour. In sociology, Auguste Comte and Emile Durkheim laid out sociological method in a positivistic framework; their aim was to construct a science of society in which predictions and generalizations could be made about social phenomena in the same way as natural phenomena. Anthony Giddens and others have, in opposition to Durkheim and Comte, argued for the impossibility of a neutral, value-free science of society. Similar debates occur within all those disciplines classified as social sciences: history, linguistics, economics, politics. Many feminists claim that Science is not merely political, but that it is moreover a male construct: the rules of 'rational method' mask male bias behind a cloak of objectivity.

Archaeologists can comfort themselves that their epistemological dilemma is at least shared across the domain of the social sciences. Whether this makes it an easier issue to resolve is open to doubt.

4

Testing, Middle-range Theory and Ethnoarchaeology

In this chapter, we return to figure 2.1 and the gap between present and past, 'data' and interpretation, but we take a rather different route from chapter 3 in asking how we bridge this gap. We have all this stuff, this archaeological material – pots, stones, bones. It exists here in the present; how do we get it to tell us about the past?

If any statement about the past is unavoidably made in the present, it is also unavoidably *an analogy*. An analogy is the use of information derived from one context, in this case usually the present, to explain data found in another context, in this case the past.

To clarify: all archaeologists of whatever theoretical stripe make a link between present and past by using analogies. We always make an assumption that things in the past were like – analogous to – the present. Analogy underpins even the most mundane interpretation. Consider, for example, the way we assign function to objects: 'this was a storage vessel'. We argue that it was a storage vessel in the past because its form (large, sturdy, undecorated) would make it seem 'natural' to us to use it in this way in the present. Further, we strengthen our argument through other analogies. The object was found with others of the same type in the room of an ancient palace adjacent to a food preparation area, which we label a 'kitchen' or 'food preparation area' – another analogy with the present. Chemical analysis reveals the object contained food remains – again, by analogy with the present, we infer that the vessel was used to store food.

The more links we can make, the more we argue or assume that the two situations are analogous. This is an assumption that is perhaps pretty obvious but nevertheless absolutely central to the way we write about the past. And like other such 'obvious' points, the issue of analogy needs further critical examination.

Binford and Middle-range Theory

Lewis Binford addressed this issue with great force in the 1970s. While the general arguments covered in the last chapter were raging over the grand theoretical issues of epistemology and positivism, Binford suggested that such debates were in many ways secondary to a more central issue. Binford claimed that archaeology's claim to be a science rested or fell on this issue of analogy. His argument, in brief, ran like this:

Archaeological data – stones, bones, potsherds – form a *static record* in the present. We carefuly record stones, bones, potsherds and their position and arrangement in the ground in the here and now. But we are not interested in the here and now, we are interested in the past: our task is to ask questions of this material in the present, questions about the past. Specifically we are interested in the *dynamics* of past societies, that is the way past cultural systems functioned, developed, were transformed.

Further, since science is a discipline which seeks to generalize for the reasons discussed in the last chapter, we want to develop generalizing theories about past dynamics (figure 4.1, which is a different version of figure 2.1).

All archaeologists offer possible links between statics and dynamics, every time they put forward an interpretation of archaeological evidence. In practice archaeologists do this by making assumptions about the *middle range*, that is, the 'space' between statics and dynamics. For example, we excavate a cemetery consisting of a few graves with lots of grave-goods and many graves with very little (static data); from this we infer a society characterized by wealth or social inequality (past dynamics). We do so by assuming a middle-

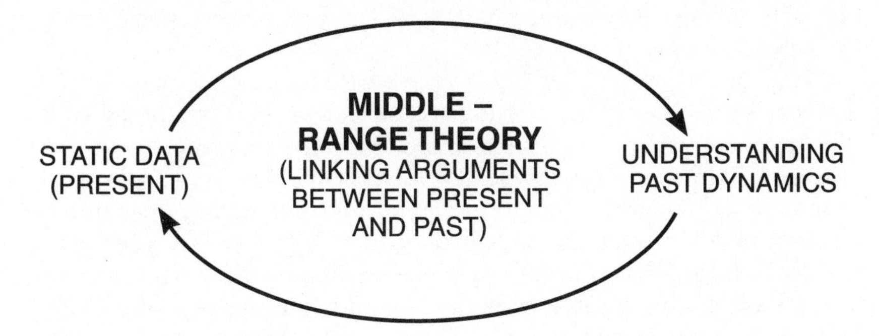

Figure 4.1 Present statics, past dynamics and middle-range theory.

range link between the number and/or value of grave goods and the social/economic status of the person buried. A second example: we excavate a pueblo in the American Southwest and discover that it increases in size and number of rooms through time. We infer population increase from this. Again, we make a middle-range assumption, namely that settlement size, measured in terms of the number of rooms in a settlement, correlates positively with population size.

Right or wrong (and however obvious they may look at first sight, the assumptions in both of the examples above can be debated), these statements can be called *middle-range* assumptions. Such middle-range assumptions guide us from observation of the static archaeological record (burials in excavated cemeteries, data on settlements derived from surveys) to general statements and theories about the past (social structure and ranking, population estimates, possible links between these variables, generalizing propositions about links between rank, population size, and social complexity: figure 4.1).

Such propositions are called middle-range by Binford because they link, in his words, statics to dynamics, and particular observations of the archaeological record to general theories about the past. In much of 'practical' archaeology, Binford argues, many propositions are often not theorized and remain implicit, as they have an apparently common-sensical, banal or trivial nature: 'the larger the settlement, the more people are likely to have lived there'.

Now many middle-range propositions may be banal or trivial, but *any good scientist should make his or her disciplinary assumptions formal and explicit* however obvious or common-sensical they might be. If such assumptions remain implicit, untested, taken-for-granted, then we can never do more than tell untestable stories about the past, because the criteria for deciding that this argument is good and that argument is bad are never made clear, let alone objective and rigorous. Binford therefore suggested that we should consciously develop an explicit 'middle-range theory' (MRT) to link present statics with past dynamics.

Now the only place that we can see a definite, certain, measurable link between a set of activity patterns or dynamics and what they look like archaeologically is in the present. We can never see a Neolithic farmer making a flint arrowhead with the debris flying in all directions, or a Palaeolithic hunter skinning and butchering an animal, leaving bones to kick around in the dust, be gnawed by dogs and finally be buried and enter the archaeological record. But what we can do is look at comparable activities – manufacturing of stone tools, hunting and butchering activities, the gathering, winnowing and sowing of seeds – in the present.

In the present, we can make a detailed and accurate record of how particular activities or systems of activities give rise to particular patterns of archaeological debris. We can look at how modern peasant societies prepare and process their grain, or how modern hunter-gatherers butcher their kills. We can observe and measure precisely what sort and how much debris then enters the archaeological record as a result of these activities, and what then happens to that debris as a result of attrition and decay (figure 4.2). We must therefore look at the *ethnographic present* for the source of an explicit middle-range theory. Binford wrote: 'My aim was to study the relation between

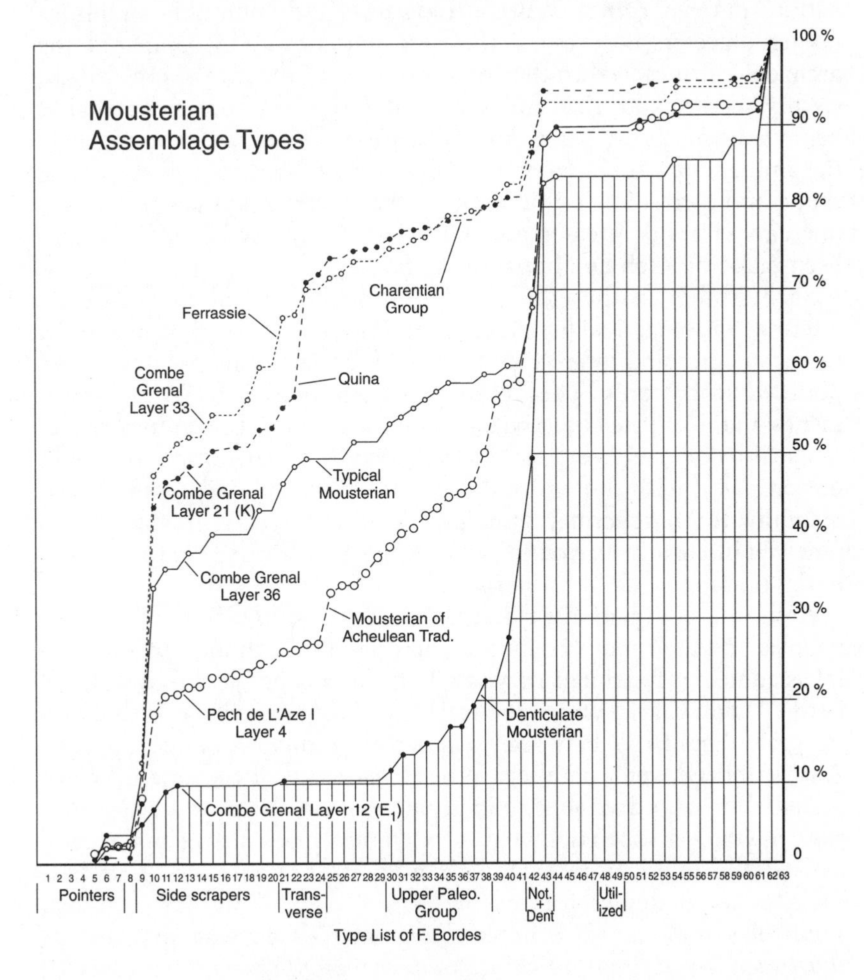

Figure 4.2 Bordes' Mousterian assemblage types, as redrawn by Binford (1983a).

statics and dynamics in a modern setting. If understood in great detail, it would give us a kind of Rosetta Stone: a way of "translating" the static, material stone tools found on an archaeological site into the vibrant life of a group of people who in fact left them there' (Binford 1983a: 24). In other words, just as the Rosetta Stone had the same inscription in three different ancient languages enabling the modern linguist to use the stone to translate from one language to another, so we should be trying to find things that enable us to translate from the observed archaeological record to the past.

Binford called such ethnographic studies *actualistic*; that is, observation and recording by archaeologists of ethnographic situations taking place in the actual, the here and now. He compared the archaeological record to that of a footprint in the forest. One might, seeing a particular size and shape of footprint, conjecture that it belonged to a large, heavy animal without having any clear idea of the animal concerned. Later, one observes a bear making that precise shape and form of a footprint; from that observation in the present, one can say with greater certainty that the previous footprint had been made by such an animal in the past.

Such studies in the ethnographic present thus led to a surge of interest and activity in *experimental archaeology*. For example, there was growing interest in the manufacture and use of flaked and polished stone tools. The debris produced at each stage of experimental manufacture could be compared with the debris in the archaeological record; microscopic traces of wear on prehistoric tools could be compared with those on modern tools that had been used experimentally for butchering, scraping hides and so on. It also led to renewed interest in *ethnoarchaeology*, or the study of material culture in the present by archaeologists.

Archaeologists had always been interested in the study of modern peoples and their material culture, and had used ethnographic material as analogies for things they saw in the archaeological record. Long before David Clarke wrote about the Iron Age lake village of Glastonbury, the huts there had been compared to huts of 'natives' in East Africa. Indeed, such parallels were at the heart of the emergence of archaeology as a discipline. Nineteenth-century ideas of social evolution, in which all societies went through the same fundamental stages, carried the implication that we could use present day 'primitive' societies as analogies for the prehistoric past. Thus, for example, Lubbock's famous 1866 book *Prehistoric Times* was subtitled *as illustrated by ancient remains, and the manners and customs of modern savages*. It contained illustrations of artefacts from both prehistory and from contemporary groups such as the Inuit.

Binford and others, however, suggested that such 'ethnoarchaeological' work had to be done primarily not by ethnographers, but by archaeologists with a specific eye to the analogies between present and past. We could not rely on ethnographers collecting relevant material for us, since their aims and purposes were different – ethnographers were concerned with a range of issues, and were not specifically interested in the link between human activities and archaeological material.

For Binford, the development of 'robust' middle-range theory was far more important than metaphysical debates about the status of archaeology as a science. While colleagues were arguing about the finer points of philosophy and epistemology, then, Binford set off for Alaska to study the Nunamiut 'Eskimo' hunters.

Interpreting the Mousterian

Binford's account of why he did so (related most accessibly in *In Pursuit of the Past*) is instructive. Binford had been interested in the 'Mousterian Question' for some time. The Mousterian period at the junction of the Middle and Upper Palaeolithic could be found in different contexts in the Old World, but had been most closely analysed in southern France; it was named after the French cave site of Le Moustier.

The Mousterian was defined and characterized by certain distinctive types of stone tools, which had been classified by the French archaeologist François Bordes. Bordes had then looked at the different proportions of different stone tool types in different layers, and shown that these could be classified into different patterns or assemblages: 'typical Mousterian', 'Charentian', 'Mousterian of Acheulean tradition', 'denticulate Mousterian', and so on (figure 4.2).

How might we interpret this pattern found in the present in terms of past processes? Bordes had assumed that different stone tool assemblages reflected the presence of different cultural groups. That is, he followed the assumptions of other traditional archaeologists in assuming that certain artefact types and assemblages represented distinctive 'cultures'. Others disagreed in how this 'interassemblage variability' might be interpreted. Binford, for example, suggested that different assemblages were not the detritus of different cultures, but should be seen within an adaptive framework – as different 'tool-kits'.

Binford wanted to test his hypothesis. He collected huge numbers of statistics from Mousterian assemblages in France and put them on to a computer. (We see here the stress on grasping variability and on quantitative methods characteristic of New Archaeology.) He expended a huge amount of labour feeding the information in, and found that there were some interesting patterns in the material he had collected. But herein lay the central problem. Binford found that there was nothing he could do with them.

Binford had no secure idea what activities or processes might have created those patterns. Bordes's suggestion that different proportions of tool types were reflective of different cultural groups, Binford's argument that different groups of tools were different 'tool-kits', and reflected different kinds of cultural adaptation, and other Palaeolithic specialists' interpretations might all be appropriate explanations, all of which appeared to be 'satisfactory' explanations of the data, no matter how many statistics the computer churned out.

Using Binford's own terminology, he had lots of information about statics in the present, but lacked the means – the middle-range theory – to translate these into past dynamics. As a result his ideas of what his patterns meant could be contrasted with the ideas of others such as Bordes, without being able to test between the two. The arguments of Binford and Bordes remained just different stories, with no clear way to judge which was the more accurate.

Binford's work with the Nunamiut, then, was animated by a desire to produce middle-range information that would give him a 'handle' on this question. The Nunamiut, as a group who practised hunting of deer in an environment similar to that which pertained in southern France during the Mousterian period, offered a chance to attack the question of what these patterns might mean. Observation of the Nunamiut could answer the question: 'what kinds of hunter-gatherer activities give rise to what kinds of archaeological assemblages?'

Before we can consider whether Binford's Nunamiut work gave him this secure handle, we must consider its underlying theory a little more.

Uniformitarian Assumptions

Binford lays down two conditions that middle-range theory must satisfy. Middle-range theory must be:

1 Formally *independent from* our development of *general theory*. Remember that science is about testing things, and the importance of keeping method separate from theory. How can we test between two general theories if our middle-range theory is based

on one of them? This would give rise to the danger of a circular argument.

2 Based on a *uniformitarian assumption*. In other words, we have to assume that conditions in the past were like those in the present. If conditions in the past varied, all bets are off; anything could have happened; actualistic studies in the present offer no secure guide to what might have happened in the past.

Consider this assumption for a moment. We can assume that physical properties and processes (gravity, the structure of molecules, geological processes such as soil formation and sedimentation) were the same in the present as in the past. Indeed, it was this assumption that was central to the development of modern geology, and hence stratigraphy in archaeology, in the nineteenth century. The geologist Lyell had argued against ascribing geological features such as layers of sedimentary rock to catastrophes and cataclysmic events such as the biblical Flood, events that had no parallel in the present. Instead, we had to assume that features such as layers of sedimented rock were created by processes observable in the present (such as marine sedimentation). Of course, a few physical processes and conditions are demonstrably not uniform – the proportion of carbon-14 in the atmosphere has varied over the millennia, for example.

Physical processes may have largely been the same in the past, but human behaviour is much more diverse. Uniformitarian assumptions about human behaviour are much more difficult to make. The law of gravity applies regardless of time and place, but different human cultures do things in very different ways. This difficulty is particularly apparent for the Lower and Middle Palaeolithic periods where we are dealing with extinct hominid species that are not *Homo sapiens sapiens*. We can debate whether 'human nature' or 'basic human needs' are constant for other periods, but at these early times we are dealing with hominid species that are not our own. We cannot therefore assume that practices we might suppose common to all human groups were even present at that time. Binford himself has made the point that practices such as 'home-base behaviour' (regular return to a 'home' such as a transitory camp) may be 'natural' or assumed for modern humans, but cannot be assumed for the hominids of the Lower Palaeolithic.

Somewhere in the middle, between the physical and human worlds, are assumptions about the behaviour of animals and plants, or ecology. Plant and animal ecology is not quite as 'hard' and invariate as the laws of physics and chemistry, but not as 'soft' and variable as cultural behaviour. For example, modern sheep will herd when threatened by a predator, whereas other species will scatter; in so far as this behaviour has a genetic basis, this has obvious implications for which species were easier to domesticate in the Neolithic.

It follows that the development of middle-range theory may be relatively plausible for areas of the archaeological record that are governed by or dependent on physical or biological processes, but less so in other areas. Let's consider some examples:

1 The preparation of grain for human consumption can only be performed in certain ways: harvesting can only take place during certain times of the year, the wheat must be separated from the chaff, the grain must be dried, and so on. The different processes involved in the harvesting and processing of grain give rise to certain recognizable by-products like chaff or charred remains. The processing of crops can readily be explored through ethnoarchaeology and experimental archaeology (figure 4.3).
2 Ageing of animals. We can assume that measures of animal age such as tooth eruption sequences did not vary in the past, and further assume that mating and breeding patterns took place in the same seasonal rhythm. It is therefore possible to take a collection of bones and determine not only age at death, but at what time in the year animals were being killed. This in turn might lead to secure inferences about whether animals were being bred for meat or dairy products, and so on.
3 As a more marginal example to explore the limits of the uniformitarian assumption, we can differentiate between 'kill sites' and 'residential sites' on the basis of the bones found at each site. We can safely make the uniformitarian assumption that the ratio of meat to bone remains constant for an animal's body part, and therefore reason that hunters will carry back the meat-bearing parts of the animal while leaving behind less 'meaty' parts of the animal. Whether a site is a kill site or a home base will therefore be reflected in the different kinds of bone left on site, and much ethnoarchaeological research has gone into establishing just how this might work.

   (But this might not work because of 'cultural' factors. A group might have cultural taboos against a part of an animal, or conversely a part might be prized for its 'ritual' properties. A high cultural value placed on part of an animal that did not correspond to its calorific or protein value might confuse these signatures. We shall explore this problem further below.)

Many of these studies can be grouped under the heading of *taphonomy*. Taphonomy is the study of how the archaeological record is

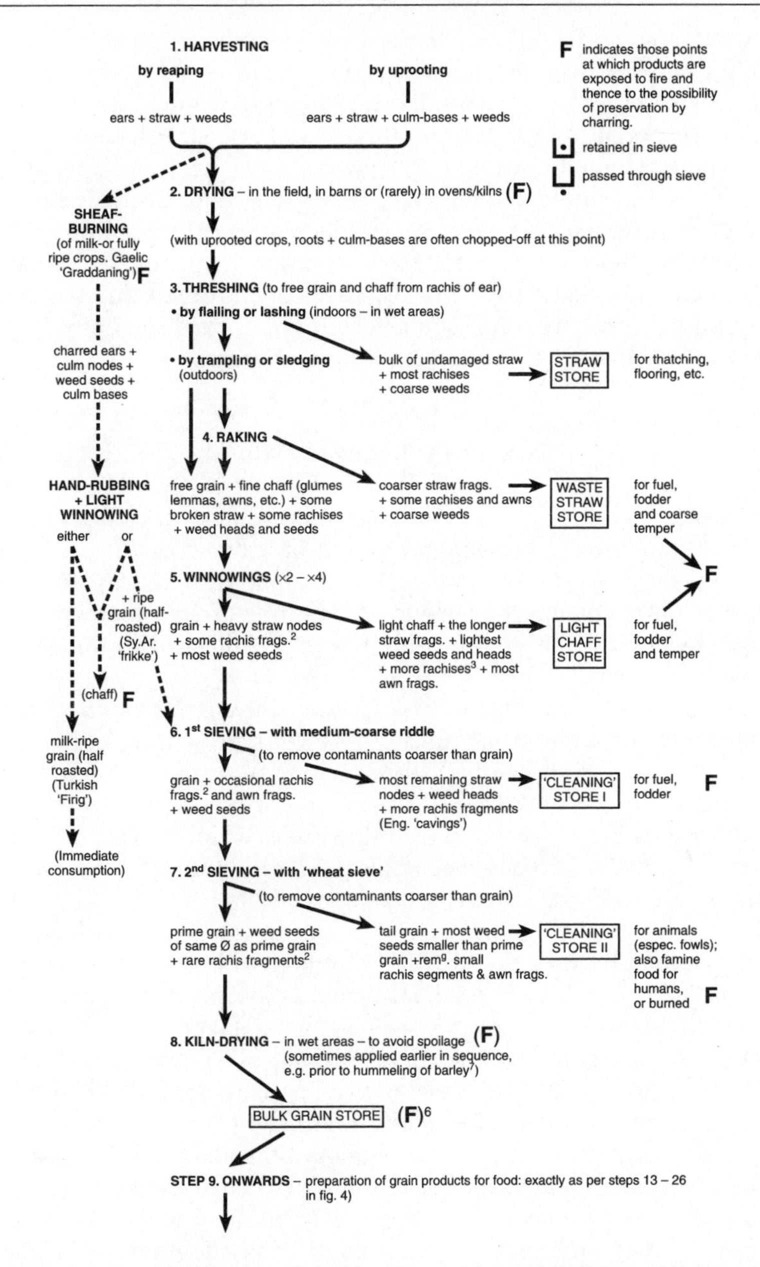

Figure 4.3 Part of Hillman's (1984) ethnoarchaeological model of grain processing, derived from ethnographic research in Turkey, with F indicating those points at which products are exposed to fire and therefore preservation by charring. After Hillman (1984: figure 2).

created from 'cultural' and 'natural' behaviour. It stresses how we cannot make easy connections between what we find in the archaeological record and past activities, and is most strongly developed in areas like botanical and faunal remains and animal behaviour.

To take one small example: the gnawing of bones by dogs. Sebastian Payne has shown how gnawed bones will more easily decay than complete bones. Sites, therefore, on which dogs are present may have many fewer bones, and perhaps different sorts of bones, than sites where no dogs are present. The negative conclusion of this is that we may misinterpret the very similar economy of sites whose only real difference is that dogs are present at one of them.

Case Study: Bones at Olduvai

To be successful, then, middle-range theory must not only develop propositions linking present statics and past dynamics. It must then take those propositions and use them in a formal way to judge between different interpretations of the same archaeological assemblage. Let us look at a case study to see whether such a judgement actually happens.

In the last chapter of his book *Bones: Ancient Men and Modern Myths*, Binford claims that 'my analysis will represent the application of a methodology developed from control information obtained in actualistic studies' (1981b: 253). In other words, he will use his ethnoarchaeological work to help determine which process gave rise to which pattern in the archaeological record. Does it?

Binford develops a series of propositions from his Nunamiut material, thereby predicting the static results of certain dynamics. For example, he proposes that if tool-using hominids were living in base camps, hunting and killing animals and transporting some parts of the kill, then one would expect a home-base assemblage similar to that of modern hunter-gatherer residences. Among other things, one would expect the hominids to be bringing back parts of the animal with lots of meat, and leaving behind parts with little meat. If, on the other hand, the hominids are only scavenging, other hunting animals will have taken off the high meat-bearing parts, leaving only low-utility parts for the hominids to pick over, resulting in an inverse situation.

Binford then looks at different sites, dividing them into sites where the animal caracasses have also been scavenged by other animals and sites where this has not happened ('ravaged' and 'non-ravaged'). He treats unravaged sites in detail, arguing against the association of hominids with the animal remains. He concludes that there are some less noticed assemblages 'consistent with the removal of essentially marrow-yielding bones from the already ravaged kills of other predator-scavengers', an interpretation reinforced by stone tool evidence.

In my view, this is an intersting and logical argument, but not a formal example of the application of middle-range theory. One would expect a series of formal propositions correlating statics with dynamics, then an observation of the statics, and finally a formal analogy with the dynamics. (To pursue Binford's own analogy, first we propose that bears leave certain prints, then see a print, and conclude that it was made by a bear.) But Binford does not do this. Instead, the evidence is explored *contextually*, with the Nunamiut work serving in a looser role than that of formal analogy. For example, the wolf-kill parallel is not even mentioned in the initial set of formal propositions. So Binford's use of ethnoarchaeological data is interesting and even rigorous, but not a formal use of middle-range theory if we adopt the strict criteria that Binford himself laid down.

We might extend these observations to the Mousterian case study outlined above. It might be expected after Binford's work that secure inferences could be drawn about how the Mousterian might be interpreted. But in fact the debate has simply gone on; in so far as it has been resolved, Paul Mellars's suggestion that different stone tool assemblages reflect different time periods currently carries the day. The conclusion we can draw from this is that while middle-range research can help us think about the archaeological record in new and interesting ways, it is difficult to see it working in practice to formally judge between alternative hypotheses. What other reasons are there to be sceptical about the value of middle-range theory?

Middle-range Theory: Problems

In my view, Binford is quite accurate in suggesting that archaeology stands or falls as a 'science' as conceived in the last chapter on the successful development of middle-range theory. If we can reliably relate present statics to past dynamics through the use of middle-range propositions, then we really can isolate archaeological reasoning from its social and political context and stop just telling stories about the past. If we cannot do so, then the aim of developing archaeology as a neutral science looks doomed.

Two basic problems can be raised with respect to the debate over analogy and middle-range theory:

(1) An analogy, whether based on the rubric of middle-range theory or not, doesn't prove or test anything. We can never know whether the uniformitarian asumption discussed above is in fact correct. If I interpret an excavated feature as a storage pit, and show that the feature shares five, ten, fifteen characteristics in common with ethnographically 'known' storage pits, there is still a possibility that the feature could be interpreted in some other way.

This criticism gets stronger the more sceptical one is about general theories of cultural evolution. If human cultures really do all go through the same stages, and cultures at each stage of cultural evolution are basically similar to one another, it follows that features from excavated, prehistoric contexts will probably be very like those known from ethnography. A uniformitarian assumption based on cultural similarity will therefore be very strong. To put it another way, if Inuit Eskimos really are just like all hunter-gatherer groups, then the use of their material culture and patterns of activity as an analogy for past groups is very plausible.

If on the other hand one believes that all cultures are historically unique, and cannot be compared one with another or lumped into evolutionary stages, then there is no reason to accept that this feature was a storage pit merely because it looks like one from another culture two thousand years later, three thousand miles away and from a completely different cultural context. Perhaps we should treat the Inuit as unique, and if so, be very cautious about arguing that any patterns derived from their means of living can be used in any way as a template for any other hunter-gatherer group past or present. We might certainly point to the fact that groups such as the !Kung San are not 'pristine' hunting and gathering groups, but have complex histories of their own. Here is a case where it can be argued that middle-range assumptions are not in fact independent of general theory; on this argument, they are inextricably linked to general theories, in this case views of social evolution.

Advocates of middle-range theory would reply, following from the last chapter, that it does not matter where ideas come from – what matters is how they are tested. Of course we shall never be absolutely sure that this feature was a storage pit, but we can evaluate its plausibility against alternative hypotheses. In his later work, Binford suggested that we don't absolutely test a proposition one way or the other, but we can focus on where the archaeological record is ambiguous.

An analogy can be strengthened if some form of cultural continuity can be demonstrated between two groups. It has been argued for example that the modern Hopi tribe of the southwestern United States are the cultural descendants of what archaeologists have called 'Anasazi' populations. Now on Anasazi sites we find semi-subterranean circular chambers, very similar to the ones found on modern Hopi pueblos. It is, therefore, plausible to refer to modern Hopi rituals in their own kivas. Again, such a link does not conclusively 'prove' anything, but it does derive interpretative strength from such a link because continuity in cultural ideas and practices is probable.

An important element of traditional archaeology in North America was the *direct historical method*, where one started by delineating groups of Native Americans in the present and then tried to trace their cultural antecedents to effectively prehistoric groups. Such a method has no direct parallel in European archaeology, though Christopher Hawkes once suggested we should write prehistory backwards, working from 'known' historical groups back to the Iron and Bronze Ages. Such an approach also underlies recent European interest in 'ethnogenesis', or the study of the creation of ethnic identities.

Both Alison Wylie and Ian Hodder have stressed a distinction between *formal* and *relational* analogies, suggesting that the latter are stronger. Formal analogies rest simply on the notion that if some elements of the two situations are similar, others must be also. Obviously such analogies are weak, though they tend to be stronger the more points of similarity that can be domonstrated between the two contexts. Relational analogies rest on a cultural or natural connection between the two contexts, as with the direct historical method, where connections based on cultural continuity can be suggested.

For example, we might interpret pits on African prehistoric sites as grain storage pits, citing a range of ethnographic examples. As it stands, such an analogy is pretty weak, though it might be strengthened with the number and range of parallels we might draw (are the pits of the same size and shape? Do we consider past and present societies to be at the 'same level of social development'? Do the ethnographic examples come from the same kind of environment, settlement type, economy?). An understanding of the relations between different variables would make the analogies still stronger. Do the ethnographic examples come from African societies with direct historical links to the prehistoric culture we are studying? Can we ask *why* grain is stored in this way, citing 'natural' reasons (the most efficient way in this type of climate) or 'cultural' factors?

In practice, of course, formal and relational analogies are two ends of a range of analogical arguments of lesser or greater strength.

(2) The issue of cultural continuity leads on to the second objection. It can be argued that people are influenced by cultural ideas in their

behaviour. These ideas don't just affect obviously 'cultural' things like religious beliefs manifested in burial practice or other 'ritual' practices. They also affect apparently mundane activities such as the organization of household space and attitudes towards rubbish. They therefore affect archaeological deposition, and must be taken into account when considering the formation of the archaeological record.

Take for example Henrietta Moore's ethnoarchaeological study of the Marakwet in East Africa. Moore found that the way Marakwet houses and compounds were laid out related to their ideas of gender – what it meant, culturally, to be a man or to be a woman in Marakwet society. Different areas of domestic compounds were thought of as 'male' and 'female'. This set of cultural ideas affected where individual residences lay and how the compound was laid out.

Again, Ian Hodder looked at the distribution of pig and cattle bones in different settlements of the Nuba. He found lots of pig bones in the compounds of one tribe, but very few in another. Hodder suggested that this was due to different cultural attitudes. In this culture, women were associated with pigs – women were responsible for the pigs' feeding and maintenance. In one area, there was a strong (male) belief that women were polluting: hence, by association, compounds were kept clean of pig bones and other debris. In another area, such pollution beliefs were weak, the people of that area seemed not to care that their compounds were left covered in refuse. Hodder argued that an archaeologist excavating different compounds would need to understand something of Nuba beliefs in order to interpret the faunal remains 'correctly'.

Conclusion

As a result of the above debate, current work in ethnoarchaeology has diverged along two very different paths. These two paths are in many ways mutually contradictory.

Much ethnoarchaeological and experimental work continues on the relationship between statics and dynamics. A particularly strong area is the taphonomy of bones, but other areas include plant remains and site economy in general. Such work tends to concentrate on problems raised by the archaeological record of the Palaeolithic and early farming communities. It tries to focus on very specific archaeological questions.

A general term often used for this work is *behavioural archaeology*, a term originally coined by Michael Schiffer. Behavioural archaeology is the study of how artefacts move from their 'systemic context', that is, their use in actual human behaviour, to their 'archaeological context' in which they are excavated. Schiffer drew attention to the intervening factors between these two contexts: for example, 'depositional processes', 'reclamation processes', 'disturbance processes' and 'reuse processes'. The most famous example of behavioural archaeology is the Tucson Garbage Project initiated by Bill Rathje, where the link between behaviour and material debris is examined in the present through study of the garbage the modern people of Tucson throw away. Part of the aim of this project is to generate links between behaviour and the archaeological record that will help us look at such processes in all times and areas.

The project of behavioural archaeology is obviously very similar to that of middle-range theory and taphonomy. Binford himself rejected this term and much of Schiffer's philosophy; but behavioural archaeology, taphonomy and middle-range theory can be considered as closely related bodies of thinking.

On the other hand, work such as Moore's had led to a renaissance of 'material culture studies' in which the symbolic meanings of material culture are explored in the present or relatively recent past. It is often difficult to see any distinction here between archaeology and anthropology – whether, that is, we are looking archaeologically at material culture in its social context, or anthropologically at society with a theoretical emphasis on the importance of material things. Indeed, a new journal edited by this 'school' (the *Journal of Material Culture*) aims to bring together archaeologists and anthropologists in this very way.

Which approach offers the more convincing way forward depends very much on the general theory of society that one finds convincing. Can one generalize between societies? Are societies to be seen as systems fundamentally adapted to their environment, or is symbolic meaning important? These are questions we will examine in the next chapter.

5

Culture as a System

In the last two chapters, we have seen how different forms of archaeological theory differ in their approach to questions of epistemology (the nature of knowledge claims) and questions of testing (analogy and middle-range theory). We will now look at how theories differ in the approach to social forms and social change.

How do human societies work? How do human beings relate to one another? How can any human being have the power of command over a hundred, let alone a thousand or a million, others? Were social groups in the past formed through consent and co-operation, or through conflict and power? Is social change a gradual, cumulative process, or does it arise violently through the clash of ideas and groups, through conflict and contradiction? How do the day-to-day actions of ordinary individuals making pots or feeding children relate or add up to long-term, large-scale changes like the origins of agriculture or the rise of modern capitalism? These are some of the core questions within disciplines that deal with humans and the relations between them, not just archaeology but particularly sociology and cultural anthropology.

Archaeologists try to talk about ancient societies and how and why they existed and changed as they did. They are thus immediately locked into the sociological and anthropological questions raised above. Yet again, we cannot choose to avoid theory in this regard. 'Atheoretical' archaeologists, for example, will not address such questions explicitly, but they do use metaphors that imply a particular view of how societies work.

We have already seen one such metaphor in action: the aquatic view of culture, in which ripples of diffusion spread across the cultural lake, cross-cutting one another. Another popular metaphor is that of society as a body. For example, we might talk about societies or social stages reaching 'maturity' or use other bodily metaphors, of social 'sickness' or 'disease'. (Supposedly descriptive and atheoretical accounts of the rise and fall of the Roman Empire are full of such metaphors.) The bodily metaphor often involves organic rhythms of 'youth', 'maturity' and 'decline'. I have just read a work of traditional history that speaks of 'the birthpangs of Protestantism'. Architectural metaphors are also popular: a society 'collapses from within', or a particular archaeological phase or event 'lays the foundations for' certain subsequent changes. Other metaphors still see societies as physical embodiments of a Big Idea, as in: 'the spirit of the Anasazi', 'the ethic of *Romanitas* still held sway', 'the inner essence of the Celtic peoples', or 'the medieval mind'. The title of a popular television series on archaeology, *The Blood of the British*, seemed to combine bodily and spiritual metaphors. To repeat, all these ideas, whether implicit or explicit, and whether right or wrong, are theoretical ideas and need to be examined and criticized as such.

You will recall from chapter 2 that more traditional forms of archaeology have a *normative view of culture* in which a culture is defined as a set of shared ideas. These ideas are imperfectly expressed in material culture; the varied forms of artefacts imperfectly reflect different norms (figure 5.1). In this view, one tends to stress the *particularity* of cultures – why and how they are different from the adjacent group. Culture history can also be seen as an *idealist* view, in that it is ideas and norms that are seen as being important in the definition of cultural identity.

There are two problems with the culture-historical view of how human societies work. The first problem is that it tends to be *mentalist*, that is, it explains why a culture is the way it is primarily by reference to what people are thinking The identification and criticism of mentalist explanation can be found time and again in archaeology and the human sciences generally. The fatal objection to a mentalist explanation is as follows: a culture decorates its houses this way because of its cultural norms. But why does it have these cultural norms? Why not a different set of norms? Again, why is this pottery decorated in this way? Because of the norms inside the potter's head; the potter wanted it to look that way. Why did the chicken cross the road? Because of what was inside its head: it wanted to get to the other side.

Traditional archaeology is full of arguments that can be criticized as being mentalist. They are especially prevalent and pernicious where religion is involved, since here the author can implicitly appeal to an unspecified inner spiritual need that the reader is lulled into assuming is 'natural':

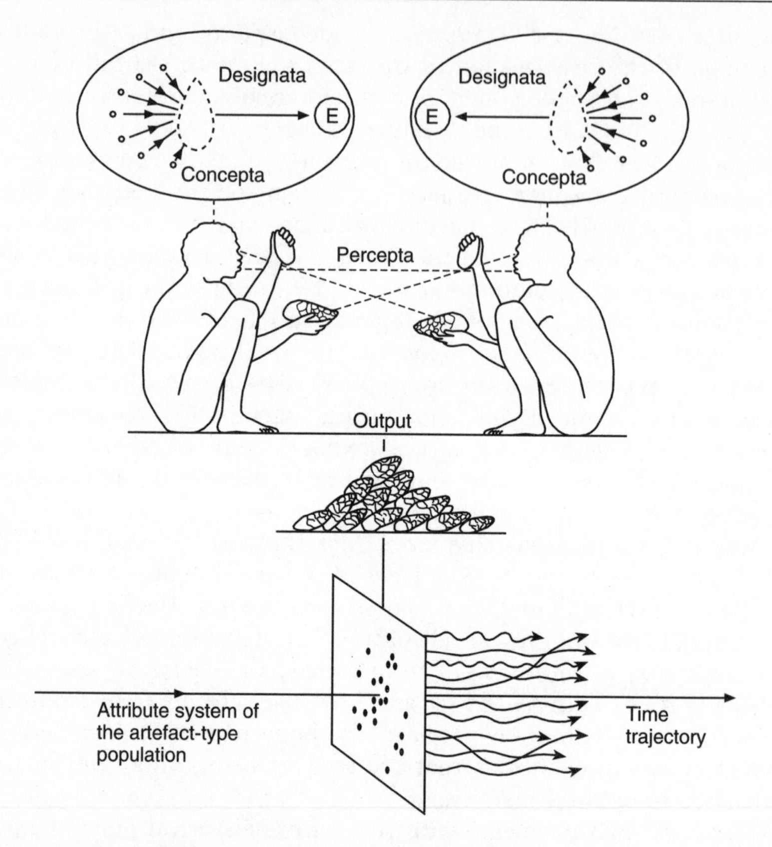

Figure 5.1 David Clarke's (1976) diagram of the normative view of culture. Members of a group produce handaxes. Each has an idea of what a handaxe should look like; by observing others and communication this idea approximates to the group idea or norm. Individual handaxes are imperfect representations of this norm, being flawed, or made with more or less skill.

> No system such as [the minster system], being designed to economise both in buildings and clergy [*why was it designed this way? Because clerics wanted it to be this way?*], could hope to meet the needs of every Christian believer [*why not? What are these needs? Are these needs really self-evident if one is not a fundamentalist Christian?*] And it was inevitable that, alongside these centres, a network of private chapels, or oratories, should very quickly have developed [*why was it inevitable?*]. (Platt 1981: 1; comments mine)

The answers to the questions in italics can only follow if the 'need' for churches is taken as self-evident, in need of no further explanation. Why did people have certain ideas inside their heads that led them to 'need' more churches? Why were the old belief systems, pagan or otherwise, now deemed inadequate? And who deemed them inadequate – why did the religious élite assume that the common people 'needed' these ideas? Were changing 'needs' of this kind anything to do with contemporary socio-economic changes, and if so, what were those changes?

In short, to explain an archaeological feature or historical phenomenon by reference to a untheorized need or intention in someone's head is to explain nothing at all. Mentalist arguments of this kind can be found lurking implicitly within most traditional archaeological and historical syntheses: they can even be built into the core of their assumptions. At the start, not the conclusion, of a major research project the academically prestigious Royal Archaeological Institute defined the castle as 'a fortified residence which might combine administrative and judicial functions but *in which military considerations were paramount*' (cited in Saunders 1977: 2; my italics). How did they know this before they had even started the research?

The second objection raised by New Archaeologists to the normative approach to culture is that culture is just treated as a rag-tag assemblage of ideas. Why do ideas fit together in a certain way? What, if anything, does the zigging versus the zagging on the pottery have to do with varying settlement and house types? Why, in short, do certain things fit together in the way they do?

The New Archaeology's definition of culture was therefore very different. For New Archaeology, culture was a *system* (figure 2.4). A system was defined by David Clarke as 'an intercommunicating network of attributes or entities forming a complex whole' (Clarke 1978: 495). For Flannery and Marcus, systems were characterized by exchanges of matter, energy and information among their components.

This is a very different view of culture. Instead of looking for shared norms, systems thinkers look for different elements or *subsystems* and study the relations between them. Instead of looking 'inside' at what people thought, what was going on inside their heads, at centre stage, they often prefer to look 'outside', at how their cultural system was adapted, to an outside environment.

Systems Thinking: Summary

There are six aspects of systems thinking that it is important to grasp.

(1) Systems are, at least in part, the way they are because they are *adapted to an external environment*, whether that is the surrounding

natural environment or that of neighbouring, competing social systems. We have seen how Lewis Binford defined culture as 'Man's extrasomatic means of adaptation'. Much systems thinking from the 1960s and 1970s thus tended to have close intellectual ties to ideas of adaptation. Many thinkers have tried to move away from this stress on the external environment in recent years, as we shall see.

(2) Systems, systemic thinkers suggest, are more or less *observable*. Obviously you cannot dig a cultural system up directly – you will never see a 'trade' or 'subsistence' subsystem in the archaeological record. You can argue that they are observable, however, in the sense that they depend on systems of energy and information flow rather than on thoughts or norms.

To clarify: you can't see 'norms' inside the mind of the potter; it's difficult to think of a way of 'testing' what was going on inside his or her head, particularly if he or she has been dead for several thousands of years. On the other hand, you can think of possible ways to measure the 'trade' subsystem for a given archaeological group. You might, for example, look at the presence and proportion of traded pottery from excavated contexts. Again, you can't dig up a 'subsistence subsystem', but you can measure and quantify the area of land suitable for arable cultivation round a site, or the meat weight and calorific value represented by the data gleaned from a faunal assemblage. So one can see how an archaeologist might begin to construct and measure a link between, in this example, subsistence economy and trade – and might then 'test' this hypothesized link by reference to the archaeological record.

(3) Such systems can be modelled and are amenable to being simulated on a computer. In this way, they can lead to generalizations about cultural processes. As we saw in chapter 3, New Archaeology moved away from formal covering laws towards much looser generalizations. Systems thinking is especially amenable to this 'softening' of the generalizing approach.

(4) Subsystems are interdependent; subsistence, trade, ritual, social subsystems are related one to another. As a result, change in one part of the system will affect the whole leading to *positive* or *negative feedback*, *homeostasis* or transformation. What do these terms mean?

Many systems thinkers have suggested that cultural systems can be seen in fundamentally similar terms to other kinds of system in the natural world. Natural systems in ecology, for example, tend towards a state of balance. When they are affected by some external change, such as a change in climate or the introduction of a new predator, the whole system will, after a period of fluctuation, tend to reach a new state of overall balance through modifications in the relations between the subsystems.

So, by analogy, an environmental change (say an improvement of the climate) will affect the subsistence subsystem (making farming more productive). This will enable farmers to produce more agricultural surplus, and to use that surplus to engage in more trade in prestige goods, thus changing the trade subsystem. The new prestige goods may also affect the social subsystem; accumulation of such prestige items might bolster the position of élites, increasing the social distance between élites and commoners. The changed social and trade subsystems will then of course react back on subsistence – newly powerful élites might encourage or insist on further agricultural intensification, or initiate large-scale projects like irrigation. With negative feedback, the system reaches a new balance; this tendency towards a new equilibrium is called homeostasis. On the other hand, positive feedback might occur – for example, the new flow of prestige goods produces a transformation in the social system, new forms of ranking that are unstable, which reacts back proportionally on trade and farming as new social groups demand more surplus and trade goods.

(5) Subsystems are linked to one another and explained by *function*. For example, if you want to explain ritual elaboration in a particular period, it might be explained in terms of the *function* of religious systems in giving legitimization to social ranking ('we are of high status because only we have access to the gods').

Again, an intensification in agricultural production (that is, producing more food) might be linked to the need to produce a surplus for prestige purposes – again one subsystem is explained by reference to its function in terms of others.

This is important because it suggests that we can look at the significance of certain practices in the archaeological record without worrying about their symbolic meaning, which in this view is untestable. In this case, we see ritual elaboration, say through the size and form of temples and religious paraphernalia, and interpret it as legitimating an élite. We don't need to worry about what this or that religious practice 'meant', what the form of the temples symbolized.

(6) Archaeologists can examine the links between subsystems in terms of *correlation rather than simple causes*. We might observe, for example, that over time in a particular context intensification of subsistence agriculture goes hand-in-hand with population rise. Arguing about which 'caused' the other is pretty fruitless, being a

chicken-and-egg argument. The systems thinker, however, can note the correlation between the two and build it in within a larger model of systemic change or stability.

Example: Systems around the North Sea

In his book *Dark Age Economics* Richard Hodges developed a systemic interpretation of the rise of towns, trade and social complexity in post-Roman northwest Europe. Again, Hodges's arguments must be seen in context. Hodges was working against a backdrop of traditional archaeological thought that had spent a great deal of time excavating trading sites and analysing documentary evidence. Much ink had been spilt trying to determine the exact date of settlements, very often in an attempt to prove that this or that settlement was 'the first' and that urban life spread outwards from that centre. This work, however, had done almost nothing in *explaining* the re-emergence of towns and trade before AD 850, had treated the evidence in a particularistic manner and in ways that were riddled with mentalist arguments (reference to innate 'rekindling of the spirit of trade' or 'the trading spirit of the Frisian peoples').

Hodges suggested that the whole of the North Sea area should be seen as a system, within which social complexity, the rise of urbanism and the growth of trade were linked in positive feedback loops. He suggested that as with chiefdom societies in general, the position of the chief or king at the apex of society depended on his ability to control the production and circulation of luxury or 'prestige' goods. The more successful the chief was at controlling this flow, the more he could reward his followers with gifts that in turn created reciprocal obligations.

The rise of a limited number of towns in the seventh to ninth century AD could be seen as an attempt to control this production and flow; Hodges drew attention to the planned nature of these settlements, suggesting that planning reflected central control and their royal origin. He also pointed out their location: on estuarine or riverine sites suitable for long-distance trade, away from existing centres of authority.

Note that this explanation *generalizes*. It puts early medieval Europe within a general classification of 'chiefdom societies' and seeks to understand them in that light. Now 'chiefdom societies' can be seen in Polynesia, the Americas, the Bronze Age in the Aegean; that is, in a variety of ethnographic, ethnohistoric and prehistoric situations spanning the globe. In all these areas other scholars have drawn attention to the importance of the flow of prestige goods, the links between prestige and chiefly power, the processes leading to greater social complexity. Citing this literature, Hodges criticized traditional scholars who had emphasized the uniqueness of northwestern Europe, suggesting memorably that we should not consider the underlying processes of cultural change to be any different in this context just because a few Northern European monks took it into their heads to write down what they thought of current events.

Such an evolving social system is more or less *observable* in the archaeological record. We cannot directly see trade or urbanism, but we can develop archaeological indexes of trade through statistical studies of artefacts. We cannot see social ranking directly, but we can develop an index of it in terms of burial practices, the richness or paucity of grave goods.

Systems Thinking: Strengths

It has been argued by some writers that we are all systems thinkers. We all think of societies as functioning units, and as we have seen many 'traditional' writers use the metaphor of bodily systems implicitly. Much systems thinking is implicit within explanations, even if the writer does not use the appropriate jargon or is even consciously aware of the intellectual background to what he or she is doing.

There are three strengths of systems thinking which are worth outlining:

(1) It avoids the problems of mentalism discussed above. Hodges tries to explain the rise of towns and trade; he does not take the easy and fallacious route of ascribing it in mentalistic fashion to some indefinable 'Viking spirit'; it is linked to other processes within a total picture of an evolving social system.

(2) It avoids *monocausal explanations*, in other words explanations that try to single out one or other cause for an event. In so doing systems thinking can combine the strengths of such explanations and avoid their weaknesses.

One example is the study of the collapse of civilizations. In studying why civilizations suddenly collapse, much fruitless academic argument has been spent in arguing over single, specific causes. The eruption of Santorini and its relation to the collapse of the Minoan civilization, the 'Classic Maya collapse', or the attribution of collapses to sudden invasions of vast hordes of barbarian peoples, are classic examples (see below).

Systems thinking directs our attention away from sudden invasions and disasters towards an understanding of *why* certain stresses or events were or were not critical (figure 5.2). For example:

(a) The fall of the Roman Empire. Traditional accounts are often consumed in endless detail on this or that barbarian invasion. A systems thinker asks: Why was this barbarian invasion a fatal blow rather than easily repulsed? What internal systemic factors lessened the ability of the Empire to respond? Conversely, what systemic factors underlay the barbarian invasions?
(b) The collapse of the Minoan civilization. In the past, many looked to specific causes, such as chance invasions of barbarians or the eruption of the volcano of Santorini. In all these cases, practical arguments raged back and forth – for example, Spyridon Marinatos's suggestion that the Santorini eruption was primarily responsible was brought into question by new dating evidence. But thinking more broadly, pointing to particular events does not help us understand the underlying process. Why should particular events like invasion or natural disaster lead to irrecoverable decline rather than rapid regeneration?
(c) The 'Classic Maya collapse'. Many of the great monuments of the Maya civilization of Central America were suddenly abandoned, apparently almost overnight. Again, traditional explanations looked to specific historical causes such as earthquake, invasion or natural catastrophe to explain this 'collapse'. Systemic thinkers redirected attention to what they saw as more fundamental underlying factors – the relationship between population rise and agricultural productivity, for example. By modelling the Maya civilization as a system, they draw attention to relationships between changing 'variables'. Analysis of these variables made an apparently sudden collapse explicable as the culmination of certain long-term processes.

(3) Systems theory is a potential source of *optimism* for archaeology. If all aspects of a culture are functionally linked one to another, we need not be restricted in what we talk about as archaeologists. Indeed, there is no reason why we cannot infer the rest of society from the meagre archaeological record. This is what I call the fairycake argument (with apologies to Douglas Adams): if all parts of the universe are linked to one another, the argument goes, we can infer the entirety of the universe from one small piece of fairycake. Binford used this argument when he wrote: 'granted we cannot excavate a kinship terminology or a philosophy, but we can and do excavate the material items which functioned together with these. . . . The formal

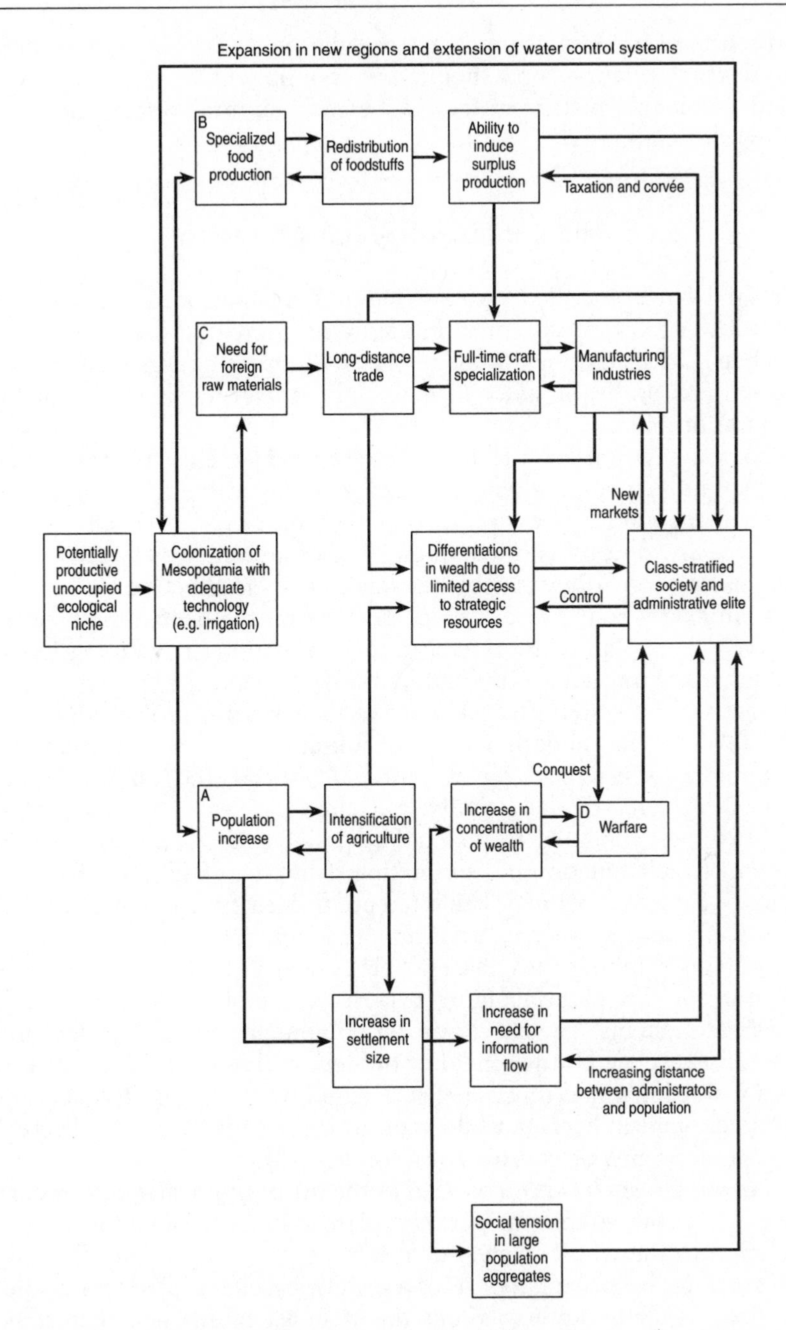

Figure 5.2 A systems model of the 'rise of civilization' in Mesopotamia. After Redman (1978: figure 7.7).

structure of artefact assemblages together with the between-element contextual relationships should and do present a systematic and understandable picture of the *total extinct* cultural system' (Binford 1964; his emphasis).

The Context of Systems Thinking

So far I have described systems thinking in isolation. However, it is important to place systems thinking in its context. As with so many archaeological theories, a lot of the intellectual background to systems thinking lies in associated disciplines sharing the same fundamental problems.

As we saw earlier, the links between subsystems are *functional* ones. The system as a whole is seen as comparable to an organism such as the human body or any other complex organism – there is an *organic analogy*, to use a common piece of jargon. We explain different parts of an organism by reference to their function within the system as a whole. For example, the form of the heart – a powerful pump – is explained by reference to its function in pumping blood which takes oxygen around the body. We explain subsystems within modern social systems by reference to their functions. For example, the form of the modern state – an administrative bureaucracy – is explained by reference to its economic, social and political function(s). Systems thinkers similarly explain past subsystems by reference to their function; for example, religious subsystems are seen in terms of their function in legitimating social hierarchies, or the presence of élites is explained with reference to their function in managing complex activities such as irrigation agriculture.

Systems thinking thus shares a great deal in common with other schools of thought, including cybernetics, ecological systems and General Systems Theory. I want to highlight one particular link here, however: with the school of thought within the human sciences as a whole known as functionalism. I don't want to give a full account of functionalism here, but I do want to make some of the intellectual links and origins of systems thinking clear.

Functionalism has been defined as the proposition that cultures are like organisms, so that the part is explained in terms of its function in relation to the whole. Cohen defines it as 'the notion that all of the institutions, beliefs and morals of a society are interrelated as a whole, so that the method of explaining the existence of any one item in the whole is to discover the law which prescribes how this system coexists with all the others' (Cohen 1968: 34).

Functionalism developed in the later nineteenth century with the rise of the human sciences as a whole. Different versions were expounded by Auguste Comte, Herbert Spencer, Emile Durkheim, Radcliffe-Brown and Malinowski (note that many of these thinkers were also associated with early attempts to fashion anthropology and sociology in a positivist mould).

We can understand functionalism better if we think about its intellectual and social context. British social anthropology in particular went hand-in-hand with the training of administrators for the Empire. Thus the one very powerful implication of functional thought was that the apparently irrational, weird and wonderful customs of native peoples, such as belief in magic and witchcraft or elaborate rules surrounding exchange systems, were functionally connected to the workings of the group as a whole. Would-be administrators were taught to think about the customs of their subjects in context and not to apply a simplistic moral or evolutionary scale. Customs should not therefore be thought of as simply irrational, relics from a previous stage of social evolution, or as the perversions of savage life.

If customs were not irrational, neither could they be satisfactorily explained as relics of previous societies. Evolutionists had often suggested that certain customs were 'hangovers' from previous stages of the evolution of a society. Functional thinking was *synchronic* – that is, it examined how different elements of society fitted together at one particular slice of time. In other words, it said 'Never mind about historical origins. How does this or that institution or custom function here and now, at this particular moment in time?'

Systems Thinking: Drawbacks

Systems thinking therefore appears to be a very strong way of thinking about cultures in the past. It avoids many problems of traditional approaches, provides convincing explanations, and allows us to generalize.

Yet in many theoretical circles, particularly in Britain, the terms 'systems thinking' and 'functionalism' have become virtually dirty words. When I first put together an outline for this book, one colleague said that systems thinking was 'intellectually moribund' and that I need not even bother discussing it. Why?

First, there is a series of well-rehearsed criticisms of functionalism. These criticisms, some argue, can equally be applied to systems theory. They include the following:

(1) There is, it is argued, a fatal flaw at the heart of functional explanation. If we explain something by reference to its function in keeping a total system going, this does not explain where it came from historically. An over-simplified example: we explain the rise of élites in state societies by reference to their managerial functions in co-ordinating agricultural activities. But where did these élites come from?

One possible answer is that it was a conscious decision; but it is difficult to see a cultural group sitting down round the hearth and saying 'OK, we're having problems co-ordinating large-scale irrigation agriculture, so we'll invent an élite and believe in them as gods. They will then function in the following ways to keep our system in equilibrium . . .'.

A more plausible answer is to link functional with adaptive explanations; that is, to say that societies that happen to have developed such élites, for example through historical accident, are better adapted and compete more effectively within their environments. In the long run therefore they tend to be 'selected for' in the Darwinian sense, and in the long run they are the ones we will find in the archaeological record. *Systemic arguments are therefore often closely related to adaptive explanations*, in terms of the way they are expressed and the sort of archaeologists who put them forward.

(2) Systemic arguments depend on functional linkages. But these links are always open to doubt in specific terms. There may be alternative strategies available to individuals and cultures that are not considered.

For example, one of the classic systemic linkages is that made between increasingly marginal environments and agricultural intensification. As an environment becomes more difficult to live in, it is argued, human groups will elaborate and intensify their efforts to cultivate food. At Chaco Canyon in northwestern New Mexico, archaeologists have found that in the period AD 700–800 there is an upsurge in the building of ceremonial monuments, and a transition from pithouses to stone pueblos. This activity is taken as indicative of the development of a higher level of social complexity. This level of complexity often has been understood in systemic terms. The environmental record suggests that at this time the climate at Chaco was getting drier. A drier climate, it is argued, meant that if agriculture was to be successful crops had to be irrigated rather than rely on rainfall. The large-scale co-ordination of labour needed to run such systems required a managerial élite.

However, alternative strategies were available: why not simply abandon the area? Or adopt population control? Why adopt this form of agriculture rather than that form? Why, specifically, does the management of irrigation agriculture require an élite; can it not be run through egalitarian co-operation between groups?

It is objected, then, that alternatives are always available: that systemic thinking fails to explore why this particular strategy was adopted rather than that particular strategy. Such choices between particular adaptive strategies may depend on the particularity of cultural groups, or on cultural preferences.

(3) Functionalism cannot, it is objected, explain *change* adequately. A functional or systemic model can explain why a system remains stable. However, why do societies become increasingly complex?

For example, Kent Flannery wrote a classic early study of the origins of agriculture in Mexico, explaining the transition from a hunting and gathering way of life as part of a wider systemic change. He treated 'Man and the southern highlands of Mexico . . . as a single complex system, composed of many subsystems, which mutually caused each other'. Culture being adaptive in this view, change was seen in terms of 'gradual change in procurement mechanisms', regulated by seasonality.

The strengths of this argument were (a) it directed attention away from the rather tedious search for the earliest example of agriculture in the form of 'the first corncob'; (b) it thus tried to explain the origins of agriculture merely than describe its diffusion; (c) it directed attention to agriculture as part of a gradual change in culture rather than a sudden invention; and (d) the important role of a changing environment could be stressed.

One weakness, however, was the assumption that 'without external change, [the development of agriculture] might never have occurred' (Flannery 1973a). I would argue, therefore, that systemic models always require an external 'kick' to start them off. Again, this has led to an interest on the part of many archaeologists, particularly those working on the origins of early states, to explore how change and conflict might be 'built in' to systemic models (see below).

(4) The political implications of systems thinking can be seen as objectionable. Suppose for a moment that systems theory were 'true'. What would its lessons be for us today?

(a) That the nature of social stability and transformation is inflexible, composed of long-term processes beyond the consciousness or control of mere individuals, who are only pawns in the game. These long-term processes are very complex and can only be understood with lots of impenetrable jargon (mutual causal deviation amplifying processes). However, such processes are scientifically understandable. The only people, then, who really understand how society works and are therefore in a position to make judgements on how we should organize it are scientists, 'men in white coats'. Ordinary people, it is further implied, are not qualified to make critical comments on the judgements of 'experts' who should therefore be left in sole charge of social management.

(b) That history is about harmony rather than conflict. If each subsystem is functionally related to the next, it is difficult to see where conflict between groups might come from. In addition, if the moral of functionalism is that all parts of the system are adapted to one another and that there is a 'natural' tendency towards balance or homeostasis, then by definition we live in a well-adapted system. Rather than think in terms of class conflicts and contradictions between groups, systems theory encourages us to treat social discord as something that can be 'managed away' by the white-coated experts mentioned above. One person's systemic management problem is another's revolution.

This is an over-simplified version of an argument developed by Jürgen Habermas and others within the 'critical theory' school of social philosophy, namely that *systems theory is an ideology of control.* In this view, systems theory is an authoritarian political statement masquerading as neutral science. It must be opposed, in this view, on basically political grounds.

(5) Systems theory is an attempt to understand society from the outside. Regardless of whether one is studying Neolithic Europe or Formative Oaxaca, systemic thinkers still seem to divide up their cultures into the same subsystems – subsistence, trade, social, ritual... Right or wrong, these are general categories imposed by the archaeologist on to particular cultures. And, of course, they are specifically Western, bourgeois categories.

Now it may be that we should be trying to understand culture from the inside. To clarify, if we want to understand why cultures changed in the past in may be necessary to understand something of 'their' worldview, 'their' ideas of how the world works. Now their ideas may not have divided the world up into such neat little blocks, or they may have divided the world up into different blocks.

This distinction between 'outside' and 'inside' views of a culture is one that is made time and time again in different areas of the social sciences. The anthropologist Marvin Harris describes such a distinction in terms of *emic* (inside) and *etic* (outside); sociologists talk of a distinction between *behaviour* (what can be objectively observed) and *action* (what the behaviour means to the participants). The argument that it is necessary to look at 'their' view of 'their' world is one that is central to 'cognitive' and 'postprocessual' views of archaeology.

Systems Thinking Modified

The force of the criticisms raised above was felt greatly by most scholars, and has meant that traditional forms of functionalism and systems theory held little popularity in archaeology after the late 1970s. Most current versions of systems thinking are heavily modified, and have developed partly in response to some of the criticisms above.

In practice, two responses can be taken:

1 Some archaeologists reject all systemic models and have tried to adopt entirely different ways of thinking about societies (most obviously within 'postprocessual' approaches; see chapter 7). In this attempt they have followed the lead of sociologists, most notably Anthony Giddens. They have managed to distance themselves from thinking in terms of systems with varying success.

2 Others have tried to separate modified, looser versions of systems thinking from much of the intellectual and historical 'baggage' of functionalism. Several propositions are involved here:
(a) We can separate functional explanation from the sins of functionalism as described above.
(b) Systemic models can incorporate conflict and contradiction within their parameters.
(c) If (b) holds, then change from *within* the system can be modelled systemically. We don't need to rely on an external 'kick' as Flannery did in his early work; we might, for example, look for class or gender inequality within a system, and view that as a source of tension that leads to change within the system. Systems models can therefore, on this argument, model change, and are correspondingly less dependent on ideas of adaptation to an external environment to explain where change comes from.
(d) We can look at cognitive factors ('their' view of 'their' world) within a systemic model, either by modelling 'cognition' as a separate subsystem or by some other means. Watson, LeBlanc and Redman for example, after having spent most of their book *Archaeological Explanation* examining systemic and 'scientific'

approaches, discuss 'ideational archaeology' with the conclusion that 'cognitive archaeologists may provide some of the most exciting results of scientific archaeology' (1984: 274). 'Cognitive archaeology' will be further discussed in the next chapter.

As a result, there has been a more recent body of work that has been generalizing and loosely systemic but has involved these considerations. Much of this work has come from North America, and often concentrates its study on early state societies.

(1) Heterarchy, or the examination of competition within systems, a term originally set out by Carole Crumley. Elizabeth Brumfiel expressed this move in systemic thinking well in the title of her review essay: 'Breaking and entering the ecosystem – gender, class and faction steal the show' (1992). In her view, we can still use a broadly systemic model but with many qualifications from earlier versions. In particular, we can look at conflict between different elements within systems, and competition between factions. Such conflict and competition can be modelled within the system, and can lead to social transformation. Heterarchy is an idea that is useful in thinking about how these early states mobilize power through competition. So instead of seeing systems as monolithic, a stress on ideas such as heterarchy and factional competition leads us towards a much more dynamic idea of systemic change – and further, one that is much less dependent on ideas of adaptation.

(2) 'World systems theory' claims to unite elements of systemic and Marxist thought. We shall discuss Marxism in the next chapter, but Marxist models clearly involve many of the factors that early systems thinking in archaeology had been criticized for ignoring: class conflict, contradiction, inequality, exploitation.

World systems theory had its origins in the analysis of the origins of modern capitalism; it is associated with the work of Emmanuel Wallerstein. Wallerstein pointed out that capitalist social formations involved more than the nation-states of Western Europe. Rather, if we wanted to understand how capitalism emerged in the fifteenth, sixteenth and seventeenth centuries, we had to look at the way different societies across the globe were brought together into a single *world system*. Such a system had a *core*, in this case of the nascent capitalist states of early modern Europe, and a *periphery*, the other ends of the developing trade routes with Africa, Asia and the Americas. Core and periphery were related through trading networks that had social implications at each end of the link: thus capitalist development in Europe was transformed through the arrival of increased quantities of gold and of traded commodities, while 'native' societies changed rapidly, often developing new élites and nascent states, partly in response to the influx of European goods. The entire globe, taken as a whole, could be modelled systemically, with stress on the interdependence between core and periphery, so that change in one could be seen to lead to change in the other, often many thousands of miles away. The social systems of both were understood by reference to functional linkages.

Archaeologists have suggested that we can use a world systems model to explain a variety of ancient social networks. In particular, they have looked at the interaction and networks of dependence between core state societies and peripheral pre-state societies in a variety of contexts (Bronze and Iron Age Europe, pre-Hispanic Central America, for example). Santley and Alexander, for example, develop a generalizing typology of units (the 'dendritic political economy', the 'hegemonic empire', the 'territorial empire') and then a set of processes involved in transformation (disenfranchisement, population redistribution, labour organization and power).

(3) Simulation and mathematical modelling: from the late 1970s onwards Renfrew and others argued that systems could be simulated on computers, and that moreover we could build chance, historical contingency and human decision-making into these models. This led in turn to an interest in new models of the natural world being produced by natural scientists. For example, chaos theory looks at how apparently random and small-scale phenomena can trigger much larger patterns. By analogy, many systemic thinkers have explored *stochastic* models (that is, models with elements of chance or random variation built into them) and asked how systems might be set off on different trajectories by *contingent* or chance events.

These strands of thought are very different one from another, but what is certain is that over the last thirty years there has been a 'softening' of systemic thinking. Cultural systems are no longer seen as monolithic structures and contingency and historical accident is allowed for; room has been made for cognition (see next chapter); and heterarchy and conflict have become popular buzz-words.

Have these modifications strengthened systems thinking? Alternatively, have they so changed the way archaeologists think about social change that we should abandon the term 'systems' entirely? It may be that systemic analysis has 'died the death of a thousand qualifications' – that is, that its basic premises have now been so hedged around with exceptions and qualifications that it cannot really be called systemic anymore.

Systems Thinking and the Individual

Stop – you've finished before discussing the most important criticism of systems thinking of all. Human beings don't act like this. They're not just pawns in a system. They are irrational and unpredictable. Systems theory can never work because human actions are random. You can't fit human beings with all their idiosyncrasies and peculiarities into a model.

Ironically, the one criticism of systems or functional thinking that is most popular is also the one that, in my view, is utterly misconceived.

Are human beings unpredictable? Almost certainly not, though we like to think so (figure 5.3). Cupid is supposed to be blind, but the vast majority of us manage by some amazing coincidence to find partners of very similar ethnic and social origins to ourselves.

In any case, unless you are a methodological individualist (see Glossary), you cannot reduce the understanding of long-term social processes to what we do as individuals. This is a classic debate not just within archaeology, but within the human sciences as a whole.

Consider an example from the present: the suicide rate. The reasons why individuals commit suicide are as varied as they are tragic, but the overall rate of suicides within society as a whole rises and falls with other factors (such as the unemployment rate, whether the country is at peace or at war). A social scientist cannot predict individual suicides, but can, given sufficient data on contemporary social trends, predict rises and falls in the suicide rate, more often than not with a great deal of success. Consider also powerful individuals. We may seek to explain events in terms of powerful or charismatic people – emperors or great leaders – but this always begs the question of where their power comes from, what makes their power possible.

If such a view works for the present, it is surely even stronger in prehistory, where we manifestly have to deal with trends and processes that span hundreds and even thousands of years, rhythms of time than are beyond the compass of any individual.

We have an emotional attachment to the idea of 'the individual' that is simply not borne out by the reality of the world around us, and still less is a valid basis for thinking about the past. We can't say in advance whether individuals were or were not important in the past. Other cultures have had different ideas about individuality and the importance of the individual versus the community. We may find these ideas strange, even disturbing, but this is no excuse for taking

Figure 5.3 Gary Larson's view of the individual.

the modern Western 'cult of the individual' as self-evident, or true for all times and all places.

There is a more sophisticated argument within postprocessual archaeology and related strands of thought, namely that we have to understand social *agency* and the individual subject. Pots are made by people, and I believe that the archaeological record is as much about the detritus of individual actions as it is about long-term aggregates or processes. There is also a moral or philosophical argument that 'freedom' is a meaningful term to use in historical analysis, but only in the presence of the absence of freedom, for example in discussions of slavery. But before we can consider such ideas, the Romantic notion of unqualified individual freedom has to be firmly squashed. It may sell Hollywood blockbusters (count the number of mentions the word 'freedom' gets in *Braveheart*) but it is no basis for a serious analysis of past societies.

6

Looking at Thoughts

The last chapter mentioned in passing the development of 'cognitive archaeology', or how we might understand or account for the thoughts of people in the past. Looking at thoughts in the minds of people long dead is obviously very difficult. Is it necessary?

The question 'do we have to look at thoughts in the past?' is embedded in deeper questions, for example:

1 What are 'thoughts', anyway? Are these conscious or unconscious? The major influence of Sigmund Freud on the human sciences was to show that our conscious thoughts were only the tip of the iceberg; human mental processes were much deeper, more complex and more difficult to understand than the 'rational' surface. Should we take a 'deep' view of thoughts or a 'shallow' view?
2 Are all human beings united by the same cognitive systems, or are these diverse? To use some common jargon, are we justified in making *essentialist* claims about the nature of cognition, or is human knowledge of the world *socially constructed* and therefore variable between different societies? If it is variable, how can we be justified in making assumptions about the individual or group psychology of prehistoric cultures on the basis of studies of modern populations?

These are all very deep questions that are not exclusive to archaeology. They are questions that all 'human sciences' have had to grapple with in different forms.

In this chapter, I want to expand on this theme and look at some of the ways theory in the human sciences at large has coped with this problem. I will do this to set the background for the origins and development of a new set of concerns in archaeological theory, loosely termed 'postprocessual' or 'interpretative' archaeology. These themes are, first, the move towards cognitive approaches, second, the influence of the structuralist tradition of thought and third, the influence of Marxism.

Looking at Thoughts

Do we really have to look at cognition, at thoughts? Many would say 'No'. A large number of positivists both within archaeology and within the human sciences in general argue that you can never test thoughts. They give two reasons:

1 You can never scientifically verify what is between someone's ears. Thoughts are therefore untestable. They are consequently beyond the domain of Science. This is a common view of some though not all positivists.
2 We don't study human actions, we study the archaeological record – a mute collection of stones and bones, matter arranged in time and space (back to figure 2.1). We can explain what we see in terms of past cultural systems; their dynamics of change, how they were adapted to their environment. We do not need to do this with direct reference to mental factors. Reference to mental factors would involve the error of mentalist explanation in any case (see chapter 4). Forms of this argument have been advanced by Binford and others.

Many traditional archaeologists also argue that it is difficult if not impossible to use the archaeological record to recover past beliefs. Archaeologists like Christopher Hawkes argued for seven levels of archaeological inference ranging from the relatively straightforward to the very difficult. Archaeological material, said Hawkes, could be used with reasonable security to tell us about technology in the past. Economic inferences were more difficult; inferences about cultural and religious life were almost impossible except in exceptional circumstances.

Whatever orientation one takes, there are clearly immense difficulties in recovering thoughts. Behavioural psychologists argue that we can never 'know' what someone else is thinking in the present; we can only record their behaviour, which can be externally measured and observed. How much more difficult to recover the minds of women and men not just long dead, but members of an extinct culture, with an utterly different view of the world! Such a task is difficult enough for archaeologists of historic periods; prehistorians have to do so using material remains, with no documentary records to assist.

Why, then, should we be trying to get at past thoughts and beliefs? In my view, to argue about whether or not it is *difficult* to do so is to miss the point. It is simply *necessary*. I suggest there are three reasons for this.

(1) We all actually make assumptions about past thoughts whether we like it or not. Take, for example, a dry, straightforward typology of pots. When we classify decorations of a certain type together, we do so on the assumption that shared design must have something to do with shared meanings in the minds of the makers and the users of the pots.

What a lot of archaeologists do in practice is assert that we can never recover past thoughts, but do so in practice by slipping assumptions about mental attitudes back into their arguments as 'common sense'. Thus, for example, putting fireplaces and chimney-stacks in houses rather than rely on open hearths is common sense because it makes the house warmer, less full of smoke, more 'comfortable'. The problem with such arguments is that they depend on assumptions about what is 'natural' or 'normal' in human beings: in this example, a desire for domestic comfort is assumed as 'natural'. It is 'common sense', then, to satisfy those desires. These assumptions tend to fall apart when closely examined, since one can always point to the diversity of human practice; in particular, different ethnographic examples where the practice is not 'normal' or 'natural'.

The problem with common sense in this context is that what is 'common sense' to 'us' may not have been common sense to 'them'. Anthropologists study other cultures in the present that have very different cultural attitudes. For the Azande, when some unfortunate accident occurs, it is common sense to go to a witch-doctor or diviner to find out who was responsible for the magic behind it. It is logical to assume that other cultures in the past may have had other common senses.

Lurking in the wings behind the common-sense argument are implicit beliefs in *essentialism* and *ethnocentrism*. Essentialism is the belief that there are certain attitudes or emotions (such as the desire for privacy, for domestic comfort, or the sex drive) that are 'natural' or biologically endowed, either to humans in general or to a specific sex. Thus the statement 'in prehistory, men must have been more warlike than women as they lacked the mothering instinct' is an *essentialist* statement since it assumes that 'the mothering instinct' is endowed naturally or biologically to all women. Now there may or may not be certain 'human universals' of this kind; that is a matter for debate; I am sceptical about most of the possible candidates.

Whatever the case, however, such essentialist statements need to be argued through rather than assumed.

Ethnocentrism is the belief that the values and attitudes of one's own culture are normal and universal. Thus an assumption that, for example, witchcraft belief is 'irrational' is ethnocentric, since it assumes that Western logic is the only form of rationality around. Belief in witchcraft must therefore be irrational since it fails to satisfy the criteria of Western logic. (Of course, Western logic fails to satisfy the criteria of Azande witch doctors.) Again, belief in the human desire for privacy is ethnocentric, since it assumes that the high stress on the individual and hence his or her right to privacy in Western society is universally normal and natural.

(2) Any archaeologist working outside the deeper recesses of prehistory (that is, before ethnohistorically attested, protoliterate or literate societies) has to deal with evidence that is strictly 'historical' in nature; that is, with documentary or textual evidence in some form. But such documents are nothing if not statements of thoughts – however mundane or 'obvious' those thoughts are. If we are therefore going to relate archaeological to documentary evidence, then, some critical attention must be given to the mental attitudes and ideas that played their part in producing that evidence.

(3) There is a philosophical point to do with the way we study human societies. As we explored in relation to criticisms of systems thinking, it is almost impossible to describe human behaviour without referring to mental concepts. Imagine trying to describe – to get a third person to 'understand' – the actions of a woman cashing a cheque in a bank solely with reference to physical movements and actions. This is a point made most elegantly by one of my favourite and most entertaining writers, the sociologist Erving Goffman:

> Take... an act which is tolerably clear: a man driving through a red light. What is he doing? [Goffman lists 24 different reasons, including] 1. Where he comes from they have signs, not lights. 2. The daylight was bad and he couldn't see. 3. He's lately become colour-blind. 4. He was late for work. 5. His wife is giving birth in the back seat and he'd like to get to a hospital. 6. The bank robber in the front seat is holding a gun on him and has told him to run the light... 15. He's an inspector testing the vigilance of the cops on duty... 22. He was drunk, high. 23. His mother has a lamentable occupation, and he has a psychiatrically certifiable compulsivity with regard to red lights...' [He concludes]:
>
> So our man has passed through a red light. But at his hearing when the judge asks him what he was doing running a red light, he will provide an argument as to what was really happening. *Obviously, what*

> *makes driving through a red light a discernible, isolable event is that a rule stipulated in regard to the light was broken. The objective 'fact', then, must be as variable as is the individual's possible relation to the rule* (Goffman 1971: 132; italics mine. Note in passing that we understand the action by reference to its *context*, a point developed in postprocessual or contextual archaeology).

The belief that thoughts and ideas are more important than the material world is called *idealism*. Postprocessual archaeology is not claimed to be an idealist philosophy by its advocates, but it has been profoundly influenced by idealist notions. Historically, the idealist tradition of philosophy is a long one, including the names of such philosophers as Plato, Vico, Berkeley, Kant, Descartes and Hegel, through to the linguist Ferdinand de Saussure and anthropologist Claude Lévi-Strauss.

Cognitive Archaeology

Many of these points were taken on board by archaeologists within a processual mould. They accepted that early processual models did not take account of people's thoughts, and that such models were therefore limited. These archaeologists therefore began to explore ways of looking at cognition within the general assumptions and framework of processualism. Recently, these attempts have coalesced into a school of thought labelled *cognitive archaeology* or *cognitive-processualism* by its advocates.

These authors look at 'mind' in a variety of ways. Renfrew and Zubrow have argued that, for example, we can identify religious or cult behaviour in the archaeological record. They have suggested that there is no contradiction between a broadly scientific view of archaeological theory and an insistence that we need to look at cognition. Kent Flannery and Joyce Marcus, for example, have looked at functional linkages between the 'ideological subsystem' and other areas of cultural subsystems, and stressed the compatibility of their work with subsistence and settlement analysis:

> Own own first effort [in cognitive archaeology: Flannery and Marcus 1976] was an attempt to understand the ancient Zapotec Indians more fully by combining their cosmological beliefs with a more traditional analysis of their subsistence and settlement.... We simply tried to show that one could explain a higher proportion of ancient Zapotec subsistence behaviour if, instead of restricting oneself to a study of agricultural plants and irrigation canals, one took into account what was

known of Zapotec notions about the relationships of lightning, rain, blood sacrifice, and the 'satisfizing ethic'. We also stressed that we could only do so because the 16th-century Spanish eyewitness accounts of the Zapotec were so rich. (Flannery and Marcus 1993: 260).

Flannery and Marcus identify the study of cosmology, religion, ideology and iconography as legitimate areas of cognitive analysis, stressing that all such work must be empirically grounded. Recently, still other sources of inspiration have come from psychology. In particular, Steve Mithen has talked of 'thoughtful foragers' – looking at how we might model the decision-making processes of hunters and gatherers within an adaptive framework, yielding a range of cognitive inferences (Mithen 1990: see also chapter 9, this volume).

The argument of all these authors is that we can look at thoughts while retaining the essential components of a processual approach: belief in scientific objectivity and 'testing', adherence to a loosely systemic model. But other archaeologists have claimed that the need to look at thoughts has led them to question the very basis of processual archaeology.

Two schools of thought have been particularly influential in this rethinking: structuralism and Marxism. I shall discuss each in turn before looking at their influence on 'postprocessual archaeology' in the next chapter.

Structuralism

One of the key ways in which idealism has affected archaeological thought is via the school of thought termed structuralism. Like both functionalism and Marxism, this theoretical current has developed and changed as a critical tradition over the years. It has few adherents in its original, classical form today, but (like systems theory) has had such a profound influence on archaeological thought that it cannot be ignored. Like Marxism also, structuralism is a term much misused and abused, referring more to a vague impression of pretentious Paris intellectuals sitting in cafes on the Rive Gauche than a given set of ideas:

> *People* magazine was showing only the other week not only how many leading Structuralists like to dine at Sardi's these days, often on very experimental diets, but how they probably started the entire Perrier revolution... there is talk of a major film set among Deconstructionists, exploring their complex thought-practices, laid-back life-style and complex sexual mores and what happens to them when they quit Paris

> and hit the trail for Texas; Robert Redford is said to be interested in the Derrida role. (Bradbury 1987: 2; ten years later, they have moved to Islington in north London and dine at Granita and the River Café)

I am going to go back to the roots of structuralism so that its present influence can be more easily understood.

For functionalists, culture is like an organism, different parts of the body/society performing different functions and the whole adapted to its environment. For structuralists, culture is *like language*.

Structuralism was originally a body of thought developed in linguistics by Ferdinand de Saussure. The most important point for our purposes is to observe that for Saussure, *language is composed of hidden rules* that we use but don't articulate. As I write and you read this sentence, I use a set of grammatical rules to compose my text. You know that set as well. Your knowledge of that set of rules enables you to decode, to 'read' what I write. You can do this even though each sentence that I produce is unique; each sentence is one that has never been composed before in the history of the English language. Indeed, I can generate a theoretically infinite set of different statements or sentences from a fairly simple set of grammatical rules.

Both of us, however, understands those rules at a deep, *implicit* rather than surface, *explicit* level. We both have a pretty hazy idea of what a gerund or a subjunctive clause is. Neither of us puts those rules 'into words' though we 'know' and use them constantly and habitually, and in general we both get them right. (Otherwise, if we did not get them right, we would not be able to decode each other's utterances and understand each other.)

In short, the rules that govern language are *hidden*, deep inside the human brain. If you want to explain the different forms of language, then, you need to refer to the hidden (cognitive) rules that generate sentences.

Archaeologists influenced by structuralism suggest that the same is true of the material things that we find in the archaeological record. They see artefacts as another expression of human culture in general. If you want to explain culture, then, you need to uncover the hidden (cognitive) rules that generate cultural forms.

Structural models have been used to produce classifications of different kinds of archaeological material. Henry Glassie, for example, used the analogy of 'grammar' to examine the layout of ordinary houses in eighteenth-century Virginia. He proposed that ordinary people designed these houses by taking a series of basic spatial units and applying a system of grammatical rules to those units to produce different house plans. He called this scheme a *transformational grammar*: that is, it described the way in which units were transformed through a series of cognitive stages into houses. Similar exercises have been performed for other classes of material, for example Palaeolithic cave art and schemes of pottery decoration.

But the implications of structuralism are deeper than simply offering tools for fresh classifications. So whereas a functional or systemic thinker's immediate instinct is to ask 'How does this practice/this subsystem function within the culture as a whole? And how does this help the system to work, to be better adapted, within a wider environment?', the structuralist will ask 'What are the underlying rules governing this structure? And what do those rules tell us about the way this culture sees the world?' For functionalists, culture is fundamentally *adaptive*; for structuralists, culture is fundamentally *expressive*, a system of (hidden, cognitive) meanings.

Marxism

> It is impossible at the present time to write history without using a whole range of concepts directly or indirectly linked to Marx's thought and situating oneself within a horizon of thought which has been defined and described by Marx. One might even wonder what difference there could ultimately be between being an historian and being a Marxist. (Foucault 1980: 53)

A second school of thought that has had a profound effect on archaeological thought is that of Marxism. Like structuralism, Marxism has developed almost beyond recognition since its original formulation and development by Karl Marx in the nineteenth century. I want to highlight a very few aspects of Marxist thought that are of relevance to archaeological theory.

In its original form, Marxism is a *materialist* philosophy. That is, it proposes that material things are more important than ideas. If so, then human history is about the growth of human productive power, the growing human ability as history unfolds to produce material things: Gerry Cohen suggests that 'history is, fundamentally, the growth of human productive power, and forms of society rise and fall accordingly as they enable or impede that growth' (Cohen 1978: x). In Karl Marx's own phrase, humans are what they do rather than what they think: 'it is not the consciousness of men that determines their being, but on the contrary, their social being that determines their consciousness' (cited in McClellan 1977: 389).

At any time, Marxists argue, people produce things in a certain distinctive way, which Marx calls the mode of production. Marxist have spoken of 'tribal', Asiatic, Ancient, feudal and capitalist modes of production among others. The ancient mode of production, to take one example, is distinctive for Marx because it relies on slave labour at its base, whereas feudalism depends on the labour of unfree peasants or 'serfs' tied to the land. Each different mode of production results in a different kind of class antagonism: in ancient societies between slave and master, in feudalism between peasant and feudal landlord, in capitalism between proletarian and bourgeois.

The mode of production, Marx argues, can be split into the *forces of production*, that is the raw materials, apparatus, labour power, and the social *relations of production*. For example, the forces of production in capitalist society consist of the machines and hardware of the factories, while the relations comprise the factory system – the division into workforce and management.

For Marx, there will always be antagonism and conflict between these two elements: 'the forces of production, the state of society, and consciousness, can and must come into contradiction with one another, because the division of labour implies the . . . fact that intellectual and moral activity – enjoyment and labour, production and consumption – devolve on different individuals, and the only possibility of their not coming into contradiction lies in the negation in its turn of the division of labour'. For this and other reasons, there will always be conflict at the heart of human societies. Contradictions and class antagonisms will tear at the heart of any social formation, developing slowly or quickly in different circumstances. Eventually, however, they will bring the whole structure crashing down, and a new social formation will rise on its ruins.

This 'classical' model has been much criticized; the road from classical to modern Marxism is too long to pursue here. I do want to pick out three key points that emerge from this account of classical Marxism, however, that have direct relevance to the development of archaeological thought:

(1) Marx's account, if it works, provides a *scientific basis to communism*. In this sense classical Marxism shares many parallels with the belief in a positivistic basis to Science that was discussed in chapter 3. Contrary to positivism, however, Marx argues that *intellectuals cannot divorce academic thought from political action*.

Archaeologists influenced by Marxism, then, have seen a close link between archaeology and politics. They have seen archaeological practice and interpretations as partly or wholly political in nature, and in turn have often seen their own archaeological work as in part a wider political exercise. And they argue that to try to deny this is to bury one's head in the sand.

(2) The process of historical change in the Marxist model is *dialectical*. A dialectical model is one that depends on the development of contradictions and conflict within a entire social formation or totality. These contradictions can only be understood within that total social formation. For example, the terms 'peasant' and 'landlord' do not have the same meaning regardless of time and place. We can only define and understand peasant and landlord classes within a total understanding of the feudal social formation. When that formation breaks down, it leads to a completely new formation and the development in their turn of new conflicts.

A dialectical model of social process contrasts with the systemic model discussed earlier. In systems thinking, change is often presented as a smooth process of accretion and adaptation. The dialectical model also leads us to question social categories and definitions that claim to be true for all times and all places.

Marxism has thus led archaeologists to question either/or oppositions such as subjectivity and objectivity. They point out that such terms only oppose each other within a total framework, and it is that total framework that they seek to question and transform.

The third point is perhaps the most crucial of all for understanding Marxism's contribution to cognition and to archaeological thought in general: the concept of ideology.

Ideology

Later Marxists (or 'neo-Marxists') have focused attention on the role of *ideology* in this model. For Marx, the forces and relations of production were the 'infrastructure', the heart of the system: the political and legal system sat on top of this, along with a set of ideological beliefs. In a simple view, while social foundations are creaking and society becomes increasingly unequal and unjust, people's beliefs act to 'paper over the cracks', to make the existing system appear legitimate.

'Vulgar' ideology is obvious: in our society, one might cite flag-waving, advertising, appeals to patriotism, motherhood and apple pie. But Marxists believe ideology also works on a far more subtle level than this. In particular, ideology:

1 naturalizes; that is, it makes the existing social order with all its inequalities appear timeless, God-given, or without any conceivable alternative;
2 makes interests that are sectional (for example to the upper classes) appear universal (of benefit to everyone);
3 masks what is 'really going on', for example by denying that social or economic inequalities exist.

To take a straightforward (and therefore overly simplistic, 'vulgar' and easily decoded) example, a Marxist would argue that we only have to open the pages of most newspapers to see ideology at work ('competition and the rules of the free market are not arbitrary human constructions that can be changed, they are out there in nature; look at how cold, wet, miserable life was in the Middle Ages, in other words, before the benefits of capitalism'). Sectional interests are presented as universal (wage rises are presented as 'harming the nation' rather than just harming the profits accruing to the wealthy capitalists). An ideology of equality ('anyone can become President, everyone is equal under the law, I want to build a classless society') masks what Marxists see as very real divisions and inequalities in gender and wealth.

This interest in ideology has led to the detailed exploration of how ideology works, and a stress on the unmasking of the relations behind ideology. Paradoxically, then, Marxism started as a materialist model, but has ended up influencing Anglo-American archaeology through its analysis of ideological beliefs. This move away from materialism is one of the key points behind the Frankfurt School of *critical theory.* The Frankfurt School sought to look behind the mask of ideology, to show how modern Western systems of belief were not neutral or objective, but actually ideological constructions that legitimated modern capitalism.

Of course, interest in ideology in archaeology has two aspects. One can look at ideology in the past, how for example a particular belief system legitimated the position of an élite in ancient societies. But one can also look at the present – how archaeological writing is itself ideological. For example, Bruce Trigger has written extensively on how different interpretations of North American prehistory served to ideologically portray Native American cultures as backward and unchanging.

All this is very interesting, but we've heard very little in this chapter about archaeology. How, precisely, do the different views lead to concretely different archaeological explanations?

I'll be discussing some more practical examples in the next chapter, but here is an 'interim summary' for the time being.

For the processual tradition, the artefacts we find are evidence of different parts of a cultural system that existed in the past. For some, artefacts form a *fossil record* of human behaviour. Many processualists argue that as we cannot see thoughts scientifically, so we can't explain artefacts in terms of the ideas in the minds of the makers – though following Flannery and Marcus, we can include 'cognitive variables' in our analyses, if used with caution. Instead, we look at different parts of past cultural systems and the links between them, often using language derived from systems thinking. Processualists claim to have the ability to test between alternative hypotheses about the way those systems worked through the development of middle-range theory.

For structuralists, artefacts are evidence of systems of belief in the broadest sense, evidence of 'mind-sets' or 'worldviews'. Just as language is structured by rules that remain hidden, so is material culture. Structuralists look at oppositions in the particular form of artefacts, the placing of artefacts within graves, for ideas about the constitution of gender, oppositions between nature and culture, and so on. Since we can never prove the existence of hidden rules, this tradition suggests that we can never really 'test' any single interpretation of the past; there is a tendency towards developing multiple, complex interpretations rather than trying to reduce culture to one single pattern.

Marxists look for contradictions and inequalities in culture. For example, is burial practice legitimating or masking what happens in life? Marxists ask: how does the belief or worldview expressed by this piece of material culture relate to what is really going on? For example, does an egalitarian burial practice mask inequalities in society?

Conclusion

In the second part of this chapter, I have picked out developments within two schools of thought within social theory as a whole – Marxism and structuralism. I could have looked at other profoundly influential movements treated elsewhere in this book (feminism, the reaction against social evolution). Both Marxism and structuralism, however, give some flavour of the intellectual currents that came to influence archaeological theory in the 1980s.

Marxism gives us: an interest in conflict and contradiction; a stress on ideology; an insistence that academic discourse is fundamentally also political discourse in the present; and a model of structure and agency. Structuralism gives us: an interest in the hidden workings of language; an interest in cultural meanings and in culture as expressive.

All these themes were taken up into a group of new theoretical strands in the 1980s, that came to be known collectively as 'postprocessual archaeology'.

7

Postprocessual and Interpretative Archaeologies

'Postprocessual archaeology' grew out of a very specific context that it is important to understand. Part of that context within the human sciences as a whole – developments in structuralism and Marxism – was presented in the last chapter. Now, I want to look briefly at developments *within* archaeology in the 1980s.

In the late 1970s and early 1980s, a number of archaeologists became increasingly dissatisfied with the direction archaeology was taking. It seemed to them that the New Archaeology was 'drying up' in intellectual vitality in various ways. In particular, they pointed to the need to address cognitive factors, the difficulties of positivist epistemology, and the problems with developing middle-range theory – issues dealt with in chapters 3 to 6.

One such archaeologist was Ian Hodder, and his intellectual development epitomizes this shift in many ways. Hodder's early work was very much within a processual mould. Hodder was heavily influenced by the 'New Geography' and the work of New Archaeologist David Clarke on spatial models in archaeology. Hodder used statistics and computer simulation to develop a series of spatial models, particularly relating to trade, markets and urbanization in Iron Age and Roman Britain. This period was seen very much as an evolving system, with trade and urbanism being linked as part of an overall process of 'Romanization'.

But as time went on and the research progressed Hodder became more and more doubtful that such models and simulations did really 'test' or 'prove' anything. The same pattern or trace in the archaeological record, for example a pottery distribution or network of urban centres, could be produced by a range of different simulated processes. Therefore, a given pattern in the archaeological record could be satisfactorily interpreted or explained in different ways, with reference to a number of different possible processes. Hodder felt that there was no way to test absolutely between these alternatives. This is often referred to in subsequent literature as a problem of *equifinality*.

A reading of Hodder and Orton's *Spatial Analysis in Archaeology*, published in 1976, shows this shift. In case after case – attempting to simulate trade patterns and settlement systems using computers – Hodder and Orton showed how difficult or impossible it was to 'prove' or 'test' anything.

A good example was the study of goods used in prehistoric trade. Goods such as obsidian flakes or polished greenstone axes were often found on sites thousands of miles from the original source of the raw material. Such finds clearly represented trade or contact in some form, but ambitious New Archaeologists wanted to go further than this. Renfrew and others had suggested that different forms of trade would leave different traces in the archaeological record. If, for example, 'down-the-line' exchange was occurring, with community A collecting the material at source before giving community B half, the community B keeping half and handing half on... then different quantities of traded material would be present in site assemblages than if everyone was going back to source and making their own collation of material.

Hodder found that if 'down-the-line', directional or other modes of exchange were modelled by computer simulation, similar rather than different curves were produced. Different forms of process left the same archaeological trace: in other words, they were equifinal (figure 7.1).

Lessons also came out of Hodder's ethnoarchaeological work. Hodder realized that however many archaeological facts you collected on a computer, the only way to get a handle on what they meant in terms of past activities is to look at the relationship between pattern and process in the present. This, of course, was Binford's perception of the problems underlying the 'Mousterian debate' as discussed in chapter 4. Like Binford, Hodder decided to turn to studies of 'archaeology in the present' to try to establish correlations between behaviour in the present and archaeological patterning. So Hodder went out to East Africa to examine, among other themes, how real living 'cultures' could be mapped archaeologically, what factors affected refuse disposal, and so on.

What Hodder found, again in a variety of instances, was that to understand patterning on the ground it was necessary to refer to people's attitudes and beliefs. We looked at Hodder's work with the Nuba in chapter 4. This led him to:

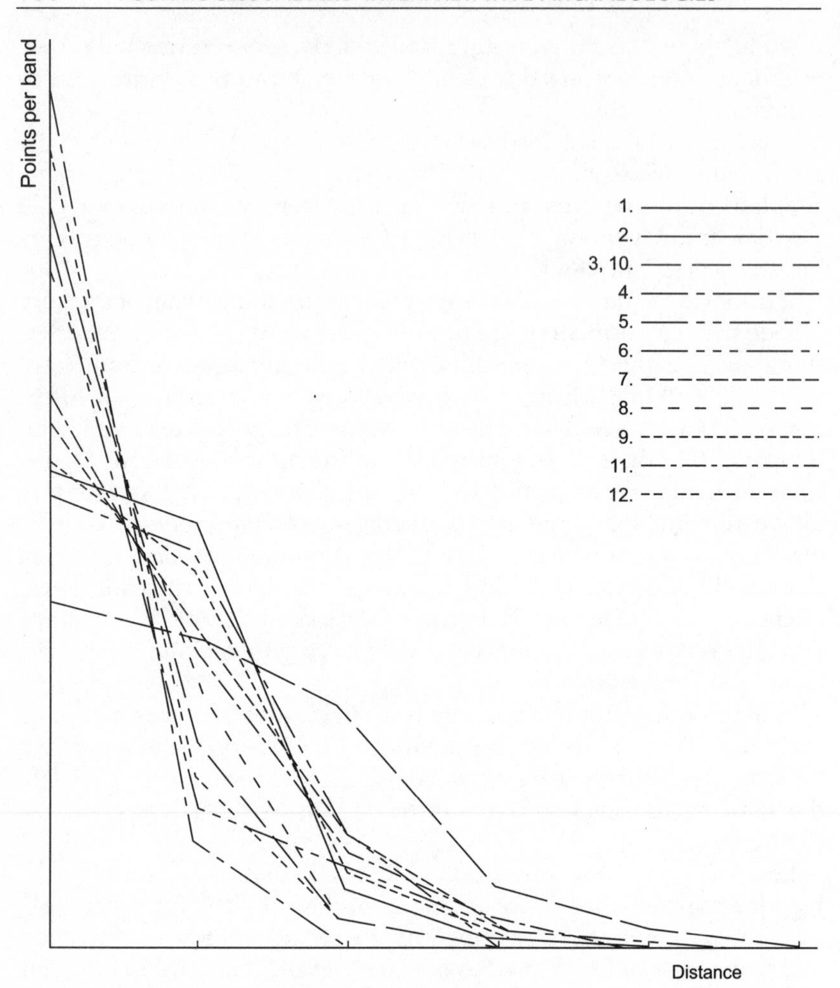

Figure 7.1 The results of Hodder and Orton's simulation exercise showing that 'different spatial processes can produce very similar fall-off curves', implying that 'this advises great caution in any attempt at interpretation' (Hodder and Orton 1976: figure 5.35 and p. 145.

1 a rejection of Binford's confidence in the success of middle-range theory as a neutral arbiter between different explanations;
2 a belief in the importance of people's thoughts and symbolism, and with this a belief that cultures could not be viewed purely as adapting to an external environment: 'their' view of 'their' world was important;

3 a belief that material culture was actively manipulated by people; that is, that people used things in different ways as part of particular social strategies, rather than material things being a passive reflection of a set of rules.

For a small but growing group of archaeologists in the early 1980s, a key buzz-phrase was 'material culture should be seen as meaningfully constituted'. That is, artefacts were more than just devices to cope with the environment. If we wanted to understand why this pottery had that decoration or why this farmstead was laid out in that way, we had to look at the cultural meanings behind their manufacture and use.

How might we do this? Several theories of 'mind' were looked at in the previous chapter. In the early 1980s a new generation of students, many of whom were studying with Hodder at Cambridge, and others with Mark Leone as part of the *Archaeology in Annapolis* project, turned to these theories. Many turned to structuralism as a way into understanding the mind. Others 'read around' Marxist and neo-Marxist texts and in particular critical theory. Others were influenced by feminist thinking, while others still looked at the writings of figures like Clifford Geertz in 'interpretative anthropology'. Together, these very diverse strands of thought coalesced into a loose cluster of traditions that came to be known by both supporters and critics as 'postprocessual archaeology'.

Postprocessual Archaeology

There is no such thing as a 'postprocessual archaeologist'. Whenever I see the phrase 'the postprocessualists' used in the archaeological literature I expect some gross over-generalization of theoretical attitudes to follow, and I am rarely disappointed. Just as New Archaeology was actually a very diverse set of concerns and ideas that coalesced around certain slogans, so the catch-all term 'postprocessual' conceals a great diversity of viewpoints and traditions. Indeed, many of those associated with this label have recently preferred the term 'interpretative archaeologies', the plural indicating the stress on diversity.

So instead I shall try to characterize postprocessual thinking in the form of eight key statements. Again, like the New Archaeology, not all of those associated with the postprocessual 'label' would fully endorse all of these. What is important is that these statements convey the *flavour* of postprocessual traditions, a way of looking at and thinking about the world. They should also indicate the debt owed to the intellectual movements described in the previous chapter.

(1) *We reject a positivist view of science and the theory/data split. The data are always theory-laden.* Postprocessualists reject the claims of Science as a unique form of knowledge, for the reasons advanced in chapter 3. Generally, they align themselves with other non-positivist conceptions of what science is or does, particularly *social constructivism* whether in its 'strong' or 'weak' forms.

Or to put it another way, postprocessualists do not argue that 'we should not test things'; rather, they suggest that in practice neither scientists not archaeologists ever test things in ways that satisfy positivist criteria. They would point out, for example, that Renfrew's 'testing' of his territorial model of megaliths in figure 2.6 was no such thing; the territories delineated are far from uniform, with many megaliths centred within totally unconvincing territories; we simply agree (or disagree) that Renfrew's is a convincing argument. Postprocessualists suggest that we can never confront theory and data; instead, we see data through a cloud of theory (figure 7.2; contrast with figure 4.1).

(2) *Interpretation is always hermeneutic.* This is a variant on Proposition One. Hermeneutics is the study of meanings. When we

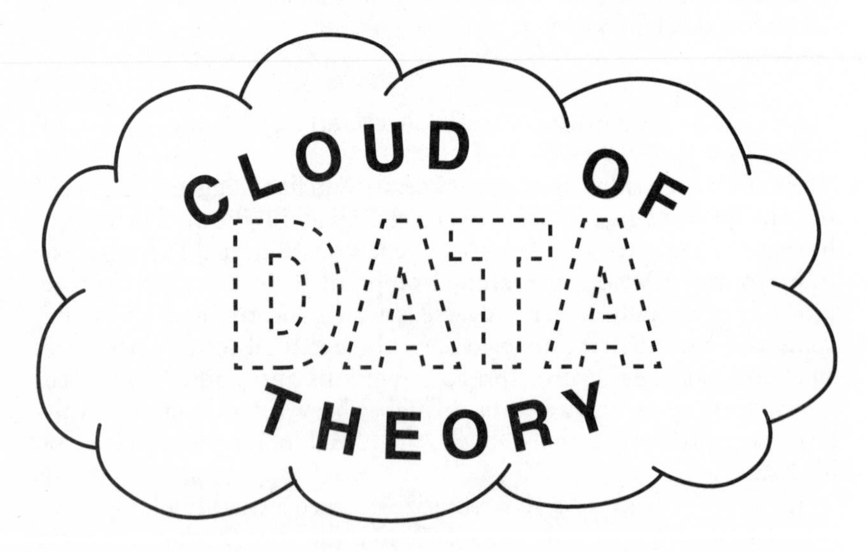

Figure 7.2 The relationship of theory and data in postprocessual archaeology; data exist, but are perceived fuzzily through a cloud of theory (contrast with figure 4.1)..

interpret things, it is argued, archaeologists do this by assigning meanings to them, meanings that we assume were also in the minds of the ancient peoples who made and used them.

Postprocessualists argue that all archaeologists do this whether they overtly admit it or not. They deconstruct accounts of 'scientific' testing to show that even Binford and others implicitly assume meanings and values in the minds of ancient peoples. Hodder (forthcoming), for example, looks at the day-to-day process of reasoning during an archaeological excavation and argues that this is always a 'hermeneutic circle' regardless of whether or not the excavators consider themselves theorists.

(3) *We reject the opposition between material and ideal.* We have seen how normative and culture-historical approaches were rejected by processual archaeology as idealist, and how processual archaeology introduced a materialist emphasis. We have also looked at the idealist approach taken by structuralism, and at how Marxism moved away from a purely materialist base.

Many postprocessualists claim that we should reject the whole opposition between material and ideal in the first place. A good example is the idea of landscape. On the one hand, a materialist view of landscape tends to stress how it may be seen in terms of a set of resources, for example for hunter-gatherer or early farming groups. This leads one to turn, for example, to optimal foraging theory and other economic models for an understanding of how people exploited the landscape 'rationally'.

Postprocessualists like to argue that landscapes are always viewed in different ways by different peoples. They reject the 'rational' view of 'landscape-as-set-of-resources' as that of our own society and one that is ideologically loaded in its own way, loaded towards ideas of commodity and exploitation found in our own society. They suggest instead that ancient peoples would have had different views of what was 'real' in that landscape.

On the other hand, an exclusively idealist view of landscape does not work either. Postprocessualists like to stress that such an understanding of landscape was not formed in the abstract – that the way people moved around and used that landscape affected their understanding of it. They argue that ancient people's understanding of a landscape was not just a set of thoughts they happened to possess; everyday movements through the landscape, farming, domestic activities were all media through which understanding of the landscape was perpetuated and transformed.

(4) *We need to look at thoughts and values in the past.* The most coherent example of this proposition is Hodder's advocacy of R. G. Collingwood's position of *historical idealism*. Collingwood was a philosopher by training, though he also practised history and archaeology. He argued that, in practice, historians always try to rethink the thoughts of the past. Take for example a classic historical question: why did the British naval leader Lord Nelson not change into plain dress before the naval battle of Trafalgar? (In the battle Nelson's medals and gaudy appearance made him a natural target for snipers, and he was fatally wounded.) Historians, says Collingwood, explain that it was considered dishonourable for a commanding officer to go below deck once battle had commenced; and that Nelson had no such opportunity before the first shots were fired. So, argues Collingwood, when historians 'understand' or 'explain' Nelson's actions, they explore by definition the culture and assumptions of a British naval officer, they rethink his thoughts – in other words, they use *empathy*.

Hodder, following Collingwood, argues that archaeologists do this all the time no matter what theoretical pose they claim to adopt. When, for example, traditional archaeologists 'explained' the placement of Roman forts on the northern frontier of Britain, they did so in terms of an evolving military and political strategy – in other words, they ended up trying to rethink the past thoughts of Roman commanders and emperors. Again, the argument is that all archaeologists actually practise empathetic thinking whether they admit it or not.

(5) *The individual is active.* Postprocessualists dislike the way they feel 'the individual' is lost in most archaeological theory. Individuals, they complain, are just pawns in some set of normative rules or adaptive systems or set of deep structures. They argue that all these different views of the world portray people as passive dupes who blindly follow social rules.

Instead, postprocessualists want to look at *agency*. Agency is a term used to refer to the active strategies of individuals. They suggest that women and men are not passively duped by the system around them. Some archaeologists borrowed the idea of a *recursive relationship between structure and agency* from the sociologist Anthony Giddens. Giddens suggested that there are social rules in the world around us, but that people understand these rules and manipulate them creatively rather than follow them passively. In so doing, they reinforce or alternatively transform the structure itself – the relationship is therefore recursive, or back-and-forth. Giddens's ideas are often referred to as *structuration theory*.

A different way of saying a similar thing was borrowed from the work of the French anthropologist Pierre Bourdieu. Bourdieu was reacting to the orthodox structuralist anthropology of his time, in which he felt humans were simply seen as passively acting out a set of structural rules. Bourdieu showed how in different ethnographic situations different actors had their own ideas about social rules and situations. He argued that we needed a theory of practice – a theory of how individual social actors actually practised living in, reproducing and transforming the culture around them.

In terms of interpreting the archaeological record, then, we need to look at rules that are not just followed, but are creatively manipulated by social actors. A good example of such manipulation comes from an unpublished anecdote from Hodder's work with the Nuba. In one area, there was a cultural belief that women were associated with the 'inside' of the domestic compound, and with the hearth; also, that women were 'polluting'. Women were therefore enjoined to dump the ash from the hearth inside the compound, rather than outside where it would pollute the male sphere. But Hodder once saw a woman self-consciously gathering up the hearth ash and dumping it outside, some way from the compound where all the men could see it. Now in so doing she was acknowledging that rule existed, but deliberately breaking it. We cannot understand her action and the archaeological signature it produced without (a) understanding the cultural system of rules, but (b) understanding her position towards those rules.
Postprocessualists also claim to take:

(a) A 'bottom-up' rather than 'top-down' view of society. Postprocessual work has often taken an interest in the routines of everyday life, the way ordinary people would experience the landscape around them. Indeed, many argue that such routines embody what society is rather than a series of abstract rules.
(b) A conflict-driven rather than consensus model of society. Where systems thinkers often look for élites who manage a system, postprocessualists look for conflict between social groups, for example along gender or class lines.

(6) *Material culture is like a text.* How do we understand the meanings of material culture? Think about the way you read any written text:

(a) A text can mean different things to different people, and different people can read texts in different ways.
(b) These meanings can be actively manipulated. We all do this with material culture in obvious and trivial ways, most obviously

with clothes (we can define the formality of a meeting according to whether we put on a skirt or a tie, for example).

(c) Such manipulation is often implicit and unspoken. We don't consciously think through grammatical rules as we read a text; similarly, we don't consciously think through rules governing material culture.

Consider for example the action of coming into a room without knocking; we might consider somebody doing this to be 'impolite'. At the same time we might deliberately break the rule, for example not knocking if we thought the room was 'our' space and we wanted to make that point to the person currently occupying it. Underlying this grammar of actions are assumptions and cultural values about the nature of space, rules of 'privacy', respect for the individual, and so on. We know what those rules are in our own society, and we manipulate them, though we do not consciously articulate them – we would not give a lecture on cultural anthropology to someone breaking that code, we would simply ask them to be more polite in future.

Postprocessualists suggest similar things go on with ancient material culture in general. They point to ethnoarchaeological studies in which the meanings of space in houses and compounds are rarely overtly discussed, for example, but which are manipulated by social actors with reference to certain rules.

(d) If the meanings of material culture are really this complex, then its different meanings can never be definitively or finally tied down in some final 'conclusion', a single all-embracing analysis. Therefore there can be no 'final' reading of a text – each generation, and even each individual, brings fresh readings to a Shakespeare play, and each reading has its own validity. There can also be no 'right' or 'wrong' reading of a text in any absolute sense. A text can always be deconstructed and shown to contain hidden meanings opposite to those on the surface, as we have seen in the last chapter. Similarly, the meanings of a pottery design or a burial rite can never be finally tied down; there is no one 'right' or 'wrong' reading.

Postprocessualists therefore encourage experimentation with multiple interpretations, and deny the necessity of coming up with one final conclusion that explains 'everything'. Chris Tilley writes: 'Understanding of any "data" in the human sciences does not conclude. It just stops when we get bored or do not have anything else to say' (Tilley 1991: 172).

(e) The meanings of a text are outside the control of its author – the 'death of the author'. If a text is open to multiple interpretations, some of these may be quite at odds with the reading that the author might consciously prefer. We cannot therefore refer to the author's intention in producing a text, whether literary or archaeological, as the only correct reading.

(7) *We have to look at context.* For Hodder, context is the central and defining feature of our discipline. For this reason, postprocessual approaches are often referred to as 'contextual archaeology'.

How do we get at different meanings? Through looking at the context of the artefact or the practice we are discussing. Let's return to our burial. We see that a particular grave good, say an axe, has a particular meaning through its context – where it is buried in the grave, the person it is buried with, the objects with which it is associated. We then widen that context and look at other axes in other graves from the same cemetery. We find that the axe is used differently in different contexts – it is associated with different assemblages, or is placed in a different position in the graves of women and men. We infer differences in meaning from these differences in context.

We might then expand our argument contextually by looking at axes within our ancient culture generally – whether they are deposited in other contexts such as 'domestic' or 'refuse', or by looking at how they are used in domestic arenas. Gradually, we build up a whole web of associations and placements for the axes.

(8) *The meanings we produce are always in the political present, and always have political resonance. Interpreting the past is always a political act.* For postprocessualists, if scientific neutrality is a myth, then our statements about the past are never cool objective judgements detached from the real world. They are always made here, in the present, with all its heady and complicated, jumbled mixture of political and moral judgements.

Note that this does not mean that individual archaeologists are insincere in their attempts to be objective. If the meanings of a text are outside the control of its author, then readings of a text can proliferate in ways never consciously intended by its 'author'. It has been argued for example that some New Archaeologists working on Native American sites stressed that the value of their work lay in their ability to use this material to generate cross-cultural generalizations, that is statements that were true about all human populations in all places. By doing so, some argued, these archaeologists implicitly devalued the importance of looking at Native American tradition in its own right – the implicit message could be read as 'the only valid way to look at this archaeology is to stress its relevance to white people'. Such a 'reading' is not to argue that such archaeologists were being consciously racist; indeed, many such archaeologists were active campaigners for Native American rights.

Case Studies: Rock Art and Medieval Houses

In *Material Culture and Text: The Art of Ambiguity* Chris Tilley (1991) explores the interpretation of a group of rock carvings in Nämforsen in Sweden (figure 7.3). At this site, figures and motifs were pecked into the stones in the third millennium BC. This material was recorded by the Swedish archaeologist Hallstrom around the turn of the century; many of the carvings have now been destroyed. Tilley does not choose to organize his analysis in an orthodox way, with chapters on approach preceding those on material. He starts instead with a consideration of the material itself and of Hallstrom's recording of it, moves on to develop a grammar of design form, and then tries to understand that form through its 'structural logic'. Having developed such a logic and explored different ways in which that might relate to the communities that produced the figures, Tilley moves on to look at different ethnographic parallels, both of a direct historical nature with modern groups such as the Saami and of other traditions such as the Australian Aborigines.

Thus, two-thirds of the way in, we have reached the critical point of the book. Tilley has given us an interpretation of the meaning of the carvings. But in the final third of the book, he proceeds to deconstruct his own interpretation. Tilley refuses to give the reader one 'pat' answer to the meaning of the carvings: 'the point I am really trying to make is that these rock carvings invite a response from us. . . . There is no fixed meaning and we must remember that images cannot in fact be reduced to words, "read" . . . I do not present a proper conclusion because this is an impossibility' (1991: 172). Tilley, then, has given us one final answer, but has then deconstructed that answer and shown that it is not final at all.

On the basis that one should practise what one preaches, I want to talk about an example from my own work: the interpretation of the rural house in the later medieval period in England (*c.* AD 1350–1530).

In southern and eastern England, thousands of ordinary houses built during this period still stand and are used as modern homes, albeit usually heavily modified. Their plan varies, but invariably has one central element: a large hall or central room, open to the roof. This room was usually heated by a central open hearth, the smoke rising to and dispersing in the rafters and thatched roof (figure 7.4).

Traditional archaeologists had done much work identifying these buildings and assigning dates to them, often on the basis of technological, stylistic and typological features. We knew much also about who lived in them. Such houses had been built by socially middling groups – tenant farmers, often combining farming with rural industry. We had analysed the technology and building practices embodied in the houses – the carpentry and framing techniques. Much work had also been done on the economic background to these houses – how and why such non-élite groups could afford a substantial, permanent house for the first time.

These questions were interesting, but I wanted to ask why was the hall the *form* that it was and what *meanings* did that form have for those that built and lived in it? Many previous writers had claimed that the hall was simply a matter of common sense: the openness to the roof space was needed to allow smoke from the open fire to disperse among the rafters. I felt this was not the whole story – chimneys had been known in this society and used at upper social levels in buildings like castles and palaces for several centuries. The peasants occupying such houses were wealthy enough to afford chimney-stacks if they so desired; they simply chose not to have them.

The hall was an open space, but was divided into upper and lower ends by a series of architectural features. The doors were symmetrically placed at the colder, draughtier, 'lower' end, which also offered access to 'service' rooms. At the other, 'upper' end there were often fittings for a raised chair or bench to seat the master and wife; the area was lit by a large window. The bay in the upper end was often one rather longer than that in the lower; the bench at the upper end was fixed by pegs to the wall.

It was easy enough to see the hall, then, as a piece of ideology. Upper and lower ends reflected upper and lower social divisions. The hall presented the social divisions of the household as fixed and immutable through the architecture. The master and wife occupied the upper end and the chamber beyond; servants worked in and around the lower end. At mealtimes, the hall acted as a microcosm of the social order. Everyone ate in the same place, stressing the household as community, but at different ends, stressing differences in social status between different elements of that household.

But the interpretation of the hall could not be this simple. There were other divisions in the late medieval household that cut across the upper/lower divide and could not be fitted into a single pattern so easily. Women occupied important and powerful economic positions

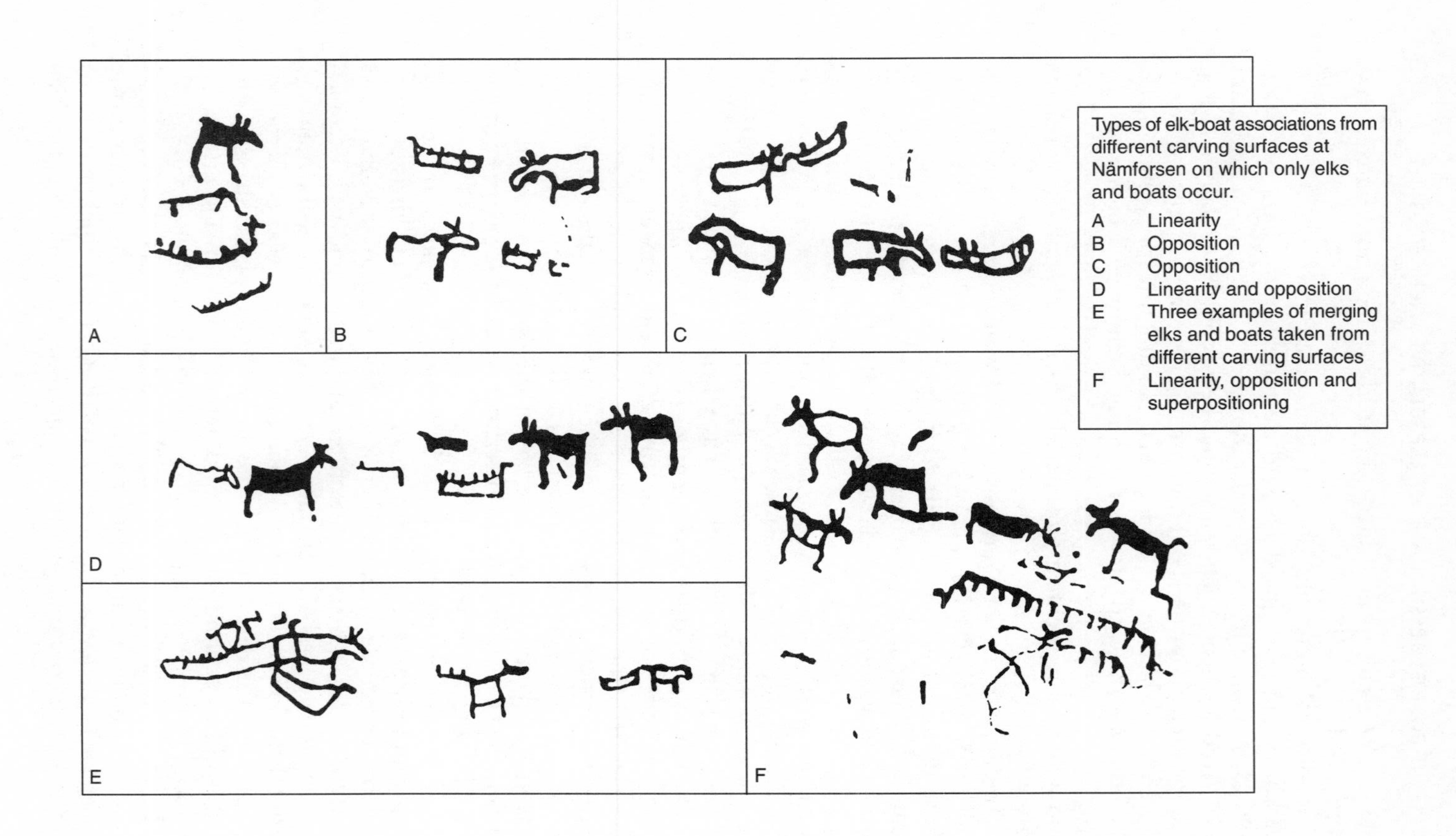

Types of elk-boat associations from different carving surfaces at Nämforsen on which only elks and boats occur.

A Linearity
B Opposition
C Opposition
D Linearity and opposition
E Three examples of merging elks and boats taken from different carving surfaces
F Linearity, opposition and superpositioning

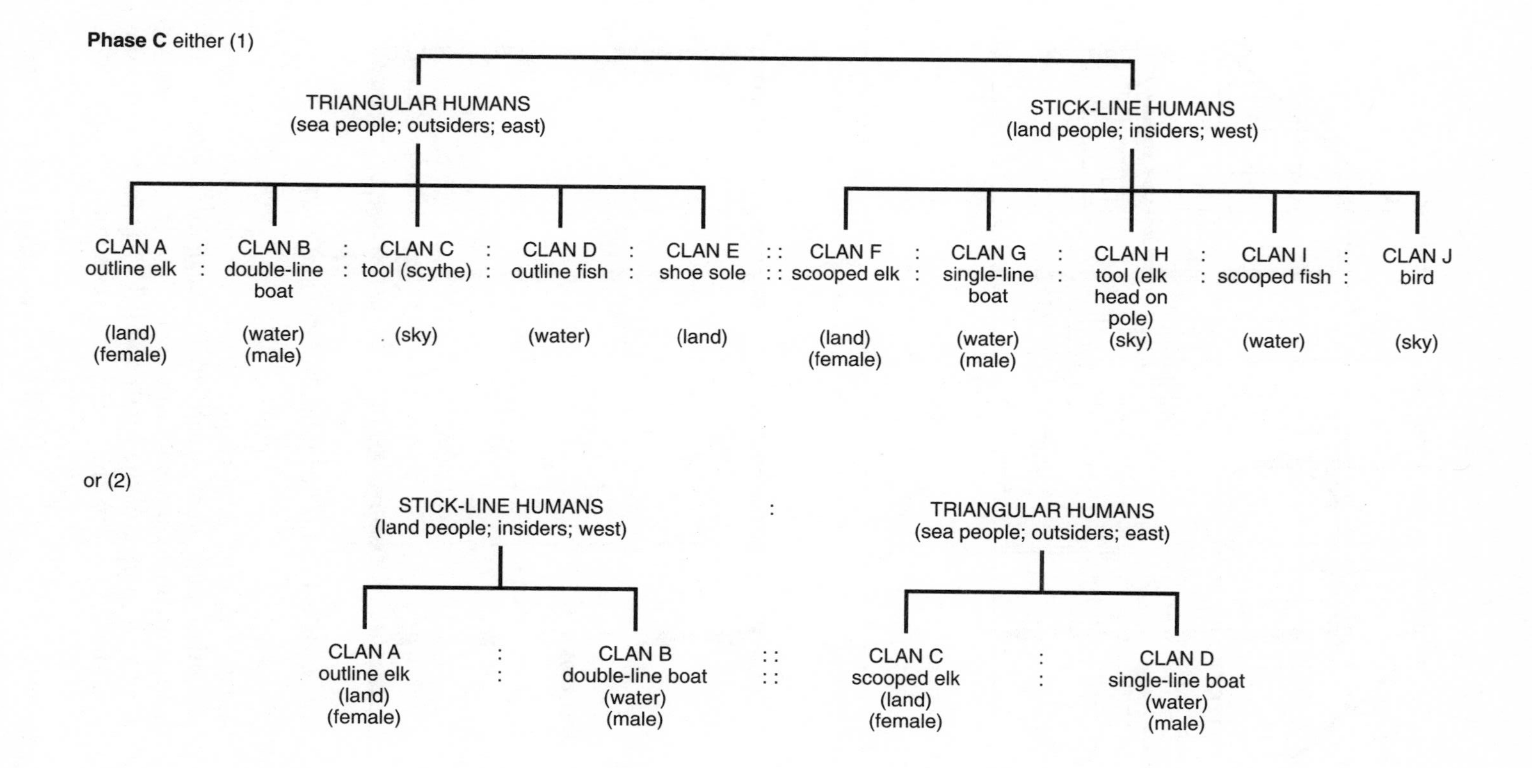

Figure 7.3 Above: carvings from Nämforsen, with below, part of Tilley's structural scheme for interpreting the carvings.

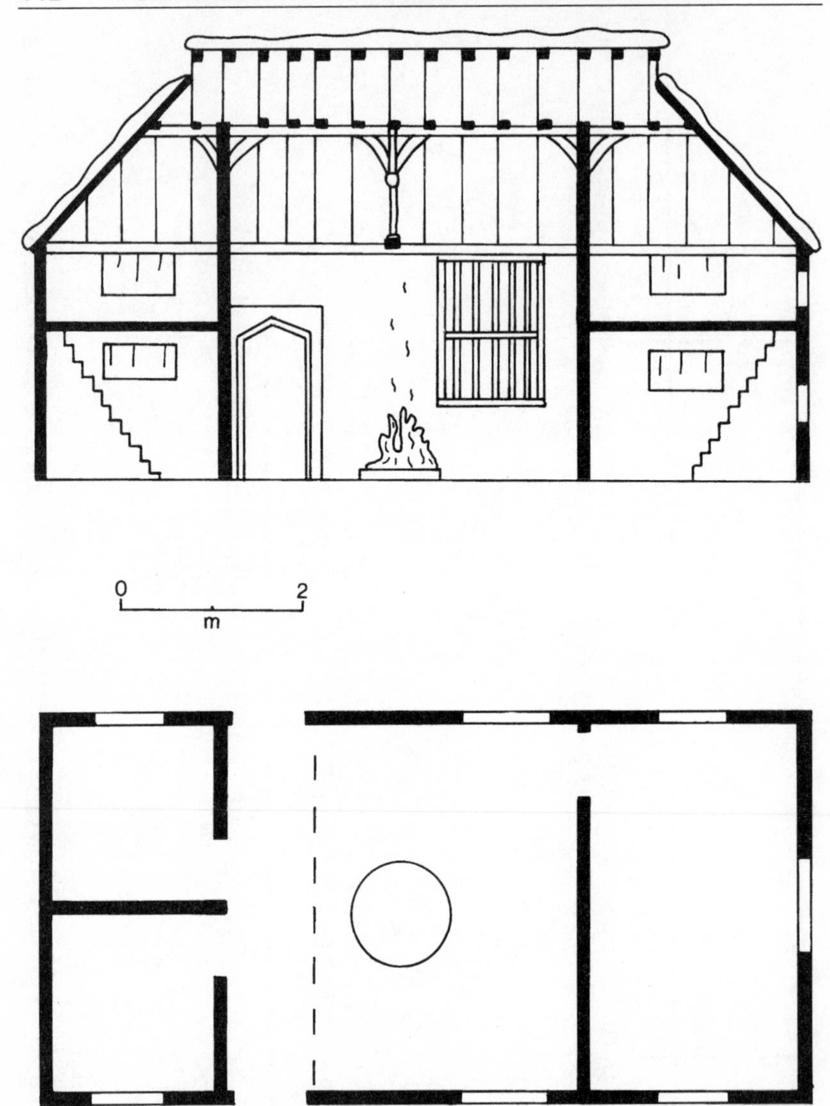

Figure 7.4 A medieval hall (after Johnson 1989: figure 2).

within the late medieval household: they controlled brewing and dairying activities, and were identified in idealized religious and political texts with the 'domestic' side of the house as opposed to the 'public' outside sphere of the roads and fields. There was tension and conflict, then, between the important economic position and everyday routine of women's lives and the formal ideology of patriarchy. So I tried to explore how other groups, women and servants in particular, may have had different 'readings' of the same space. These different 'readings' were rarely overtly articulated; they were, rather, implicit.

I also tried to look at the context of the open hall by looking at other kinds of use of space in the same period. First, I looked at fields, and argued that just as the open hall was open to all but in fact subdivided, so it was in the 'open field': medieval fields were often unbounded and farmed co-operatively, but divided into strips. Then I looked at churches, and suggested that ritual space was also divided, between the nave and chancel of the parish church. So I was arguing that a series of common spatial metaphors ran across ordinary people's experiences of the world around them, that ran between the domestic, the agrarian and the religious.

The whole debate between archaeologists over the meanings of the open hall could not be seen independently of its cultural and political context. The 'vernacular house' occupies a central place in images of rural England. In particular, these images implied continuity with an essential, unchanging rural past of 'old England' in which 'the English' are seen as a traditional, conservative organic community. In the same year that I published my work, Conservative Prime Minister John Major linked 'old England' to a vision of 'British' continuity when he exclaimed that:

> Fifty years from now Britain will still be the country of long shadows on county grounds, warm beer, invincible green suburbs, dog lovers and pools fillers and – as George Orwell said – 'old maids cycling to holy communion through the morning mist' and – if we get our way – Shakespeare still read even in school. Britain will survive unamendable in all essentials. (John Major, speech to Conservative Group for Europe, 22 April 1993)

In placing these houses within a context of profound rural crisis and change, and emphasizing their different meanings to different elements of the household, I was implicitly commenting negatively on that profoundly conservative image of the English countryside and 'Englishness' in general. This political comment was unavoidable; it was there whether I liked it or not. At the time, it wasn't my conscious intention to comment implicitly or explicitly on John Major's views, but a subsequent reading of 'my' work in such a light would nevertheless be a perfectly valid one – though it is one of several possible readings.

Stop – I've lots of questions already! Can I drag you back to Point Six? Surely there are lots of problems with this analogy with text.

Yes, there are. Many archaeologists have argued within the postprocessual tradition that we should get away from this analogy, that it is fundamentally limited. In particular, it is argued that material things convey meaning in fundamentally dissimilar ways to texts.

I've emphasized text here because it is a good introduction to the underlying ideas. We all read texts, and can all grasp the analogy quickly.

Some thinkers have turned instead to traditions of *phenomenology* as developed by philosophers like Schutz, Husserl, Heidegger and others. Phenomenology is the study of conscious human experience in everyday life. For example, instead of thinking about monuments as texts being read in different ways, people like Chris Gosden, Julian Thomas and Chris Tilley have talked about how people move through monuments, what they see from different points, how the physical experience of the monument affects its perception – much more a bodily metaphor than a linguistic one. 'Thinking through the body' has become a buzz-phrase of the late 1990s.

One of the advantages of such a bodily metaphor is that it stresses the falsity of the opposition between material and ideal mentioned above. The body is undeniably real and physical – as Shakespeare said, 'there was never yet philosopher / That could endure the toothache patiently' – and yet at the same time undeniably constructed according to certain ideas – different societies have different ideas of the individual, of gender, of how the body works.

So postprocessualists deny the value of testing. Doesn't this mean they are open to the charge of relativism?

Well, to repeat, they don't 'deny its value'; they claim that, in practice, no archaeologist whatever their theoretical stripe actually rigorously tests theory against 'raw data' in such a way.

Well we certainly can't 'test' people's thoughts. How can we ever understand what people were really thinking? Not only are they now dead, but their culture and values were almost certainly very, very different to our own. It's striking that the two examples you chose (Nelson and Roman forts) were from military history.

It is very difficult – but archaeology is very difficult. It's certainly true that to my mind many of the most exciting and fruitful 'postprocessual' case studies have been done in historical archaeology, where there is plenty of documentary and ethnohistoric data to bring to bear on questions of mentality (see chapter 10). This shows the importance of having plenty of contextual information.

A more complex answer to your question is that we may never be able to fully grasp the content of ancient belief systems: we will never 'know' that this figurine was a depiction of that goddess, or 'know' the stories and myths told about the goddess using the figurine as a prop. But we can move towards an anthropological description of what a figurine or architectural space might have meant at a deeper level, for example by noting that 'female' figurines are found on the left side of a temple while male figurines are on the right. Anthropologists do this as standard practice, for example moving beyond the overt stories told by a community or folk tradition to inferences about the 'underlying meanings' of those stories – underlying meanings that might be overtly denied by the community in question.

So, to give an example, we might take the story of Little Red Riding Hood and interpret it in terms of ideas about gender and fears of adolescent sexuality in Western culture. With prehistoric or ancient cultures, we will never know the stories, but we can use the archaeological material and its contextual associations to get some sense of what such underlying ideas might be.

I've heard an awful lot about 'the postmodernists' lately. Is postprocessual archaeology the same thing as postmodernism?

Oh dear, I was hoping you wouldn't ask that. This is a thorny issue that had better wait till chapter 11.

8

Archaeology and Gender

In the first two-thirds of this book, I have tried to present some of the background and content of current debates within archaeology. I have tended to present this as two distinct traditions, both drawing on a distinct strand of social theory in general and having distinct if not contradictory notions of where archaeology is or should be going.

In the process, I have had to over-simplify. I have presented these different traditions as both unitary and irrevocably opposed to one another: that all processualists think this, and all postprocessualists think that. The reader could be forgiven for thinking that the bars at archaeological conferences have a line of empty tables running down the middle of them separating two distinct huddles, one muttering into their beer about social evolution, taphonomy and middle-range theory, the other getting agitated about hermeneutics, structuration theory and political commitment.

To put it another way, 'processual' and 'postprocessual' archaeology have been *reified*. In other words, they have been converted mentally into things. Both have been presented as unified schools with a definite existence and autonomy of their own.

Theoretical practice is much more varied and diffuse than this – just as archaeological practice is also much more varied and diffuse than many practical textbooks might indicate. We can use the analogy of political parties. I could write a description of what the British Conservative Party stands for, the history, intellectual traditions of and influences on Conservatives, and list ten or twelve points of current policy. But this is not to say that all individual Conservatives have the same beliefs or agree on the same policies (indeed, as I write the reality is quite different).

First, as I stated in the Introduction, this book is very much an Anglo-American portrayal of theory. Other traditions thrive in other areas of the globe.

Second, many scholars have tried to combine different elements of both traditions. As we have seen, Colin Renfrew has asserted that a broadly systemic, 'scientific' framework can be combined with a recognition that cognition is important and scientifically accessible. Tim Earle, Elizabeth Brumfiel and others have combined elements of social evolution and a generalizing perspective with a stress on competition, conflict, gender, and so on, as I discussed in chapter 5. This 'softening' of processual thinking may be in response to postprocessual criticisms, or it may have happened anyway as part of a more general move within the human sciences. However it happened, whatever route was taken, the destination is the same.

Some have talked of an emerging consensus in theory, or of traditions at two extreme ends of a spectrum within which there is a comfortable middle position; I feel that this is not the case (see concluding chapter). Nevertheless one increasingly reads comments like the following that combine generalizing, 'processual' comments with explicit attention to meaning and context:

> Goods and ideas moving among societies had variable significance in the groups to which they were introduced... what may have been a utilitarian item near its source could serve as a badge of office within a more distant locale.... In reconstructing interregional networks, we must be able to place the objects and styles which define them within their original behavioural contexts. Treating them as the undifferentiated products of monolithic, homogeneous cultures will only obscure the socio-political significance of ancient transactions.... Determining the behavioural significance of objects and styles invariably depends on careful analyses of their contexts of recovery. (Schortman and Urban 1992: 237)

Third, there are contemporary movements and interests that cut across the battle lines of previous traditions. Recent work, for example, in feminist archaeology and the archaeology of gender, has been done from a variety of theoretical frameworks. And interests common to many archaeologists in theoretical issues such as 'space', 'agency', and 'trade and exchange' cut across the divisions presented here. Possibly the most influential book published on archaeological theory in the last decade, Gero and Conkey's edited volume *Engendering Archaeology*, includes contributions from a variety of viewpoints and backgrounds, though its Introduction does seek to establish certain theoretical alliances as we shall see.

Fourth, the view taken in previous chapters presents different traditions as competing with one another. But different traditions may be as much complementary as contradictory. For Robert Preucel (personal communication) 'theory is best understood not as a succession of different theories, with each new theory superseding the previously favoured theory, but rather as a web of interrelated theories and approaches, with each constraining and enabling the others'.

I don't agree fully with any of these views. There are, I feel, major contradictions between different theoretical views of the way the world works which are not easily resolved. It is very tempting to gloss over these differences, since we all like to feel that our own view occupies the 'middle ground', combines the best elements of all traditions, and that it is everybody else who is being 'extreme'. Archaeologists, like politicians, like to be seen to be occupying the middle ground whatever the reality is. It is equally difficult to oppose the seductive argument that each theory has its own legitimate place within the grand scheme of things, with its overtones of tolerance, moderation and 'fair play'.

To get across some of the variety (and intellectual vitality) of this activity I want to use the next few chapters to look at different theoretical approaches to a number of current themes. I have selected areas that happen to interest me particularly (gender, evolution, history). All these issues cut across the theoretical schema laid out before; I could have written a book with politics, gender, history, evolution as the core themes, and added chapters to these defining different overall traditions.

Gender

One of the most current and popular themes in archaeological theory is that of an archaeology of gender. This interest has become widespread and overt since the early 1980s. As with other interests, this rise of an explicit interest has been paralleled by a growing interest in gender issues in other disciplines, particularly sociology, literature, anthropology and history. It has also gone hand-in-hand with the growth of the feminist movement and feminist theory generally, though archaeological thought has lagged behind these other areas somewhat.

The archaeology of gender encompasses several different themes. These include: correction of male bias in archaeology; a critique of existing structures of archaeological practice; a reassessment of the history of archaeology; an examination of gender in the archaeological record; and a critique of what is seen as the male-biased nature of academic knowledge and the academic world in general. These different interests have, to an extent, succeeded one another since the early 1980s. I have also listed them in a very rough order, from less to more controversial.

Bias Correction

Interest in the archaeology of gender started, in part, with a critique of *androcentric* assumptions. Androcentrism is the belief that men are at the centre of things, either making up society exclusively or with women on the margins.

The most obvious example is what feminists see as the sexist use of language – the use of 'Man' for human, or of 'he' when 'she or he' is meant. Consider the following quotes, collated by Fiona Burtt from a study of children's books:

> The favourite subjects of prehistoric artists seem to have been animals and women. This is quite logical as both were indispensable to prehistoric man (just as they are both indispensable to 20th century man). Animals guaranteed that he survived from day to day and women that he survived from generation to generation. (Mitchell 1981: 31)

> Early man made a home in a cave.... He made scrapers and bones ....His wife used the scraper to clean the underside of animal skins. (Unstead 1953: 7; see also figure 8.1)

Or consider the following example, more 'academic', rather less obvious and as a result more difficult to disentangle, given as an explanation of the shift from the medieval castle to the Renaissance country house in England, made yet again by an avowedly atheoretical writer:

> In the late Middle Ages... the individual was left by default to establish his own position and maintain his own security by means of a personal affinity of retainers and a public display of strength. From the late 15th century onwards, however... states that were rapidly growing in authority were increasingly able to circumscribe the power of the individual at the same time better able to guarantee his freedom within strictly defined boundaries... the individual is left to make good his claims to status and authority not only through the exercise of powers bestowed on him by the state but by the cultivation of more personal distinctions. (Cooper 1997: 120)

What is missing from this passage? Is 'the individual' here exclusively male, or does it include women as well? (Note the 'as well' that the reader is seamlessly drawn into). Cooper might reasonably expect his

Figure 8.1 Prehistoric life according to children's books. From Unstead (1953: 20).

reader to 'know' (or simply to assume) that this society was largely patriarchal, and therefore he is referring largely to men when he talks of the individual. But then again, a minority of housebuilders of the period were women; the reader of the passage either mentally defines such women out of existence, treats them as surrogate men with exactly the same ideas and attitudes, or assumes they were 'exceptions' in some sense. What were women's views on this 'freedom' in a period when many of them were regularly beaten with the sanction of the state and in which they were considered in law, politics and religion to be inferior to men? Cooper does not tell us. Read the passage again, and form a picture of Cooper's individual in your mind, and I predict that you will find that it is a man.

By leaving women out of such discourses, any attempt to 'put them back' has to involve a lot of work: a complete rewriting of established common-sense terms and turns of phrase such as 'public display', 'power', 'authority'. These terms which at first reading seemed obvious now appear rather opaque. It therefore becomes very difficult to place women (or indeed men below the level of the élite, or children) 'back into the picture'; subconsciously, we are disinclined to make the effort, particularly as Cooper writes so apparently lucidly and smoothly. Women therefore become a 'problem'; the literature is full of discussions of the methodological difficulties of interpreting women's thoughts and activities during this period. But the 'problem' has in fact been created at least in part by discourses like Cooper's.

Feminists argue that it is important to isolate these androcentric assumptions because when someone tells you that, for example, male dominance is normal or natural to the human species, they refer implicitly to the way we have always been – in the distant past, or in the primate and animal world. But this argument, they suggest, is circular. When we look at 'empirical' archaeological studies of the past such as Cooper's, or ethnographic studies of other cultures, or anthropological studies of primates, we find that they have been studied from a viewpoint biased in favour of the male of the species. This bias is all the more pervasive because it is often unconscious.

Ethnographic studies are a good example. Various cross-cultural studies have suggested that 'male dominance' is universal. But consider for a moment the nature of this information. Much of it was collected in the nineteenth century by predominantly male ethnographers with literally Victorian attitudes towards such issues. Ethnographers would 'naturally' choose to ask the men of the tribe about the nature of its political system rather than the women, and tend to interpret the varying and ambiguous replies that they got back in terms of their own Victorian expectations and preconceptions. Therefore, feminist anthropologists argue that such information derived from ethnography needs to be questioned and theorized rather than accepted blindly and uncritically. The same point goes for what we 'know' from other disciplines.

Another example of androcentrism is the history of archaeology itself. Read most traditional textbooks and you will find that archaeology developed via the discoveries and intellectual insights of, in the main, 'great men'. Many have argued, however, that the contribution of women to archaeological thought has been systematically minimized by historians of archaeology. Figures such as Dorothy Garrod or Jacquetta Hawkes tend to be left out of many such narratives, or treated as somehow less important. An important recent strand of feminist archaeology has consisted of the rediscovery and rewriting of the history of archaeology to reflect the achievements of these women. The motivations for this rewriting may include a simple desire to 'tell the past as it really was', or to provide an inspiration for young women archaeologists in the present. It is striking that in response to this critique, successive editions of standard textbooks have been heavily modified (compare, for example, successive editions of Willey and Sabloff's *A History of American Archaeology*, or the first and second editions of Renfrew and Bahn (1996)).

Critique of Archaeological Practice

Feminist archaeologists question the position of women within the archaeological profession. Overt and implicit sexism in recruitment policies, academic funding and promotion have all been questioned, very much in line with the general questioning of discriminatory practices in Britain and North America generally.

For example, Joan Gero (1988, 1991) analysed the granting of research funds to different people. She found that men were statistically more successful at getting grants for excavation and 'fieldwork' in general, whereas women were statistically less likely to be awarded financial help, and more likely to be awarded grants for what Gero termed 'archaeological housework' – pottery and small finds analysis, environmental material. Was it then any surprise, she asked, when the interpretations produced by this fieldwork emphasized stereotypical images?

Note that many of what Alison Wylie (1993) calls these 'chilly-making activities' are not dependent on overt bias, openly chauvinist attitudes or political discrimination as such, but are dependent on deeper and less obvious practices such as the use of language, hidden assumptions about career trajectories, even patterns of writing and conversation. This observation has two implications. First, it can be argued that we all participate in sexist practices however consciously we oppose sexism in principle. Second, the minutiae of everyday behaviour links in to wider practices – 'the personal is political'.

Much of these first two points is fairly uncontroversial – few dispute the fact that past interpretations have reflected the conscious and unconscious sexism of their time, or that women remain discriminated against in contemporary society in a variety of ways, and that career development in archaeology reflects this. The next two points move on to more disputed territory.

Archaeologies of Gender

The third point is a desire to look at different constructions of gender in the past, as revealed in the archaeological record. If we think it is legitimate to take societies long extinct and look at 'social ranking', at trade and exchange, even at cognitive factors, why can't we also look at different gender roles in the past?

These gender roles, it is argued, vary from culture to culture. A theoretical distinction is made by theorists between *sex* and *gender.* Sex is, it is argued, biological – most of us are born men or women, and our biological makeup does not vary (though even this can be questioned; see below).

There is a difference, however, between being born a biological male or female, and the experience of being 'gendered', of being a woman or a man in a given society. It can be argued that there is nothing 'normal' or 'natural' about acting like a man or a woman. For example, it was considered manly in the Middle Ages for élite men to weep and swoon on a regular basis; by the nineteenth century, the women were doing the weeping and swooning while the men were keeping a stiff upper lip. In some cultures women are sexually assertive and men are expected to be passive; and so on.

Gender, then, is culturally constructed, even if we accept the argument that gender is usually assigned on a biological basis. Gender varies from culture to culture. There is much debate about the extent of this variation (is it completely variable? are there some cross-cultural universals?) and how closely gender and sex are linked.

It follows that if we are interested in the past, we cannot assume that women and men behaved in the same way in all societies. For example, we cannot assume distinctions that we often take for granted existed in the past. These include distinctions between domestic and public, between hunting and gathering, between the household and the wider world.

Instead, we need to ask questions about the different roles and experiences of women and men in a given period. These may have been similar or different; but the question needs to be asked rather than particular kinds of division assumed. Indeed, we need to question the assumption often made that a rigid binary division of labour ('the men did this and the women did that') existed at all.

Many argue that in practice all archaeology is 'gendered'. They point out that many archaeologists make assumptions about gender in their work, as we pointed out above, and that there is no such thing as a 'gender-neutral' account of the past. Think of the quote from Cooper, or the way, for example, different human activities are valued. There are countless descriptions of craft specialization in the literature, but few of changing methods of food preparation. There is, feminists argue, an implicit assumption in much of the literature that specialized craft activity was done by men and is therefore important, and food preparation was done by women and is less so. Food preparation may or may not have been performed by men, women or both; whoever prepared the food, it is certainly important in the constitution of culture.

An archaeology of gender, then, has led in practice to a re-examination of the small scale such as the archaeology of the household, a widening of thinking to include areas such as an archaeology of children and an archaeology of sexuality, and the reinterpretation of the domestic as an important part of social and political life in the past rather than simply a 'domestic retreat'.

Men, Women and Knowledge

The *phallocentric nature of knowledge* is a difficult point to grasp, since it involves questioning the very basis of academic enquiry, or indeed what it is to be a student or a teacher.

Think about the way we praise an academic argument, or denigrate it. We praise 'strong', 'robust', 'well organized', 'powerful' arguments; conversely, we denigrate arguments that are weak, tentative, inconclusive. The language of archaeological theory itself is the language of battle – theories conflict and clash, different schools muster allies to strengthen their arguments. Debate is confrontational: one side gets the better or the worse of the argument. Students are taught to be impersonal in their essays – to separate emotions and feelings from academic argument, to omit personal experience from their writing.

Many feminists argue that the academic structuring of knowledge in this way is *phallocentric*. That is, the academic establishment treats stereotypically 'male' ways of thinking and acting as legitimate, and stereotypically 'female' ways as illegitimate, 'out of court'. Phallocentric discourse claims to be fair and neutral, to offer a 'level playing field'; the professor will tell you that anyone can write a first class paper if they follow the correct academic rules and have the necessary commitment and intellectual ability. In practice, however, the rules of this game are discriminatory, since (among other reasons) it requires women to think and write 'like men', at least stereotypically, if they are to suceed. If men have been socialized into this way of thinking from birth, the argument continues, is it any surprise that they are 'better' at this academic game than women?

What is needed, feminists suggest, are different rules for the game. Why can't we be 'emotional' when writing? What is wrong with multivocality – telling stories with different voices, different conclusions? Why can't we write stories about people's personal experiences? What's wrong with ending with a question rather than a final, firm conclusive statement?

In this way, much feminist critique ends up at a very similar position to that of many postprocessual archaeologists; indeed, many of the postprocessual arguments rehearsed in chapter 5 owe a profound debt to feminist thinking on this and other points (see below).

Case Study: What This Awl Means

Janet Spector's book *What This Awl Means: Feminist Archaeology at a Wahpeton Dakota Village* is a study of a nineteenth-century Native American settlement, Little Rapids, in what is now Minnesota in the Midwestern USA. Rather than attempt to write a neutral, distanced, objective site report, however, Spector consciously and explicitly sets out to explore her original, emotive reasons for wanting to be an archaeologist: 'these motives are empathetic – a longing to discover essences, images, and feelings of the past – not detached, distanced, objective' (Spector 1993: 1).

Spector breaks three rules of academic discourse in the opening chapters. First, she goes into her own past life history and explores her personal reasons for doing archaeology and coming to the Little Rapids site. Second, rather than looking at 'big questions' such as social complexity or the pattern of trade between Native and white Americans, she focuses initially on one very tiny artefact, apparently insignificant in itself – 'a small antler awl handle' (figure 8.2). Third, Spector writes a story about this handle – how it was lost, what the young woman who owned it was doing at the time, what the experience of life at Little Rapids was like. The story is backed up by Spector's extensive knowledge and understanding of the archaeological and historic data, but is self-consciously written as a story nevertheless, intended to evoke the emotions and spirit of the inhabitants of the site.

Spector contrasts the story she has told with previous archaeological work on awls. Previous typologies of awl handless present themselves as neutral classifications, Spector argues, but they are in fact biased in respect both to ethnicity and gender. Conventional typologies treat awls first and foremost as trade goods brought in by Europeans, rather than as artefacts related to Native American ('Indian') women's activities:

> An important but hidden assumption . . . is that European-produced metal awl tips are more important than Indian-produced awl handles. Built into [these] classifications and table titles, this theme leads to

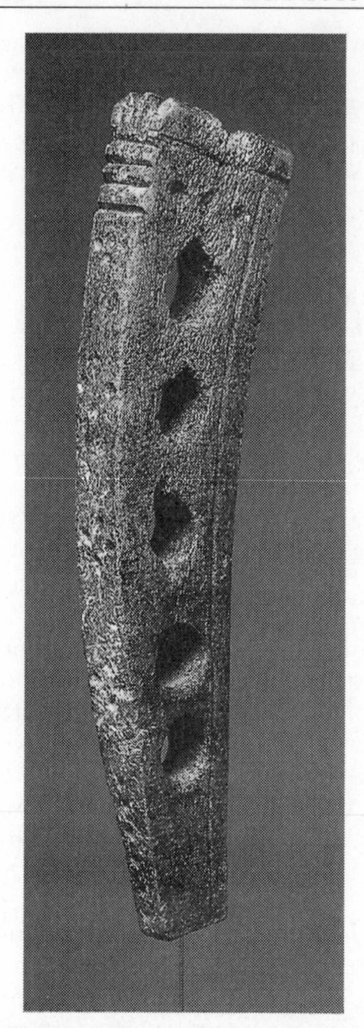
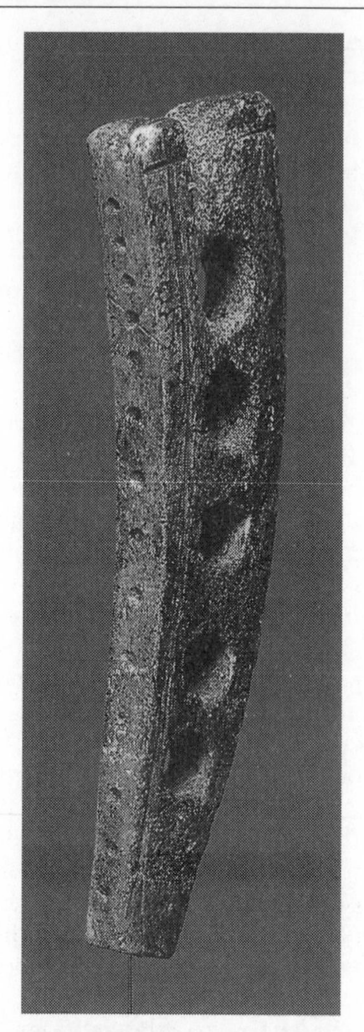

Figure 8.2 The awl handle excavated by Spector's crew. Spector's narrative links it to the young girl Mazaokeyiwin who lived at Little Rapids and may have lost the awl in the 1840s (Spector 1993).

> emphasis on metal awl tips as markers of European influence on Indians and implies the disintegration of native culture. This would have been insulting, annoying, or simply wrong to Indians who used awls, particularly to women who inscribed their bone or antler handles to display publicly their accomplishments. (Spector 1993: 31–2)

Spector tells stories also about the progress of the dig, the discovery of the awl, the experiences of different dig members, and frankly

Figure 8.3 The elderly Mazaokeyiwin working a hide (Spector 1993).

explores tensions and co-operation with Native Americans in the course of the research project. She is helped in her task by the extensive historical and ethnographic documentation of the Dakota people and of the site, that allows her to give names and personalities to many of the nineteenth-century inhabitants of Little Rapids (figure 8.3).

It is striking that Spector's openly feminist perspective leads her to accentuate the small scale and personal (what the awl handle meant to its owner, not the awl's position within wider trade networks; the personalities and excitement of the research project). It is also striking how Spector's feminist account is also immediately and unavoidably engaged in other questions of politics and identity, most obviously that of relations between Native Americans and whites.

This all sounds fine, but I'm getting a little confused over terminology here. Is gender archaeology the same thing as feminist archaeology?

Not necessarily. It is without question that interest in gender issues in archaeology grew out of the rise in feminist concerns of the last twenty years. But remember that it is pretty undeniable to assert that all archaeology makes assumptions about gender. If we need to look at gender in the past, there is no *a priori* reason why a specifically feminist perspective needs to be used.

Gero and Conkey (1991, 1997) argue that the archaeology of gender is increasingly diverse in the theoretical positions it has taken. They show that sociobiology, social constructivism, cultural and biological evolution, political economy, and agency and performance theory have all been used to structure enquiry into gender in the archaeological record. They point to the very deep differences in theoretical assumptions behind many of these schools, and assert that many studies of gender do not draw extensively or even at all on feminist critiques within the human sciences in general.

Of course, it all depends on definitions of feminism, which vary. 'I myself have never been able to find out precisely what feminism is: I only know that people call me a feminist whenever I express sentiments that differentiate me from a doormat or a prostitute' (Rebecca West 1913; cited in Humm 1992: 34). More specifically, Conkey and Gero draw on feminist critiques of science and point to four areas that they feel distinguish specifically feminist enquiry in archaeology:

1 The recognition that 'politics and the substantive products of knowledge are essentially inseparable';
2 The recognition that rationality is a 'mythical conflation that never exists in actual scientific practice';
3 'Association with a cognitive style that favours 'intimate' knowledge and nuanced understandings of data over categorical thinking';
4 A challenge to 'basic disciplinary arrangements' and the fostering of alternative views. (Conkey and Gero 1997: 427–8)

Conkey and Gero argue that feminist archaeology is, or should be, a dangerous and transforming exercise. They distance themselves from considerations 'of gender in prehistoric studies without reconfiguring archaeology in any way' and assert that

> An archaeology that takes feminist theory seriously is self-transformational and communal. Radical reappraisals – rigorous, scholarly,

> informed, and purposive – emerge from feminist theory precisely because traditional assumptions and values really do look profoundly different when viewed from a woman-centred perspective. Some have wanted to call this 'seeing gender everywhere', with the derogatory term 'genderlirium'. But 'genderlirium' is an equally apt term with which to critique Western androcentrism, with its hard-headed rules for a single way of knowing and its single vision. (Conkey and Gero 1997: 424 and 430)

For Conkey and Gero, then, archaeological studies of gender come from a variety of theoretical viewpoints, but a specifically feminist standpoint is one that questions existing archaeological practice at a very basic level.

OK, so we can't assume men and women did this or that in the past. But in that case how can we ever begin to talk about gender?

This impinges on the question of *essentialism*. In the view of some feminists, there is nothing essential to 'feminine nature'. Some attack 'biological essentialism', that is, the attempt to define cross-culturally gender roles based on biological 'facts' such as men's greater upper-body strength or women's role in childbirth and infant care. They argue that such 'facts' are socially constructed. For example, they question the way gender differences are always presented in a binary fashion in biological studies.

The problem you raise is that if we cannot say with certainty which activities were undertaken by which gender, or even that activities were or were not gendered, then we cannot say anything positive about the construction of gender in a given society, particularly a prehistoric one.

One way out of this is to construct a contextual argument. Liv Gibbs (1987), for example, has looked at which artefacts are associated with which gender in graves in prehistoric Denmark, and has then extended this argument outwards, to look at the same classes of artefacts in domestic contexts. Another way out is to rely on a limited essentialism: for example, that child-rearing does involve an association of women with domestic contexts.

You've said that gender cuts across previous theoretical categories. But it seems to me that it's closely related to postprocessual archaeology. Both movements relate archaeology to politics, both try to look at conflict and inequality, both try to write different narratives that include the personal . . .

Historically, the archaeology of gender and postprocessual archaeology have close links both with each other and with feminist thought in the human sciences. Many of the younger archaeologists in the 1980s were and remain closely involved with both movements, particularly in Britain. Specifically, we can point to (a) the widening of the definition of 'political'; (b) stress on small-scale, local and household contexts as important; (c) stress on multivocality; (d) stress on meaning and lived experience; (e) stress on conflict as being played out through everyday practice. Indeed, I suspect that when the history of postprocessual thought in the 1980s comes to be written it will be found that the role of individual feminists has been under-acknowledged.

But many would argue that bias correction (point 1 above) is a legitimate and indeed essential part of any scientific archaeology. Within science as a whole, much work has been done to correct what are seen as specific biases; for example, critiques of Charles Darwin's terminology when he attributes 'passive' and 'active' roles to female and male apes respectively.

Similarly, there is no necessary conflict between a positivist view of science and stress on recruitment and equal rights issues within archaeology. It is perfectly possible to argue for 'scientific method' in archaeological reasoning, while acknowledging that the archaeological profession needs to address issues of discrimination. But in accordance with positivist method, one's stance on 'political' issues such as equality should be kept separate from one's academic judgements.

Some feminists, particularly in the human sciences as a whole, argue strongly against what they see as the slippery nature of the way some arguments under the postprocessual banner see everything in a very multifaceted, deliberately ambiguous way, in which the very real powerlessness and exploitation felt by many women seems to them to be glossed over. Isn't it ironic, they point out, that just as women are beginning to get a small slice of the cake, making a real difference at work and so on, that it's revealed that such bread-and-butter issues are only a 'language game' anyway? Alison Wylie writes that

> strong constructivist and relativist positions embody what seem to be patently an ideology of the powerful. Only the most powerful, the most successful in achieving control over the world, could be constructed as

> they choose.... Any who lack such power, or who lack an investment in believing they have such power, are painfully aware that they negotiate an intransigent reality that impinges on their lives at every turn. (Wylie 1992b: 25)

A related argument is that of inclusiveness. Feminists often feel that their arguments are 'hijacked', made part of some 'wider argument' such as that of Marxism or of postprocessual archaeology and in the process subsumed and ultimately ignored. It is striking that Spector prefers her argument to stand on its own two feet. Her bibliography refers to very little of the 'postprocessual' literature. In practical terms, just as the majority of New Archaeologists were pushy young men, so some feminists argue that many male postprocessualists have now slid seamlessly into senior academic positions.

In short, both in the archaeology of gender and within the feminist movement as a whole, there is a great diversity of approaches and tensions between different viewpoints. Many of these tensions reflect archaeological theory as a whole; but other tensions point the way forward for new thinking in theory beyond some of the more sterile debates of recent years.

9

Archaeology and Evolution

In this chapter I want to look at the way different theoretical approaches treat the question of evolution. As with the archaeology of gender and politics, we shall find that different attitudes to evolution betray different attitudes to archaeological theory and practice as a whole. Again, we shall also find that different attitudes within archaeology are paralleled by a similar range of attitudes within the social sciences as a whole.

As with other terms, the word 'evolution' is not easily defined. Evolution has come to have an array of different meanings, some at odds with or even completely contradicting others. The best way to explain what these different meanings are is to look at the history of archaeology and of evolution.

The origins of evolutionary ideas can be traced back to the Renaissance of the fifteenth and sixteenth centuries, and in particular to the first encounters between Europeans and other peoples around the world. If we consider these origins, we find that early evolutionary ideas were closely bound up with the development of archaeology as a discipline. Before the fifteenth century, people in the past were considered to be 'just like us'; look at any portrayal of St George, a Roman soldier, in a medieval stained glass window, where he is given medieval armour and weaponry (figure 9.1). The idea that past peoples practised different ways of life, had different cultures and beliefs, and that these needed to be studied on their own terms was largely absent before the Renaissance.

Fifteenth- and sixteenth-century European explorers and colonists faced an intellectual paradox when they encountered native peoples, in particular Native Americans. Native peoples were *different*. In the view of many European thinkers, here in the forests of North America were people who practised none of the civilized arts – they went naked, had no formal code of law, no state, and above all, no

Figure 9.1 Portrayal of St George, from a fifteenth-century panel in Ranworth Church, Norfolk, England (photo: Pam Graves).

(Christian) religion. *And yet such 'savages' could act in noble and civilized ways.* This was difficult to explain within the sixteenth-century European scheme of things to say the least. One way out of the conundrum was to suggest a powerful idea: *perhaps 'we', the civilized peoples of Europe, were like this in the past.* Perhaps, in other words, such 'savages' represented some sort of earlier or lower order of human existence from which Renaissance 'Man' had evolved. Hence, for example, the portrayals by early antiquarians of 'early Britons' were often closely modelled on those of Native Americans (figures 9.2 and 9.3).

As a result of this colonial encounter and the intellectual challenge it posed to European thinkers, early antiquarians began to think about a distant prehistoric past at the same time as they began to think about the idea that is central to many versions of cultural or social evolution, namely that *different peoples in different areas of the world went through similar sorts of social changes and processes.* At its most simple, this was conceived of as a transition between 'savagery' and 'civilization', 'them' and 'us'.

In the nineteenth century this very basic idea was elaborated in the thought of, among others, Herbert Spencer and Charles Darwin.

Spencer and Cultural Evolution

Spencer elaborated the idea that all human societies move from a less to a more complex state and linked this to notions of morality and human 'progress'. In Spencer's thought, 'civilized' society was more moral than 'savagery' – look at the way both words are loaded, ambiguous terms, even today. Spencer went further. He suggested that the idea of Progress was more than just a moral belief. The new positivist Science had given us the ability to objectively measure and confirm our belief in progress. Spencer therefore gave this belief in progress a scientific mandate.

Clearly, all these ideas were popular in an age of imperialism. The thought of Spencer and others contributed to a view of the world where Europeans were fitted to govern subject peoples. Not only did Europeans have Christian religion and the moral order on their side, but they were also confirmed in their self-belief by the objective findings of the natural sciences. Native peoples such as the subjects of the British Empire might in this view aspire to progress to civilized states, but the upward progress might well be very slow, so slow as to be imperceptible to the contemporary observer, as upward progress had been slow in the origins of civilization in the first place.

Figure 9.2 A Native American chief, drawn by John White in the 1580s.

Figure 9.3 An 'Ancient Briton', drawn by John White in the 1580s.

It is worth elaborating upon this point. It has been suggested that evolutionary ideas that treat human history in terms of a 'league table' of progress have always been popular when the intellectual basis of a culture is feeling self-confident. Thus, ideas of progress were popular in Victorian Britain, but waned in the twentieth century with two world wars and the end of the British Empire; whereas in the United States, they were especially popular during the 1960s, but lost popularity after Vietnam.

Darwin and Biological Evolution

Charles Darwin is the most important figure in the intellectual history of the term 'evolution'. Darwin's views, however, have been seen by many as being quite distinct from Spencer's. This is important because, as we shall see, two very different views of evolution emerge in modern archaeology: *cultural evolution* and *biological evolution*. Cultural evolution can trace its ancestry back to Spencer and beyond; biological evolution to Darwin. Much confusion has been caused by the treatment of these two movements as one and the same thing.

Darwin's ideas were based on observation of species in the natural world. He suggested that organisms that reproduce sexually varied one from another: each individual organism is slightly different to its parents. Later scholars would explain these differences in terms of genetic mutation. Such random mutations then fared differently, in that some mutations were better adapted to the environment around them, that is, they were better able to survive and reproduce than others. To take a classic (and over-simplified) example, giraffes with longer rather than shorter necks would be able to feed themselves better by reaching more of the tops of trees in the savannah; giraffes with shorter necks would not fare so well, would not get as much food, would mate less often and thus be less likely to pass their genes on to the next generation. The natural environment, then, 'selected for' certain forms of mutation rather than others; the latter would fail to reproduce and would die out in the long run.

Darwin's theory of biological evolution in the natural world was thus centred on ideas of *random variation, adaptation and natural selection*, for which the reader is referred to the literature for a more detailed exposition. Here, I want to focus on some of the broader aspects of the impact of Darwinian thought on archaeology.

The first implication is obvious: a long timescale for human origins and consequently for many of the processes we study as archaeologists. A view of the world as starting in 4004 BC was replaced by a world and its occupants millions of years old. In this sense the views of the geologist Lyell, who interpreted the geological record as the product of very long-term processes, set the scene for Darwin's destruction of the biblical view of Creation, and the consequent implication of a long timescale for the physical evolution of the human race. By analogy, many archaeologists argued, cultural evolution might take place at a similarly slow, gradual rate. Hence *there is a close link between ideas of evolution and ideas of cultural process* discussed in chapters 2 and 5.

A second implication is a very simple and basic point – that humans were and are part of the natural world like any other species. Therefore, there is no *a priori* reason why the theories and methods of the natural sciences should not be applied to the human species. Thinkers in the Darwinian tradition are often highly sceptical of claims that humans are 'special' or 'different' to any other species in the natural world. They often regard such claims as based on metaphysical or semi-religious assertions about the 'essence' of humankind that are, in their view, value-laden and unscientific. It follows, therefore, that there were and *are close links between positivism* (the belief that the human sciences should model themselves on the natural sciences: chapter 3) *and many strands of evolutionary theory.*

A third broader implication is that whereas an idealist view of the world focuses attention on people's norms and beliefs, a Darwinian view focuses attention on reproduction, adaptation, natural selection – it can be seen as profoundly materialist. Darwinian arguments often stress that culture is 'Man's extrasomatic means of adaptation', and cultural traits are often explained in terms of the way they help humans adapt to a particular ecological setting. Cognitive factors might be important in this view, but simply as 'coping devices' for dealing with the outside world. *Ideas of evolution therefore tend to be linked with materialist philosophies* in general.

Ideas of both cultural and biological evolution, therefore, were closely linked to some of the ideas of the early New Archaeology. We have seen how the strongly evolutionary ideas of Leslie White had a very specific influence on the thought of Binford and others. Conversely, opposition to evolutionary ideas as applied to human culture can be closely linked to various strands of postprocessual thinking, as we shall see. But before we get to the point of looking at such criticisms, it is first important to look at particular forms of evolutionary theory. We shall look first at different cultural evolutionary typologies, and go on to look further at the distinction between cultural and biological evolution.

Cultural Evolution

If we go back to the Renaissance and Spencer and accept the belief that societies go through similar developmental stages, then we can see that many different schema of social development are 'evolutionary' even if they do not necessarily spell this out explicitly.

Classical Marxism, for example, proposes that all societies go through the same set of stages: primitive communist, ancient, feudal, capitalist. Marx and Engels, indeed, read and were profoundly influenced by the thought of several nineteenth-century evolutionary thinkers, most notably Maine and Morgan. In *The Origin of the Family, Private Property and the State*, a standard text of traditional Marxist thought on pre-capitalist societies, Engels argued that all three features (the nuclear family, private property and a centralized state) were absent from pre-modern societies, using (faulty) ethnographic evidence from 'primitive' societies as an analogue for the prehistoric past.

Most schemes of cultural evolution tend to classify societies in a line moving from simple to complex, on the grounds that this, empirically, is the story of human development: from 'simple' hunter-gatherer forms many thousands of years ago to the 'complex' modern states of today. For Leslie White, this move from simple to complex was explained as a tendency to harness ever more vast quantities of energy, as systems became more entropic or tightly integrated. Durkheim's and Spencer's views of evolution also specified a definite direction from simple to complex. In many versions of evolutionary theory, however, there is no *a priori* reason why social forms cannot move in the other direction in certain circumstances, that is from complex to simple. This is what is proposed with the collapse of cultural systems and their 'return' to 'simpler' forms of society, like the Ancient Maya after the 'Classic Maya Collapse' or the ancestral pueblos of Chaco Canyon. There is also no *a priori* theoretical reason why more complex forms of society are better adapted to the natural environment than less complex forms. If modern capitalist society is wiped out in, say, excesses of industrial pollution, it may well be the case that 'simpler' forms of human society based on subsistence agriculture or on gathering and hunting are shown to be more adaptive in the long run to this planet's environment than 'complex' industrial forms.

Some evolutionary schemes are *unilineal*; that is, they suggest that there is one broad pattern or trend to cultural evolution. Others are *multilinear*, suggesting a number of divergent evolutionary paths a

Fig 28a The tree of organic phylogeny with its characteristic forking branch pattern.
Source: Kroeber 1948, p 260.

Fig 28b The tree of cultural phylogeny with *its* characteristic reticulated branch pattern.
Source: Kroeber 1948, p 260.

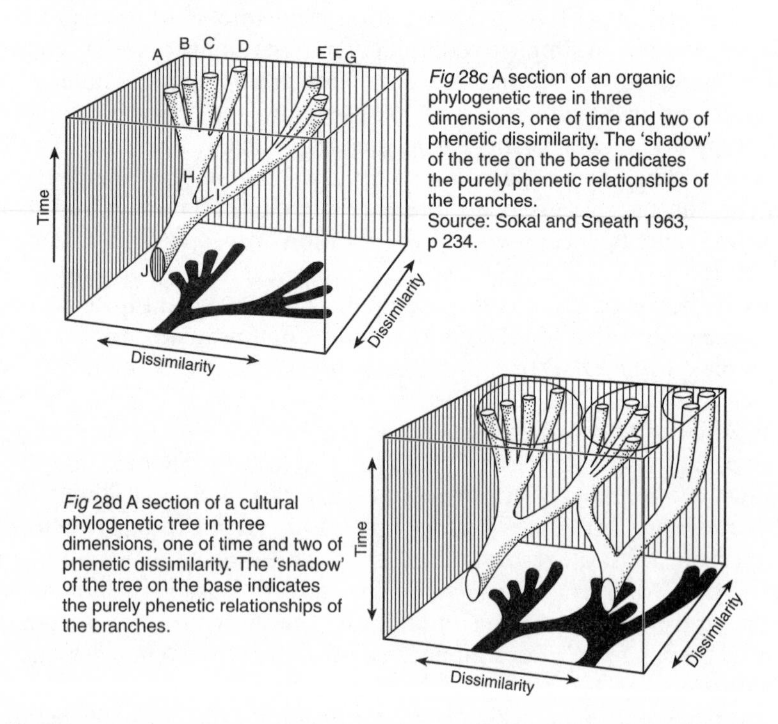

Fig 28c A section of an organic phylogenetic tree in three dimensions, one of time and two of phenetic dissimilarity. The 'shadow' of the tree on the base indicates the purely phenetic relationships of the branches.
Source: Sokal and Sneath 1963, p 234.

Fig 28d A section of a cultural phylogenetic tree in three dimensions, one of time and two of phenetic dissimilarity. The 'shadow' of the tree on the base indicates the purely phenetic relationships of the branches.

Figure 9.4 Clarke's contrast (drawn from Kroeber 1948) between organic and cultural evolution.

particular cultural sequence can follow. These multilinear schemes can diverge or converge (figure 9.4).

We might contrast for example the two unilinear schemes of the cultural anthropologists Elman Service and Morton Fried. Both have been particularly influential on archaeologists. Service gives us a fourfold typology ranging along the scale of simple to complex of band, tribe, chiefdom and state. Fried offers an alternative scheme of egalitarian, ranked, stratified and state. Note that while they differ in their terminology, the descriptions of Service and Fried share a great deal of common ground. Both start and stop at the same point (they start with 'simple' gatherer-hunter societies, though their definitions of such societies differ, and end with the modern state). They both also share a similar methodology; in other words, the methods that have been used to draw them up are very much the same.

Note that this is another example of archaeology being influenced by other disciplines. In practice, much archaeology within the tradition of cultural evolution has followed the method of ascertaining what the archaeological correlates of each stage might be, and then looking for them in the archaeological record.

For example, Service suggests that chiefdoms will have the following features among others: a settlement hierarchy; redistributive trade networks; religious complexity involving monumental construction and so on. Much archaeological effort has been spent in refining these criteria and seeking out relevant evidence in the archaeological record in a wide variety of contexts, from Renfrew's work on Neolithic and Early Bronze Age Wessex to Tim Earle's work on chiefdoms in Southern America and Polynesia.

Note also the very close parallels in much of evolutionary thought with classical Marxism. Indeed, Leslie White was attacked in the McCarthyite paranoia of his time as being a 'closet Marxist', though conversely he was accused of watering down his Marxism by others such as Maurice Bloch.

Social evolution also shares many of the problems of classical Marxism. One of these is that in its 'classical', unilinear form it allows little or no room for contact between societies. If societies evolve from one state to another, what role is there for cultural contact and diffusion? Others have argued that to propose one single scheme of evolution is simplistic. Societies might develop along different paths. Such schemes are termed *multilinear.* In recent years, evolutionary theory has responded to these and other criticisms in a variety of ways.

Criticisms of Cultural Evolution

Many of the criticisms of cultural evolution are framed in parallel to postprocessual critiques of archaeology as a whole. Shanks and Tilley, for example, write: 'The concepts of function, adaptation, and evolution have no explanatory role in a consideration of the social and need to be either completely abandoned or reduced to a simple descriptive vocabulary' (1987: 210). Why do they suggest this?

1 It is argued that evolutionary schema apply criteria from 'outside'. Polynesia, Wessex, Iron Age Denmark, the Anasazi are all treated as belonging to the same stage of evolution, and the same factors and mechanisms for change are examined in each context – class conflict, environmental stress, development of a managerial élite, and so on.

   Cultural evolutionary models, it is therefore argued, 'flatten out' past societies. Past people's own view of themselves are seen as unimportant, and the uniqueness of particular cultures is not seen as important or capable of producing generalizations. In short, they find it difficult to encompass the *particularity* of historical sequences. We have seen parallel criticisms of systems thinking (chapter 5).
2 A related criticism is that cultural evolutionary models seem to leave little room for *contingency* or historical accident. Societies seem to be on a smooth, high, inexorable road to state formation. Critics argue that history could have happened otherwise, purely by chance. A favourite variant of this claim is that all such models are implicitly *teleological*. A teleological view of history is one in which there is a strong sense of direction, of humanity moving inexorably towards a predefined and predetermined goal (*telos*).
3 Such evolutionary models tend to ignore diffusion and cultural contact. If each society goes through a fundamentally similar set of stages, what account is given of contact between societies? How might such contact alter or deflect social change?
4 The individual is also ignored. Human beings are presented as pawns, locked into an inexorable evolutionary process over which they have no control. Again, in parallel with systems thinking, evolutionary models are open to the attack of critical theorists like Habermas and others discussed in chapter 5.

As a result of these criticisms, simple models of cultural evolution have been all but abandoned. Archaeologists using evolutionary theory have taken one of two courses: they have either tried to abandon evolutionary theory entirely (such as many postprocessualists), or alternatively have developed cultural evolutionary ideas to take account of these criticisms. We have seen some of these developed forms linking up with the modifications to systems thinking discussed in chapter 5.

Biological Evolution

For advocates of cultural evolution, the basic unit of analysis is the cultural group or society. Societies rise, fall, die out, transform themselves; societies are ranked on tables; societies evolve. In biological evolution, harking back to Darwin, the unit of selection is much smaller. In many versions, it can only be the individual: it is only the individual who lives and reproduces. But as with cultural evolution, the strands of thought involved are very varied, and it is difficult to generalize about a 'school of biological evolution' as a whole.

One variant is sociobiology. Sociobiology attempts to explain features of human behaviour as being the result of genetic/biological rather than social, non-genetic causes. It suggests that certain behaviours are the result of genetic propensities that were adaptive at some point in the past. The origins of language, for example, have been sought in the primate use of grooming as an aid to primate group solidarity: in the absence of grooming, modern humans use language to create such solidarity. Sociobiology is an exceptionally controversial theory of culture, since the stress on social differences as being rooted in genes is often interpreted by its opponents as being racist or sexist. For example, some sociobiologists argue that it makes adaptive sense for males to spread their genes around widely and reproduce as much as possible; female primates, by contrast, can only have a limited number of children, and need a stable partner for protection against predators and other environmental dangers. Therefore, it is argued, women in modern Western society are genetically predisposed to stable relationships, whereas men are genetically predisposed to sleep with as many sexual partners as possible. Sociobiology is a popular school within evolutionary studies as a whole, but published archaeological studies taking an explicitly sociobiological view are rare.

A second position is that of Robert Dunnell. Dunnell rejects the entire project of cultural evolution as 'unscientific' and having nothing to do with biological models. Dunnell separates two very different strands of nineteenth-century thought: Spencer's stress on social totalities leading to cultural evolution; and the adaptationist arguments of Darwin. Only the latter, he claims, is 'scientific'. Cultural evolution is unscientific because it substitutes cause/intention for a scientific framework: 'it employs different notions of cause, lacks theory in the usual sense of the word, and employs an entirely different research strategy' (Dunnell 1989: 38). Dunnell also rejects sociobiology, on the grounds that most transmission of traits is cultural rather than genetic.

Instead of positing the individual as the unit of selection, Dunnell selects the 'phenotype'. Phenotypes are the physical and behavioural elements of organisms; 'artefacts are the hard parts of the behavioural segment of phenotypes', like shells or nests for other species. If Dunnell is correct, then we must abandon much of traditional archaeology, including what he terms 'model descriptions' of phases, cultures and periods, as well as 'behavioural reconstruction'.

Programmes such as Dunnell's have very few case studies worked through in detail to back them up; Bettinger and Eerkens note 'an unfortunate parallel between evolutionary archaeology and the weather: everyone talks about it but no one does anything about it' (1997: 177). Nevertheless, models such as these are increasing in popularity, particularly in North American archaeology.

Adaptation, Rationality and Cultural Ecology

However defined, ideas of adaptation and selection have influenced the thinking behind a raft of techniques in modern archaeology. These ideas can be loosely defined as cultural ecology. Cultural ecology is the belief that societies will be more or less adapted to their material environment, and therefore that the characteristics of those societies can be explained in terms of such adaptation.

Cultural ecology is a school of thought associated with Julian Steward and profoundly influential on early New Archaeology (see chapter 2). Many of its adherents are anthropologists working with modern societies. Examples of ideas from cultural ecology that have been taken up and used by archaeologists are site catchment analysis, optimal foraging theory, risk and seasonality.

Site catchment analysis is a body of techniques based on the mapping of resources around a site. It is assumed that people will exploit the landscape 'rationally', and they will utilize resources in such a way as to maximize returns. The technique, then, consists of drawing a line around a site's location and looking at the resources within two, three, four hours' walk of the site.

Interest in 'risk' is based on the observation that it is not so much the overall productivity of an environment that is important for understanding human adaptations, but the degree of risk within it. Neolithic farming communities, for example, may be worried not so much about producing more food as such, but about what might happen during the odd 'bad year' of disaster and famine. It is no use a village producing enough food to support 500 people nine years out of ten if there is only food to support 100 people in the tenth, famine year. Many economic, social and even religious strategies, then, can be understood as risk minimization. Extended networks of kin, trading contacts, food storage: all these phenomena have been interpreted by anthropologists and archaeologists as ways to mitigate the risk of subsistence crisis. If food is short one year, one can call on one's distant cousins; or on trade partners who owe you obligations; or on the tribe to whom you gave marriage partners. Thus, elaborate social networks such as those of Australian Aborigines or Inuit Native Americans can be explained as adaptive responses to 'high-risk' environments such as the Australian desert or the Arctic tundra.

'Seasonality' refers to an interest in how human groups survive through the year. There may be plenty of resources in an environment for most of the year, but this is of no use if people will starve two months out of twelve. Peter Rowley-Conwy looked at the Ertebølle culture of Denmark and suggested that the collection of oysters, though not important in terms of overall caloric intake, was absolutely critical at a certain time of year when few other resources were available. This observation in turn helped Rowley-Conwy explain site location and other aspects of Ertebølle behaviour.

Case Study: Palaeolithic Art

A good example of how ideas derived from cultural ecology have affected archaeological interpretations is Steven Mithen's explanation of Palaeolithic cave art. Mithen suggests that the creativity of the art is an adaptive response to an environment full of risk and fluctuation, in which there was often plenty of game around but in which sharp fluctuations could occur. He draws attention to the content of the art – images of animals that he interprets as encoding valuable information for hunters – and its distribution – in an area rich in game and possibly dense in population at this period.

Mithen suggests that the art relates to critical moments in changing hunting strategies when changes in the environment forced hunters to adapt by turning from group activities to solitary hunting. The art, then, helped prepare hunters for such changes, who Mithen suggests were aware that troughs in reindeer/red deer populations would occur, but were unsure when.

What is striking about Mithen's approach is its use of different ideas. He uses ideas of adaptation to a changing environment to explain a phenomenon – art – not normally regarded as amenable to an adaptive approach. Mithen insists that 'creativity' and 'adaptation' are not mutually exclusive; indeed, he comments:

> I am left wondering about a possible connection between the creative act of producing images and the creative thoughts about hunting behaviour that such images helped create. I feel that these must have fed off each other in a spiral of creativity leaving us today with the splendours of Palaeolithic art and enabling the Palaeolithic hunters to adapt to their uncertain world. (Mithen 1990: 13)

Cultural Ecology: Criticisms

Criticisms of ecology are difficult to enumerate. As we have seen, the school of thought itself is a varied and complex beast. Criticisms directed, for example, at Steward's cultural ecology are quite misdirected at certain forms of biological evolution or other programmes such as optimal foraging theory. As Darwinian models of evolution vary in what they consider to be the appropriate unit of analysis (individual, culture, phenotype), critique of one model is not necessarily applicable to others.

Shanks and Tilley come closest to a complete rejection of such models. They reject any kind of evolutionary or ecological theory on grounds that are basically similar to their rejection of systems thinking. Concepts such as time budgeting, risk and cost-benefit analysis are, Shanks and Tilley argue, ideas that are derived from modern economics: that is, the study of modern capitalist societies. If, as Shanks and Tilley suggest, people in the past had systems of cultural values that were other than those of modern capitalists, it follows that such concepts are inapplicable to them. In fact, we can go further: if archaeologists claim that such analyses hold any truth, then they are in fact claiming that capitalist values are true in all times and all places. Cultural ecology is therefore ideological – as we discussed in chapter 6, an ideology is a system of beliefs that makes certain values appear universal, normal and natural.

Cultural ecologists counter that, as we look at other cultures, their beliefs are indeed more or less 'rational'. Modern ethnographic studies, they claim, show that all or most cultures do in fact have a 'rational' view of their environment, and that therefore we can apply modern 'rational' concepts such as time-budgeting and risk.

This is an unresolved argument, but it is worth pointing out its roots in economic anthropology. In the 1960s and 1970s, many anthropologists working on the economics of modern non-Western societies claimed that all such societies made 'rational' economic choices that could be understood using the ideas and vocabulary of Western economists – marginal cost, energy flows, risk, etc. This was called the *formalist* school of economic anthropology. Formalists were opposed by *substantivists*, who argued that Western ideas were inappropriate for the study of the economic choices of other cultures. The 'formalist versus substantivist debate' has lost its heat more recently, but it continues to surface in debates over the claims of cultural ecology.

A related attack on evolution and ecology has come via social constructivism, the social critique of science that we discussed in chapter 3. If a culture is indeed adapted to an external environment, it is argued, what was that environment? The resources and risks in that environment are delineated by the techniques of Western Science. But if those techniques are themselves socially constructed, they cannot claim to be a 'neutral' or 'objective' mapping of the resources in that environment. A different way of making the same objection is via an attack on *essentialism*: that is, if one deconstructs the idea that the body has certain 'natural' or 'biologically endowed' needs and desires, then the landscape cannot be interpreted as a set of resources that may fulfil those needs and desires.

A third objection, specific to models of biological evolution, is that it is very difficult to specify what the 'unit of selection' is and how cultural traits are transmitted. Some argue, following Darwin, that the only valid unit of selection is the individual. It is difficult, however, to see how cultural traits are passed on from one generation to another, if we reject the sociobiological claim that such transmission is genetic also. Some evolutionists, including Dunnell, argue that the unit of selection is the 'phenotype' and not the individual, and that transmission of traits is cultural rather than genetic. This is very much an ongoing debate within evolutionary archaeology.

The debate over evolution and ecology is, in my view, a prime example of the lack of communication between different schools of archaeological thought in the 1990s. At recent archaeological conferences, one had a choice of going to sessions on 'Darwin, sex and food' on the one hand, and 'Hermeneutics of the body' on the other. One rarely sees the same faces at both sessions; yet protagonists on both sides of the debate feel that they have been proven to be intellectually victorious and do not need to address the critique of the other. Rumours of the death of either camp are probably, with apologies to Mark Twain, exaggerated.

10

Archaeology and History

For most in North America, the sister discipline of archaeology is anthropology; for many, archaeology is anthropology or it is nothing. In Europe, a straw poll of the views of most archaeologists would suggest that the sister discipline of archaeology is history.

In part, this reflects the different subject matter in North America and Europe. The archaeology of North America is largely prehistoric until the first colonies of the fifteenth, sixteenth and seventeenth centuries AD. There is a flourishing and vibrant 'historical archaeology' of the period of the American colonies and of eighteenth- and nineteenth-century North America, but numerically it is very much a minority pursuit within Americanist archaeology. In contrast, the 'historical horizon' is much earlier in Europe. Europeanists have historical texts that bear on the pre-Roman Iron Age; archaeologists specializing in this or later periods form over half the teaching staff in most British universities, and at a rough estimate over half the excavations in Europe take place on Classical or post-Roman sites. All these archaeologists deal with historical texts, and therefore with university colleagues in Classics or History departments, in some form. The full story of this divergence between Britain and America in terms of disciplinary allies, however, goes a little deeper than this. As we saw in chapter 2, this different disciplinary configuration led to the differential impact of the New Archaeology in Britain and America. It also led to the continuing flourishing and variety of 'traditional', culture-historical approaches in Britain.

In this chapter, I want to look at some of the different theoretical views taken on the relationship between archaeology and history. Before I can do this, however, we must look at different views of historical theory and practice. The theoretical positions of historians are as varied as those of archaeologists. To an extent, debates within historical theory run in parallel to those within archaeology.

Traditional History

Historians often like to trace their roots as a discipline back to the nineteenth century with figures such as the German historian Ranke. Ranke espoused what today would be seen as a narrow empiricism: his aim was to tell history 'as it really was'. The task of the late nineteenth-century historian was simply to amass piles of facts.

Coupled with an empiricist and inductivist approach to the material went a stress on history as a narrative of political events. Traditional historians told a story. Traditional history books often have a beginning, a middle and an end to their plots. Indeed, it can be argued that while traditional historians protested (and protest) that they have no theory, in fact they follow rules of narrative and emplotment that have been ably characterized by the historical theorist Hayden White.

Traditional political history of this kind continues to be written to the present day. In this century, however, there has been a widening of historical thinking in several directions too wide-ranging to even detail here. One example of this widening of approach is the Annales school of French historians (named after their journal, *Annales: Economies, Societies, Civilisations*) such as Marc Bloch, Fernand Braudel, Emmanuel Le Roy Ladurie and Jacques Le Goff. The Annales school has been much cited by archaeologists as a useful inspiration for archaeological thought, so it is worth reviewing its theories briefly.

The Annales School

First, Annales historians broadened their interests to include all aspects of past societies. They looked not just at the political machinations of the élite, but also at economy, society and cognition. In this sense the Annales school helped history become more anthropological and processual – that is, to understand total cultural systems rather than just tell stories about its political events.

Second, the Annales school broadened historical interest in the nature of time. Traditional historians tended to see time as no more than just a series of events such as battles, political treaties, births, coronations and deaths of monarchs. The task of the historian in this view is simply to describe these events. The Annales school wanted to look at longer-term processes that underlay particular events. Underneath the 'surface froth' of battles and treaties, they saw economic, environmental and demographic trends and cycles. As discussed by Fernand Braudel, history moved at three scales or rhythms:

1 that of events, *l'histoire evenementielle*;
2 medium-term cycles such as economic boom and bust;
3 the very long term, 'enduring structures' or *longue dureé* (climatic changes, physical geography).

Note the similarity between the Annales notion of the long term and the archaeological concept of process as a trend underlying specific variability (discussed in chapter 2). Note also two areas of debate prompted by Annales thinking that have parallels within archaeological theory:

1 Which (if any) of the three levels or scales of time is dominant? Each timescale might have its own logic; they might intersect at specific conjunctures. At times Braudel implied that the *longue dureé* dominated the other two levels; other Annales historians implied that the three levels interacted and that no one level was dominant.
2 Are people's thoughts important, or does the environment dominate? Some writers suggested that what they called 'mentalité' or mentalities could be just as much part of the *longue dureé* as climate or physical geography. For example, Jacques Le Goff talked of 'the medieval mind' as a mentality spanning five centuries that structured medieval people's attitudes towards economic life and the natural world. So while Braudel tended to equate environment with the long term and to treat environment as a base-line, no such equation is logically necessary.

For example, in his book *The Peasants of Languedoc* Emmanuel Le Roy Ladurie looked at the lives of peasants in southern France. He used quantitative evidence, for example on the nutrition of peasants and of daily wage-rates; he used a loosely systemic model to understand why populations grew, stabilized and contracted at certain points; he emphasized the importance of 'environmental' variables such as climate. At the same time, his book *Montaillou* is one of the most famous reconstructions of peasant mentalities in historical literature. Le Roy Ladurie's work, and Annales thinking in general, therefore incorporates many of the tensions between environment and society, short and long term, seen in archaeology and the human sciences in general.

The Linguistic Turn

In recent years, however, there has been a move taking us still further away from traditional forms of historical discourse: this has been called the 'linguistic turn'.

A good way to explain this shift is to look at the story of English 'social history'. In the 1960s, very much in parallel with New Archaeology and New Geography, and influenced also by the Annales school, historians working within the Cambridge Group for the Study of Population and Social Structure turned to new areas outside traditional history. Some writers even termed this the 'New Social History'. The New Social History sought answers to the dynamics of past societies through the use of statistics and looked at processes such as demographic cycles and fertility rates, using systemic jargon to understand the links between these. Cross-cultural analogies were used, for example between Europe before and during the Industrial Revolution and modern 'developing' societies.

But the New Social History rapidly found that key elements of the answers to the questions it was asking lay in 'sentiment' and 'mentality' – that is, in the realm of cognition. A good example is the New Social History's attempt to understand changing patterns of marriage. We could not understand statistics of changing age at marriage, for example, without looking at changing attitudes and sentiments (for example, changing attitudes towards illegitimacy, attitudes towards patriarchy, or the rise of the modern notion of romantic love).

As a result, historians turned to other forms of evidence to explore people's attitudes. These included such 'non-statistical' sources as conduct books prescribing manners and behaviour, court accounts of popular sentiments expressed at church, even literary and poetic descriptions of feeling and behaviour.

At the same time, historians became responsive to the argument that there was no one objective historical truth or 'social reality'. If the sentiments underlying 'marriage' had to be explored, these sentiments obviously varied. There was no one correct answer to the question 'What was marriage really like in seventeenth-century England?'; there were many different experiences of marriage, many possible interpretations of what people 'really thought' about marriage. And these interpretations were unavoidably subjective – any historical account of marriage was written and was read within a late twentieth-century society in which the idea of marriage seemed to be under grave threat or at the very least to be changing.

As a result, social historians saw the dissolution of objective facts to the extent that recent work has proclaimed the 'end of social history'. Many argued that we could not have 'social reality' because 'what was really going on' in any given historical situation was open to multiple interpretations; people's social lives were constructed within cultural understandings and beliefs. These beliefs, of course, were variable and could be 'read' in different ways, just as in chapter 7 we discussed different 'readings' of archaeological material. Instead of an objective society with a concrete existence, we had a more amorphous set of cultural beliefs. Behind 'social reality' lay cultural perception. So out of the New Social History was born...the New Cultural History.

This excursion into historical theory is brief, potted and incomplete in the extreme. I want to make two points with it, however:

1 *The history of archaeological thinking runs in parallel with that in history in particular and the human sciences as a whole*, though the jargon used is often different. I could have given similar potted histories of thought in sociology, economics, politics, etc.
2 There are many different forms of historical thinking, many different theories of historical method. It is not sufficient, therefore, to say 'we should reject history' or indeed conversely 'we should adopt tried and tested historical methods' without specifying what those methods are and examining those methods within their own disciplinary context. While the theories of other disciplines can be a source of useful new ideas, there is therefore *no salvation for archaeological thought in turning to the methods of another discipline*, since *the unity of methods professed by that discipline is invariably illusory* whether we are discussing the methods of the natural sciences or those of history or of literary criticism.

Unsurprisingly, we find that different schools of archaeological theory have turned to different elements of current historical practice as allies.

Jacquetta Hawkes famously wrote of archaeology: 'however scientific the methods employed, the final aims of the discipline remain historical: the description of individual events in time' (Hawkes 1968: 258). Even when she wrote, this was a description of but one form of historical practice, and a narrowly traditional form at that. It was a form that Gordon Childe modelled his early culture-historical work on also. Childe in his later life came to be critical of his earlier work and wrote critically of it in his 'Retrospect' (1958).

Recently, some archaeologists have turned to the ideas and methods of the Annales school for inspiration. In particular, they have stressed Annales interest in different timescales and its interplay of the material and the world of 'mentalities' in which no one feature is dominant. Finally, many postprocessualists including myself have derived inspiration from the methods and theories of historians involved in the New Cultural History.

Historical Archaeology

In the first part of this chapter, I looked at the relationship between history and archaeology in the abstract. I now want to look at how the two disciplines interact in practice, in different approaches to the archaeology of historic periods. My definition of 'historical archaeology' differs from that of many North American archaeologists, for whom this refers exclusively to the post-1500 period; I shall be discussing examples from Classical and medieval archaeology also.

Much traditional archaeology has found itself in alliance with traditional forms of history mentioned above. In particular, archaeologists working in Classical periods or early medieval Europe deal with areas of historical discourse that, with exceptions, are still largely traditional in scope. In many cases, the archaeologists concerned took their first degree in Classics, History or a related discipline, and came to archaeology through a desire to attack questions defined in advance through (traditional) historical methods: Who was the king buried at Sutton Hoo? What was the appearance of the Forum in Rome? When was this medieval village deserted?

Subservience to historical accounts has meant subservience to traditional models of culture history and a normative view of culture. The classic example is the story of the Anglo-Saxon settlement of England. The eighth-century historian Bede tells us that three groups of settlers came to Britain in the fifth century AD: the Angles, the Saxons and the Jutes. Bede tells us where they settled and which kingdoms they founded. A generation of traditional archaeologists looked at the grave-goods from cemeteries in these areas and interpreted them by looking to north Germany and southern Denmark for parallels. Thus, because Bede tells us the county of Kent was settled by Jutes, material from Kent were labelled 'Jutish' and stylistic parallels sought – and found – with material from Jutland in Denmark of similar or slightly earlier date.

Though this is culture history based on theories of migration rather than diffusion, the parallels with prehistoric culture history are obvious. More recent work has criticized this model, either seeking to minimize the impact and numbers involved in fifth-century migrations, to be more critical about the historical record, or to stress social change at the level of small-scale structures rather than large-scale migrations.

Historical Archaeology and the Text

In North America in the 1960s and 1970s, a group of historical archaeologists worked to adapt the tenets of New Archaeology to the archaeological study of historic periods, following Binford's insistence that 'specialists in this field should provide the most informative tests or evaluations of ideas set forth by archaeologists in general' (1977: 169). We saw one example of such an approach in Hodges's systemic analysis of Dark Age trade in chapter 3.

This work attempted to generalize and be anthropological in the sense of getting away from traditional historical descriptions of colonial and later history. It attempts to look for pattern – to define diagnostic patterns of artefacts; and tries to generalize about the societies under examination. For example, the work of Kathleen Deagan and others in St Augustine, Florida, a town populated in the seventeenth and eighteenth centuries by a number of different ethnic groups, has tried to look for different archaeological patterns associated with these groups. The aim here is in part to elaborate a more rigorous approach to the definition of ethnicity based on the definition of quantitative measures.

One way in which historical archaeology has taken up such concerns is to try to treat documents as a form of middle-range documentation. Remember that Binford argued that we could look to independent sources of information to build 'robust' arguments (chapter 4). In the Palaeolithic, he looked to animal and plant behaviour. Many have argued that in historic periods, documents can play a similar role. Account books at ports, for example, can tell us exactly what was being imported and exported and at what price, a pattern we can then match or fail to match against those goods or their containers when we find them in rubbish pits.

Conversely, many have turned to elements of postprocessual and interpretative thought for an alternative model of the integration of archaeology and history. Remember the importance of context in postprocessual thought. Documents read from this view can provide a special form of contextual information, for example on the individual or on different views of gender. We have already seen one example of this work: my discussion of the late medieval hall in England in chapter 7. As a result, many recent explorations of recent theoretical trends have come in historical archaeology, particularly in colonial contexts – South Africa and North America especially.

Historical archaeology as a whole, however, refuses to fit into the neat theoretical boxes that have very often been defined by prehistoric archaeologists. A good example of how historical archaeology simply does not 'follow the rules' is provided from the archaeology of castles.

Case Study: Bodiam Castle

There is a long-standing debate about castles in medieval England. Castles are high-status buildings, and combine accommodation for a great lord and his household with 'defensive' features – towers, battlements, gatehouses, moats and ditches.

Interpretation of castles has traditionally been dominated by scholars with a military background. Developments in castle architecture have been interpreted in terms of changing techniques of attack and defence. This narrative is a progressive one: attack and defence become more technologically sophisticated over time. Both the evidence of archaeology (the changing form of walls, towers, gatehouses) and documents (narratives of sieges) have been used to tell a story about castles, quite literally: most books on castles consist of a narrative history, with individual castles being cited as illustrative anecdotes.

In this story the documents take centre stage. Most narratives start with definitions of 'castles' based on the (usually Latin) texts within which words like 'castrum' and 'castellum' are defined. Next come the obviously military features. Residential features within the walls receive less attention, and the landscape context of castles – the villages and towns outside their walls – even less attention.

To over-simplify, these élite sites have generally been approached in 'culture-historical' ways, stressing influence, contact, diffusion of new architectural ideas. This document-based narrative is rarely questioned, let alone tested. Nothing like a 'processual' approach to castle studies has ever been proposed let alone pursued.

In recent years, some historians and archaeologists have begun to ask other questions: what of the social dimensions of these buildings? Are not their lordly functions (judicial centres, lordly residences) at least as important as their military/strategic role? Some have gone further still: what of the symbolic dimensions of these structures? Are the battlements and towers not in fact to do with military needs, but rather the self-image of a masculine military élite basing its ideology on images of knighthood?

Bodiam Castle, ten miles from the south coast of England in Sussex (figures 10.1 and 10.2), was built in the 1380s by Sir Edward Dalyngrygge, an old soldier from the Hundred Year's War in France. The interpretation of this castle has centred on the question: is this a

Figure 10.1 Bodiam Castle: photograph of the north front and gatehouse across the lake.

seriously defensively strong castle, as the military theorists would have it? Or are its features not seriously military but symbolic in some way, as more recent scholars have argued?

Military theorists have drawn attention to the proliferation of military features: gunloops commanding the approach ways, twin towers flanking the gate and other towers dominating the tops of the walls. Most particularly, Bodiam is situated within a small rectangular lake that has been artificially created. The lake is a complex piece of hydraulic engineering, and is held back on two sides by an earthern dam. It apparently forms a formidable obstacle to any would-be attacker. The main entrance to Bodiam runs at an angle across this lake, exposing attackers to fire from the battlements.

Not only is Bodiam clearly militarily very strong on this analysis: the final 'proof' of the military thesis comes from a historical document, a 'licence to crenellate [fortify]'. Translated from the Latin, it states apparently quite unequivocally that Sir Edward Dallyngrygge sought and duly obtained licence in October 1385 'to fortify with a wall of stone and lime the dwelling-place of the manor of Bodiam next to the sea . . . and to construct and make thereof a castle for the defence of the adjacent countryside and for the resisting of [the king's] enemies'. Here is a clear, irrefutable documentary statement of the military purpose of the castle. Or is it?

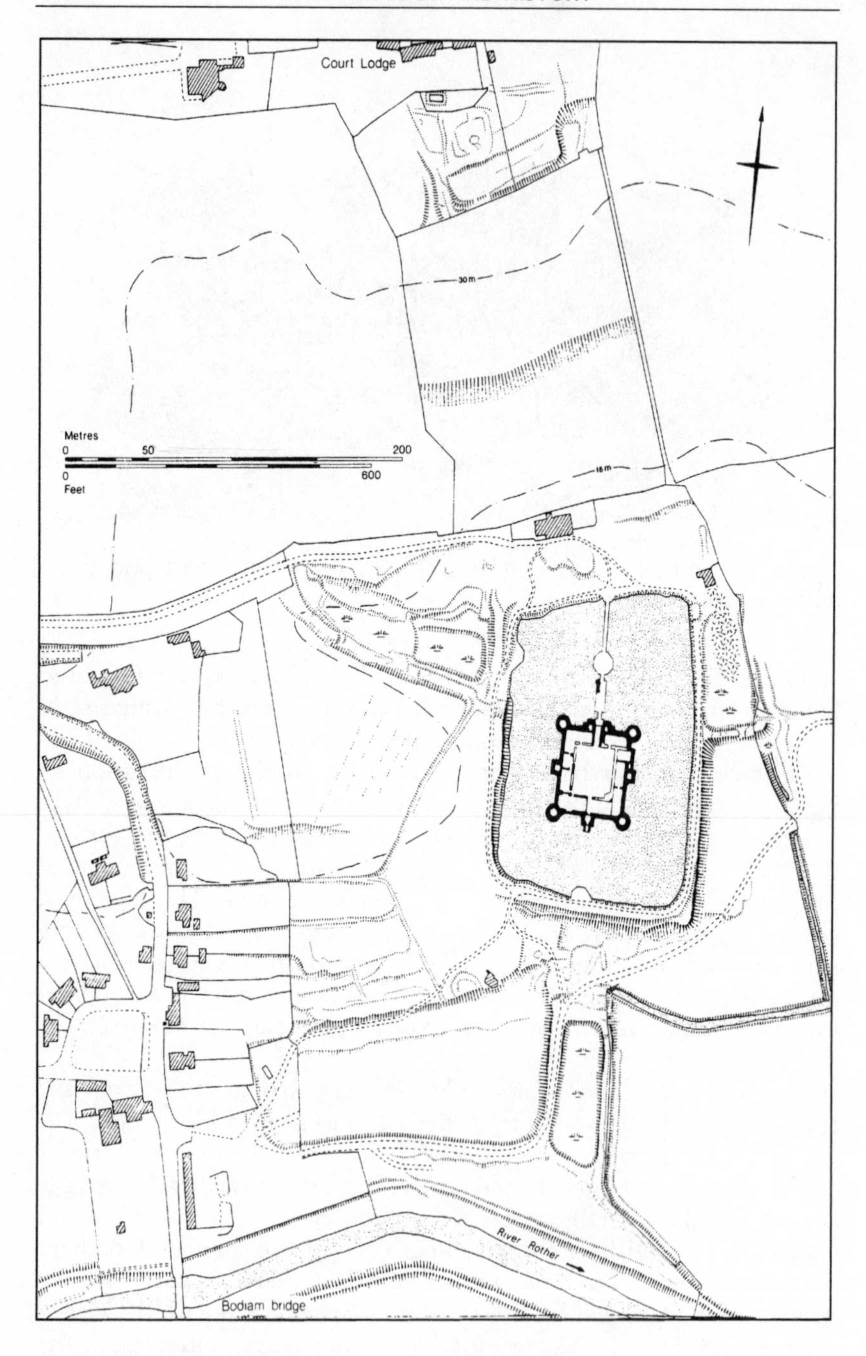

Figure 10.2 Bodiam Castle: plan of landscape context.

Disbelief in the military view of the castle has been relatively recent, and comes from three sources:

1 A reassessment of the architecture of the castle. Charles Coulson has shown convincingly that the apparently 'military' features of the castle are a sham. The gunports are not placed effectively; guns placed in them do not command an effective field of fire. Other openings are almost impossible to use by longbow or crossbowmen; the fighting parapet is not easily accessible; the list could go on.
2 A detailed survey, carried out independently, of the landscape context of the castle (figure 10.2). First, the earthwork dam is utterly undefended; in several estimations it could be cut through by a dozen workers in one night. The lake itself is not as deep as it could be; it is more a sheet of water like those of eighteenth-century ornamental gardens than a serious obstacle. Outside the lake are the earthworks of a large formal garden, including a 'platform' from which the castle could be viewed from above.
3 A reassessment of the meaning of the licence to crenellate. Bodiam is not 'next to the sea'; it is ten miles away. Documents of this kind cannot be taken at face value as prehistorians might suppose. Coulson suggests that the production of such documents was largely part of a system of chivalric honour, and the references to defensive intent part of a knightly code of chivalrous values. He writes suggestively:

> Reasoning from illusive defensive effects mechanistically back to imagined military causes has, in the case of Bodiam, led to the famous licence of October 1385 being taken at its face value.... Because no study has been done of licences to crenellate as a whole... *many misjudgments have arisen partly from lack of contextual awareness*. (Coulson 1992; emphasis mine)

Coulson's detailed knowledge and experience of late medieval documents, inductively acquired as part of his practice as a documentary historian, leads him to have a better 'feel' for the quality of the evidence than other writers on the subject.

But this reinterpretation is not simply a statement that 'symbolic is more important than military'. Coulson writes:

> The wisest course is to resist the temptation to write off any feature as 'sham', or to take any element as purely 'functional' (by which 'defensive' is intended normally). It is an artful combination which expresses ... all the complex seignorial associations of the medieval castle-image,

> which included the deterring (and, if necessary, the defeating) of attack at whatever level was appropriate... the bravado of double portal chambers, 'murder holes' and three portcullises is mere rodomontade when the lateral doors are so weak. There is no 'military' logic in trebling the main closures while leaving a short and direct approach to a weak back door (Postern) which entirely lacks elaboration. But there is a powerful psychological sense nonetheless: it is closer to Jean Froissart (and perhaps also to Franz Kafka) than it is to Vegetius or to the Sieur de Vauban. The fairy-tale element is here, allusive and romantic.... 'Fortification' was surely metaphysical as well as material; a matter of imagery and symbolism, not just of technology. (Coulson 1992: 66, 83)

What theoretical lessons can be drawn from the Bodiam story? First, the arguments are over formal rather than quantitative analysis. In other words, scholars argue not over the numbers of things, as they did over the relative proportions of different tool types in a given Mousterian assemblage as discussed in chapter 3, but over their form, whether that is of the form of the lake or of the gunloops. Such a way of debating derives in part from an existing archaeological tradition hitherto little discussed in this book. The so-called 'English landscape tradition' is a school of thought looking to the local historian W. G. Hoskins as its founder. The landscape tradition stresses close empirical analysis of pieces of landscape, a view of landscapes as both very old and as complex documents on which many phases of settlement are 'written', of the integration of history, archaeology and geography using an inductive model, and of hostility to 'grand theory'. Such an approach has both strengths and weaknesses: it stresses interdisciplinarity and close attention to detail, but is essentially anecdotal in its approach. That is, it uses closely worked-through case studies but gives little consideration to how typical the case study or 'anecdote' is of the wider context. More seriously, it is almost never consciously theorized.

This debate, and the wider landscape tradition of which it is a part, does not follow the established rules of archaeological theory. While some approaches are more or less 'culture-historical' in nature, there is no established 'processual' view of Bodiam. No one has tried formally to characterize Bodiam in terms of a settlement hierarchy. No systematic approach to the landscape around Bodiam has been taken. Conversely, Coulson is not a paid-up postprocessualist: his discussion is peppered with aesthetic value judgements appropriate to the discourse of traditional architectural history but reading quite oddly to someone trained as a prehistoric archaeologist (Bodiam is 'charmingly proportioned', 'elegant', 'nicely moulded'). Indeed, in my view Coulson's arguments could be strengthened by reference to such theory, considering for example which social groups and/or genders would have 'read aright' the symbolism of Bodiam, and considering in more depth the peasant–landlord antagonism of the period.

Conclusion

Archaeological theory has tended to be played out over certain classic 'case studies' (I almost flippantly wrote 'playgrounds') such as megaliths, cave art, the Mousterian question. These have tended to be prehistoric, for several reasons. First, prehistory is perceived as 'pure' archaeology. Second, most histories of archaeology have seen historic periods as secondary to the main story of the development of prehistoric chronology. In passing, it is worth noting that such histories themselves need rewriting; for example, nineteenth-century European medievalists were well aware of stratigraphy in buildings archaeology, and documented such stratigraphy carefully, independently of more well-known prehistoric studies of excavated stratigraphy. Third, the stress on very long-term processes within New Archaeology tended to make the shorter-term perspectives of historical archaeologists marginal to the discipline.

The story of historic archaeology shows that we do not need to stick to the notion of prehistory as 'pure' archaeology, and that the archaeology of historic periods throws up equally relevant and complex problems of interpretation. In addition, the cross-cutting influence of different disciplines (archaeology, history, literature, etc.) throws up a series of unexpected theoretical debates that enrich archaeological discourse as a whole.

11

Archaeology in a Postmodern World

I'm puzzled. We've almost reached the end of the book, but the most popular buzzword in theory at the moment has hardly been raised yet – 'postmodernism'. I've heard lots about postmodernism recently, though no one ever tells me what this means, let alone why it might be relevant to archaeology.

Well, the question of postmodernism is in many ways a red herring. But I guess I'd better try to deal with it as briefly as possible, though it may take a whole chapter to do justice to it and all its implications. Again, I'll go through the theory before discussing its application to archaeology.

The 'postmodern condition' has been defined by the French philosopher François Lyotard as *incredulity toward metanarratives*. Lyotard suggests that the postmodern condition is the condition of knowledge in Western capitalist societies.

A metanarrative is a big story, or a grand claim of absolute truth. Examples of metanarratives are:

1 A belief in scientific progress, that our ideas of the world are getting better and better through the use of rational method. In this sense postmodernists see belief in Science as a metanarrative.
2 Any total scheme of social evolution in which societies move from one stage to another. For example, a belief in a scientific Marxism – that through an objective science of society we can see grand, successive stages in human history leading inexorably towards communism. Or again, a classification of societies into band, tribe, chiefdom and state.
3 A belief in any absolute system of morality true in all times and in all places, whether that morality is derived from religious, nationalist or ethnic claims.

4 Any scheme of 'progress' in human history. Such progress may be aesthetic or artistic: for example, much traditional art history assumes that artists get better and better at representing Nature. It may be technological: that humans have more and more complex technology through time. Postmodernists argue that assumptions of 'progress' implicitly underline many apparently atheoretical typologies (for example, pre-Classical to Classical or Gothic to Renaissance in the history of art and architecture, or most 'progressive' archaeological accounts of ancient technology in which advance succeeds technical advance).

For postmodernists, all such beliefs can be traced back to the basic assumptions of the Enlightenment of the eighteenth century. Enlightenment philosophers claimed that with the use of Reason, we could study human affairs in a rational and objective manner. Enlightenment philosophy therefore implied:

(1) Belief in some kind of *Utopia*. If Reason can be applied to the study of human affairs, it follows that it can be applied to its organization. Therefore, we can reach some kind of perfectly organized state, or we can at least aim for that goal even if it is unattainable within our lifetime. It can even be a goal that we know we shall never attain but nevertheless wish to aim for as an ideal, such as perfect 'scientific' knowledge of the natural world. Examples are for Marx, communism; for Fukuyama, bourgeois capitalism; for positivists, a final theory of the physical universe.

(2) A notion of *teleology* in human affairs. A teleology is an assumption of an underlying grand process with a definite start point and end point; for example, within Marxism, the drive towards ever greater inequality and alienation, culminating in its ultimate overthrow and dissolution under communism. For the Enlightenment, this could be the steady unfolding of Reason as human history progressed, or variants thereof.

(3) A belief in essential properties of a 'real world' out there that we can study independent of the text, independent of what we write about it. If there is such a real world, then meanings can be fixed. But for critics of modernity, there is no such fixity. For Jacques Derrida, 'there is nothing outside the text'; there are just other texts.

In other words, the text apparently refers to a real world, but when we look at that real world, we find that it too consists of a set of signifiers that refer to something else. The word 'pot' refers to a definite thing made of clay with handles, but the thing made of clay with handles itself refers to other things. Any self-evident factual statement can be pulled apart by its own internal logic, since it cannot refer to a stable external world – the signifiers just go on and on. Derrida demonstrates this through the technique of *deconstruction*, in which he shows that however self-evident and factual a text appears to be, its meanings can be turned against itself.

As a result, it is argued that the postmodern condition is of a world with fluid, unstable meanings with no final reference point. Instead of looking for deep, underlying, 'core' or 'essential' features of a phenomenon, there is simply endless fluidity and play across surface meanings.

(4) A questioning of *disciplinarity*. In the eighteenth century, the study of the 'real world' was divided into different disciplines dealing with different kinds of phenomena. Thus, physics and chemistry deal with physical processes, whereas biology deals with organisms. But if all texts refer outwards, if the chain of signifiers just goes on and on rather than stopping, there is no certainty, no final reference point, in language – everything just refers to everything else; there is no final meaning or interpretation. So there can be no distinct 'disciplines' dealing with distinct fields of study. Divides between disciplines are arbitrary, depending on historical accident or contingency – how the history of systems of thought happened to unfold during the Enlightenment.

Some postmodern thinkers, for example, have deconstructed the barrier between history and literature. Since all historical documents are also literary texts and all historians write narratives, and all literature exists within a certain historical context, it is argued that there can be no *a priori* distinction between history and fiction. Reliance on 'facts', postmodernists argue, is problematic at best: it is rare to read a novel in which Washington is not the capital of the USA, or human beings do not have two arms and two legs. In practice, it is argued, 'disciplines' such as history or literature are constituted and their boundaries maintained not through 'real differences' in their subject matter, as traditional scholars would claim. Such claimed differences would owe their reality to an outside world that does not have any fixed or stable boundaries at all (the 'logocentric fallacy').

In the later twentieth century, the argument continues, Western thought has entered 'the postmodern condition'. Historically, all these grand narratives, certain distinctions and disciplinary boundaries have fallen away; we don't have any large stories or certainties left that we can rely on. The most obvious example given is that of Marxism. In 1900 Marxists could be confident that world history was on the high road to revolution and communism. They had a system for explaining the world which seemed to work and which gave definitive pointers to the way they should think and act in the present. Now things are not so certain, to say the least.

Postmodernists spread the attack more widely, however: they also point to the erosion of confidence in a single 'scientific method' discussed in chapter 3 and also in the decline of Victorian ideas of evolutionary progress (chapter 9).

Postmodernism is a way of thinking that has affected much of Western thought. Within architecture, modernists believed that creation of buildings along 'rational' principles (for example, the use of tower blocks) could contribute to the solution of social problems such as inner-city crowding and deprivation. The failure of these beliefs, postmodernists allege, reflects the intellectual failure of underlying modernist philosophies.

To an extent, then, we should talk not so much of postmodernism but of *the postmodern condition*: it is alleged that the decline of confidence in the Enlightenment, in human perfectibility, or to intrinsic Truth is not so much a position to be debated back and forth, as a general state, the way the world is at the end of the millennium.

Postmodern thought often refers to two 'heroes'. The nineteenth-century thinker Nietszche stood against the Enlightenment, arguing against the sway of Reason. In this century, they cite the philosopher Ludwig Wittgenstein. Wittgenstein started his intellectual career as a logical-positivist philosopher (see chapter 3). He attempted to create a philosophical language that was perfectly neutral, a language that described the outside world in completely objective terms. When this attempt collapsed, Wittgenstein 'saw the light' and spent the rest of his career arguing that communication was simply an endless 'language game' in which the rules were arbitrary but by which we nevertheless agree to play.

I want to pick out one contemporary thinker in particular as important in the development of postmodern thought, as he is cited more frequently than anyone else by contemporary archaeologists: Michel Foucault.

Foucault looked at many of the concrete institutions of the Enlightenment, places where Enlightenment values of Reason held sway. These included the reform of prisons, the replacement of 'barbaric' methods of punishment with 'rational', 'enlightened' penal systems; the development of modern scientific medicine and clinical practice; the treatment of madness and the development of the 'enlightened' idea that madness was an illness that could be treated medically. He tried to show that far from representing 'progress' or the rise of more rational or humane ways of treating human beings, all these institutions were bound up with new forms of oppression in what he called 'the disciplinary society'.

Foucault's second theme was an attack on *essentialism*. Human beings in the Enlightenment were assumed to have a set of 'natural' of 'normal' faculties: the possession of Reason, a certain form of sexuality, desire for privacy and for individual freedom. In each case Foucault showed how each historical epoch had its own ideas about what was 'normal' and 'natural' for the body to desire or feel. There cannot, therefore, be reference to a biological base-line for scientists such as 'the sex drive' because there can be no cross-cultural definition of such a base-line.

Great. What has any of this got to do with archaeology?

First, much postprocessual thought clearly shares ground with postmodern thinking: the loss of confidence in Science, the attack on essentialism, the stress on a diversity of readings and a lack of fixity of meaning.

I would argue against an easy equation with postmodernism, however. The postprocessual turn in archaeology *parallels* the postmodern turn in the human sciences rather than being derived from it. In other words, the changes that archaeological thought went through in the 1980s and 1990s were one small example of a wider set of changes across the human sciences as a whole. This is why I suggested at the start of this chapter that postmodernism is in some ways a 'red herring'.

Second, the postmodern questioning of disciplinarity has led to interest in breaking down disciplinary boundaries. At the same time, it also implies a fragmentation of method. If there is no one Truth 'out there' waiting to be discovered any more, it is difficult to see how there can be one 'right' or 'wrong' way of doing archaeology.

The implication for archaeology is therefore (a) can we really talk about a single 'archaeological method' distinctive from that of other disciplines? and (b) is there such a thing as a unified method in archaeology anyway?

Third, postmodernism does suggest that we need to engage with other forms of knowledge outside the traditionally conceived purview of 'archaeology' or of 'science'. At the very least, we have to think carefully and seriously about the world outside the academic and professional practice of archaeology, rather than simply dismissing other views of the past as a 'lunatic fringe'. Postmodernism suggests that if there can be no one neutral method, then other views of the past can have validity, and not simply be ruled out of court because they do not conform to established procedures of archaeological method.

For example, we may not agree with the ley line hunters, Native Americans or others who have come to their version of what the past was like by rules that are not strictly those of archaeology as an academic discipline – but we do have to take them seriously. We cannot simply continue to write about the past 'as [we think] it really was' independently of the present. In short, we have to look at the social, political and cultural context of archaeology.

Archaeology is Not in a Vacuum

Whatever their theoretical differences, most would agree that archaeological interpretation does not exist in a vacuum, isolated from the outside world. Before the practising archaeologist goes to work, he or she reads the morning papers, worries about all the wars in the world and imminent economic recession. At work, relations of status between teacher and student are constantly invoked; out on site, decisions about what to dig and how to dig it are orders from the site director, arrived at after debate between (usually senior) members of the team or crew. In short, decisions are taken and archaeology practised within a definite set of social and political relations whether we like it or not.

How, if at all, does this political environment affect archaeological interpretation? If it does, it does not necessarily do so consciously. Take, for example, the study of the rise of the Roman Empire. Most traditional historians of the Roman Empire would angrily, and sincerely, protest that their accounts of 'Romanization' were simply descriptions of 'what really happened', free of any conscious bias. More recent writers point out that these writers are certainly not consciously biased, but never see the need to ask the question: why did natives so rapidly and readily assimilate themselves into an imperial system? This is at least partly due to the fact that for the previous generation the benefits of Empire were obvious and self-evident; conversely, for our generation they need explaining at the very least.

So for some, even as archaeology proclaims its neutrality it is deeply committed:

> Archaeology is best understood as a narrative, a particular and powerful form of origin myth that began in 19th century Euro-American

> societies to take on increasing importance as a vehicle of validation for social groups engaged (and enmeshed) in industrial growth, capital accumulation, and colonial expansion. (Hinsley 1989: 79–80)

> Archaeology, as cultural practice, is always a politics, always a morality. (Shanks and Tilley 1987: 212)

Politics in this sense is more than 'party politics'. It is about power in the broadest sense, from the policies and practices of the state down to the smallest human interaction. In this view, everything that we say and do is political in some sense. When a site director gives instructions to his or her team, when we write that an argument is 'strong' or 'weak', when we choose which site projects to fund and which to ignore, when a self-confident student cuts across a more diffident and nervous student in debate – these are all political decisions and actions.

This point is an emotive and controversial one. Many students have told me that they dislike politics, and specifically chose the study of archaeology to get away from it. The Classical author Livy wrote his *History* with this aim in mind also. But we have seen many times in this book how we always return to the present in the end, whatever philosophical viewpoint we take. In chapter 2 we noted that the data are mute, that the past does not exist; rather, statements about it are made in the here and now. In chapter 6 we discussed the concept of ideology, and earlier in chapter 5 we saw systems theory condemned by critical theorists as such an ideology. Chapter 8 saw feminists criticizing archaeology and academic discourse in general for its phallocentrism.

The common point of all these critiques is very simple: when an archaeologist claims that their position is neutral and apolitical, what are they trying to hide?

Case Study: African Burial Ground

During the eighteenth century, between 10,000 and 20,000 people of African descent were buried in an area of New York that came to be known as the African Burial Ground. In one estimate, 'at least half of the present African-descent population in the United States probably has at least one ancestor buried in this area'. The area fell out of use after 1795, and the land was filled in and overbuilt. The role of slaves of African descent in eighteenth-century New York was gradually forgotten. According to Michael Blakey:

> The very existence of an African Burial Ground in colonial New York raised the issue of false historical representation. The vast majority of educated Americans had learned that there was little if any African presence in New York during the colonial period, and that the northern American colonies had not engaged in the practice of slavery. The Burial Ground helped show that these notions comprised a kind of national myth. (Blakey 1995: 546)

In 1991 the burial ground was 'rediscovered' and partly excavated by archaeologists in advance of redevelopment. Over 400 burials were excavated before public concern led to legislation to suspend excavation and to protect and display the site.

This concern had come from members of the African-American community in New York. The nature of this concern and the way it affected archaeological practice is revealing. In the first place, formal lawsuits arguing that the site should be preserved found little comfort in existing legislation, which had been framed around a narrow view of 'archaeological significance' rather than the cultural associations a site might have for specific ethnic groups. Such lawsuits were however backed up by the support of black activist groups, Mayor Dinkins and the Congressional Black Caucus. At one point, a one-day blockade of the site halted redevelopment work.

Second, the archaeological research was transformed. Initial work on the bones was done by the Metropolitan Forensic Anthropology Team (MFAT), but public pressure ensured that in late 1993 the bones were transferred to the Cobb Biological Anthropology Laboratory at Howard University. The research team, headed by African-American bioarchaeologist Michael Blakey, has already produced results pointing to excessive workloads, malnutrition and childhood disease.

The analysis of the bones was not simply done by a different team: it had a different research design that linked together political concerns (who controls these remains?) with new intellectual ideas about ethnicity and new techniques of archaeological practice. According to Terence Epperson:

> [The MFAT] approach was based upon an essentialist, bio-genetic conception of 'race'. As control of the analysis was shifted to Howard University this approach was displaced by a research paradigm that emphasizes genetic affinity and cultural identity, greatly enhancing the social relevance and scientific importance of the project. For example, the project will utilize emergent mitochondrial and nuclear DNA studies to examine genetic origins and change in the archaeological population. DNA-based genetics, anatomical structure, chemical structure, chemical signatures for environments, and cultural traits will be used to

> link individuals from the Burial Ground with specific cultural/regional origins in Africa. . . . To the extent that it analyses ethnicity as a social construct rather than a bio-genetic phenomenon, the current research design has the potential to enhance our understanding of 'ethnogenesis', the active creation and reinvention of cultural identity under conditions of domination. (Epperson forthcoming)

Not only was the research design changed; the Howard University team publicized the research design and offered it up to criticism and modification from the descendant black community. Even the name of the place and the project became a contested topic. The site had been referred to as 'The Negro's Burial Ground' before objections coupled with academic arguments led to it being renamed the 'African Burial Ground' (though at the time of writing traditionalists at the *New York Times* and the New York Historical Society continue in the former usage).

On 19 April 1993 the burial ground was designated a National Historic Landmark and plans for redevelopment were scrapped. There is now an African Burial Ground Memorial on the site (figure 11.1).

The major implication for the practice of archaeology is that while what we do is unavoidably political, changing the way we do it is far from straightforward. In this case, it was not simply a matter of rewriting a research design, but of opening up that design to scrutiny from non-archaeologists – people who themselves occupy a problematic position within their own communities. There was no one 'right' or 'wrong' way to handle the African Burial Ground controversy, though there were better and worse ways. To a great extent, sympathetic and sensitive handling of the archaeological interpretation depends on the acknowledgement that there is a multiplicity of different views.

The Relativism Question

Well, it seems to me we've reached an impasse. Postmodernism has undermined our confidence in scientific rationality. We've seen that all versions of the past are political in some sense. So it seems we just make up whatever stories suit us, are convenient in the political present.

No, that will not do. There are better and worse interpretations of the past. I do not know of a single archaeologist of whatever

Figure 11.1 The mosaic above the African Burial Ground, Foley Square, New York.

theoretical stripe who would disagree. Even Jacques Derrida writes that '[the relativist] definition of deconstruction is false (that's right: false, not true) and feeble; it supposes a bad (that's right: bad, not good) and feeble reading of numerous texts, first of all mine' (1988: 136–7).

The criticisms of an unrestrained relativism are many, various and irrefutable. It is demonstrably wrong: archaeology has 'progressed', we no longer believe in the Creation of 4004 BC. Relativism involves a logical fallacy: 'all views are of equal value – including this one'. Relativism undercuts the value of archaeology as a form of knowledge about the past, and if pursued to its logical implication would do archaeologists out of a job. For many, the most fundamental and damning criticism of relativism is that it destroys our ability to speak out against politically undesirable and even obnoxious views of the past, the classic example being Holocaust denial groups. We might wish to acknowledge the validity of different views at the African Burial Ground – but who would suggest that this means we have to acknowledge racist views as of equal value?

Modern theorists take several roads out of this impasse. Many continue to insist that most archaeological facts and interpretations are mundane, beyond politics. Politics does play a part in this view, but at a level of theory that happens 'after' primary interpretation – we can collect our pottery sherds, and worry about the politics when it comes to interpreting them.

A processualist might well write: 'Of course we are influenced by contemporary ideas. It couldn't be any other way – our hypotheses about the past processes, by definition, are framed in the present. But the essence of science is to use rigorous procedures of testing to move beyond this through observation of the archaeological record. This is why the development of middle-range theory is so important. Only by developing robust ways of testing our ideas against archaeological material can we move beyond simply telling stories about the past.

'For a scientist, you can get an idea about how atoms might work, or about physical processes, from the newspaper, from a conversation, or from a drug-crazed hallucination. It doesn't matter where the idea comes from. What does matter is that you then test that idea. That is, you set up that idea as a rigorous hypothesis and then test it against material that you observe. That is the way science works, and it is the way it has been proven to work.'

Thus, for example, Jerry Sabloff is quite happy to note Wilk's work relating different explanations of the Classic Maya collapse to contemporary political events, but takes care to suggest how this can help us do better science:

> While Wilk's correlations are interesting, they do not prove that current intellectual trends determine which views of the collapse became popular, nor is there anything necessarily 'wrong' about archaeologists letting political trends influence their thinking. However, if his correlations are valid, they indicate how careful scholars must be to ensure that current biases are not blinding them to alternative hypotheses or limiting the kinds of data they collect. (Sabloff 1990: 166–7)

In other words, the processual view will grant that everything we say is in some sense political, but by using science we can move away from just telling stories.

There has been a series of recent discussions of this problem, attempting to steer a middle course between positivism and relativism. Bruce Trigger has suggested that the course of archaeology is driven both by political context and by a progressively better understanding of the data. He advocates a modified version of middle-range theory to grasp the interplay of different kinds of influence. Alison Wylie suggests that the way we relate theory to data will vary according to the context or locality we are working in:

> The question of what epistemic stance is appropriate...should be settled locally, in the light of what we have come to know about specific subject matters and about the resources we have for their investigation. We should resist the pressure to adopt a general epistemic stance appropriate to all knowledge claims. (Wylie 1992b: 35)

The most recent discussion of this problem is Elizabeth Brumfiel's discussion of the quality of textiles in Mexico. In this period, women under Aztec rule had to produce tribute cloth; Brumfiel's feminist perspective made her sceptical that the women were ideologically 'duped' and led her to expect that through time 'the quality of tribute cloth was deteriorating...because Indian women were engaged in resistance. Indian women were deliberately turning out undersized, loosely woven cloth with thick, loosely spun thread as a form of opposition to tribute extraction'.

However, the archaeological evidence suggested that quality did not decline. 'Rejecting the hypothesis', however, 'did not lead [Brumfiel] to reject the entire framework of theoretical propositions from which it was derived'; rather she created an *ad hoc* modification of her theory: 'resistance to exploitation does not occur when activities ...are vulnerable to supervision and control by the dominant class. This enabled me to continue to affirm that proponents of ideological domination have underestimated the frequency of resistance and the importance of coercion in maintaining dominance' (Brumfiel 1996: 454, 458).

Brumfiel concludes that:

> Long before the choice between coercion and ideological domination is decided by appeals to data, the need to choose will be eliminated by a theoretical insight that clarifies the complementary relationship between the two phenomena. Even so, data will have an important role to play.... For example, these observations on the quality of tribute cloth production... have opened a new line of enquiry for me concerning how the vulnerability of men and women to state coercion may differ because of differences in the location of their work or in the kind of goods that they produce for the state. The knowledge I have gained from this enquiry will affect the way I regard ideological domination and resistance in future studies. (Brumfiel 1996: 459)

My own view is largely in agreement with Brumfiel, with one qualification: Brumfiel, Wylie, Trigger and others all cast their arguments in the form of a 'reply' to 'the postprocessual critique'. But there is little in any of their arguments that contradicts any of the tenets of postprocessual archaeology. Indeed, I know of no archaeologist who would openly declare themselves to be an unqualified relativist.

The Context of Relativism

A more interesting question, then, is why there is so much concern about the perils of relativism. I think there are several reasons for this.

1 Relativism, unfortunately, is actually a very strong characterization of much of archaeological practice. Despite the unanswerable data we all assemble in a neutral and objective manner, our opponents still refuse to acknowledge the rightness of our arguments and the wrongness of theirs; it must be sheer pigheadedness on their part. Even worse, their pigheaded refusal to acknowledge the data is not seen for what it is by the academic community as a whole. So while 'we' are receptive to the resistance of the data, 'they' view the data with cavalier disregard. I am not being entirely flippant here:

> When Gananath Obeyesekere published his book *The Apotheosis of Captain Cook*... [he] had put together such a flimsy historical case, as it seems to me, that it was sure to be taken apart by historical reviewers, who presumably would also be able to perceive the humbug he put out about my own work. I was wrong. On the

contrary, the American Society of Eighteenth Century Studies awarded *The Apotheosis of Captain Cook* the Louis Gottschalk Prize for 1992... (Sahlins 1995: ix)

2 Many of the writers involved in the attack on relativism have played large parts in the perceived relativizing of archaeological discourse. Mark Leone's stress on middle-range theory comes after his development of an openly materialist archaeology. Brumfiel and Wylie are committed feminists. Kohl has written on the politics of archaeology. Trigger's papers in the early 1980s were routinely cited as examples of the unavoidably political nature of archaeological discourse (indeed, his 1980 paper on the 'American Indian' was one of the first hints I had as an innocent student that archaeology and politics had any relationship whatsoever).

In fact, peace has broken out in the realm of epistemology. With the notable exceptions of hard-line positivists and behavioural archaeologists, few would disagree that we are unavoidably influenced by our social and political circumstances, and that 'raw data' do not exist in any unproblematic or unbiased way. Conversely, few would disagree that the data are important, and that at the very least they form a network of resistance to the interpretations we wish to put on them. Most of us would say this network of resistance is very strong, and that our methods should try to strengthen it.

Recent discussions are, I suspect, far more to do with the perceptions, fears and uncertainties of a postmodern world, in particular the uncertain place of archaeology within academic and intellectual practice. Rather than replies to or refutations of a postmodernist philosophy, they are symptomatic of the difficulties of working within the postmodern condition. All the contributors to this debate have seen through the naive certainties of positivist rhetoric to the realities of a world that is uncertain and difficult to live and write in.

12

Conclusion: Conflict and Consensus

Now just hold on a minute. There's one huge omission from the entirety of the preceding text that can't be permitted to go on any longer. What exactly is theory? You can't get away with not defining theory for the entire book.

Well, we saw in chapter 1 that there were different definitions of what theory is. Which definition one prefers depends on one's own theoretical viewpoint.

Remember figure 4.1. For many positivists, theory is a definable set of propositions that can be set up and tested against data. For advocates of middle-range theory, we have been developing over the last thirty years a set of methods that enable us to test theory against data.

In this view, theory is defined quite narrowly and precisely. It is simply a set of general propositions. These can be either generalizations about the archaeological record ('the rise of early states correlates with the emergence of redistributive trade networks') or about how we should do archaeology ('we must make testability the central criterion of our epistemology'). The data that we manipulate cannot be changed in this view: data just exist independently of the theory we are using. Many of the things we do as archaeologists (site catchment analysis, random sampling, retrieval of surface scatters of pottery) are in this view simply techniques. The questions the techniques are designed to answer may be theoretical, but the techniques and the data are outside the purview of theory.

At the other extreme, all archaeology is theoretical; theory is defined very broadly. As we have seen, postprocessualists argue that both techniques and data are 'theory-laden', and that we must theorize 'interpretation at the trowel's edge'. Many would go further and, following critical theory, argue that site catchment analysis and other techniques masquerade as neutral but are actually deeply theoretical.

Remember that for poststructuralists even a banal factual statement like 'there are 23 pig molars from Layer 346' is a statement within a text that can be deconstructed. Or postprocessualists might take another tack: 'Of course the number of pig molars is a factual statement – but why does it appear where it does in this text? Why did the site director decide to put so much emphasis on economic reconstruction at this site to the exclusion of all others? In short, the question may be factual, but we want to question the question.' So, just as feminists argue that inequality penetrates deeply into everyday life, and just as many would draw a broad and deep view of politics, so in this view all or almost all of archaeological practice is drawn within the remit of theory.

Shanks and Tilley write:

> Theory is thoroughly subjective. It is not a technical product of a specialist but a delimited and localized production, arising from a specific contextualized interaction between individuals, the experiences of these individuals, the manner in which their life and work interacts, and the way in which the archaeologist manages to arrive at a specific picture of the past based on the scraps of contingent materials ... and life experiences at his or her disposal. (Shanks and Tilley 1987: 212–13)

I have tried to be sympathetic to different positions in this book, so whichever view of theory you choose to adopt is up to you.

Defining the Middle Ground

Or is it up to you? It's your choice, but the chances are that your choice will be categorized and interpreted before you have a chance to get a word in edgeways. You will be labelled 'extreme' or 'moderate', 'suitable' or 'marginal', a 'naive empiricist' or 'slippery relativist', depending on the view that you choose. But who defines what is extreme or moderate, central or marginal? Who sets the agenda, who decides where theory is going?

Here are four views, each very different in its own way:

> Science works responsibly. We create our data in the present. We seek through pattern recognition studies to gain an insight into how the past was organized. We propose ideas as to the nature of past organizations and how they changed. At this juncture the scientist is responsible for seeking out experiences as widely as possible in order to provide reality checks on the accuracy and utility of his ideas. Responsible learning is

> dependent upon the degree to which research is designed so as to expose ambiguity, inadequacy and inaccuracy in our ideas guiding both the production of data and our attempts to understand it. The backboard for achieving this is the world of experience. The external world exists in its own right, and that includes the properties of the archaeological record.... The claim that our cognitive devices insulate us from the external world is false. (Binford 1987: 403)

> In the 1970s structuralists, poststructuralists, and then 'postprocessualists' reacted against the functionalism of the early New Archaeology, advocating greater emphasis on the ideas and beliefs of past societies and criticizing the idea of testing, since all knowledge is subjective. Processualists have responded by reaffirming the importance of testing – how else are we to choose between competing theories? – but have accepted the need to look afresh at ideas and beliefs, at the cognitive aspects of culture and to develop a methodology which can recognize the role of the individual and of agency in the inception of change. A new cognitive-processual synthesis can thus be seen to have emerged in the 1990s. (Renfrew and Bahn 1996: 473)

> The European experience shows that we can accept that the past and archaeology are socially embedded while retaining a commitment to scientific methodological rigour.... We do not need, as archaeologists, to feel that the only alternative to positivist processual archaeology is a hopeless slide towards relativity and chaos. European traditions demonstrate a range of satisfactory possibilities between the two extremes. (Hodder 1991a: 21–2)

> For the subjective idealism of scientistic archaeology we substitute a view of the discipline as an hermeneutically informed dialectical science of past and present unremittingly embracing and attempting to understand the polyvalent qualities of the socially constructed world in which we live. We sustain throughout a rejection of the past as presented in archaeological texts as objective, or alternatively, as subjective. There is no question of choosing one or another. Archaeological theory and practice as labour in the present completely transcend this artificial division. (Shanks and Tilley 1992: 243)

Where is archaeological theory going? Each of the views quoted above states a different view. Implicit in each view is a different understanding of where theory has been, where theory is now. Each defined a different 'mainstream' and different areas as marginal or peripheral. Each statement is a piece of rhetoric.

The rhetorical similarities cut across the grain of theoretical divides. For Binford and Shanks and Tilley, statements are offered on a take-it-or-leave-it basis. Science is the way it is because Binford says so. Look at Binford's best and most accessible book, *In Pursuit of the Past*: the question of different possible definitions of science and scientific method is dealt with in a footnote. In the paper cited, the word 'science' is mentioned over fifty times, but non-positivist views of science are never discussed or even acknowledged. So, as readers perhaps encountering archaeological theory for the first time and feeling uncertain about our own credentials and background knowledge, we can either take it or leave it: we can either accept or reject Binford's claim. Similarly with Shanks and Tilley. First, we must master the jargon in their quote. If we have made the investment of time and intellect required to work our way through the last 242 pages, we have done this already, but having made the effort we will be disinclined to reject their arguments wholesale.

Both Binford and Shanks and Tilley engage in a *rhetoric of confrontation.* This is the way it is. If you don't agree with Shanks and Tilley, you are theoretically moribund, an intellectual dinosaur. If you don't agree with Binford, you are simply unscientific.

Hodder and Renfrew and Bahn are altogether more subtle in their approach. Both texts take care to enlist a host of powerful allies in their respective camps. Both also engage in a *rhetoric of conciliation*: both acknowledge that other points of view have some validity, though of course other views are really marginal.

Hodder makes his claim in the introductory essay in a book entitled *Archaeological Theory in Europe: The Last Three Decades.* The essay is situated within a rhetoric of European ideals: it asserts that there has always been a vibrant European theoretical tradition, and theory is now renascent; contrast this, Hodder asserts, with what he sees as the increasing sterility of the North American scene which has been 'held back by the dominance of the methodological concerns of processual archaeology' (1991a: 9). It is striking that Hodder cites Renfrew to support his views on this point, creating a strong alliance across theoretical boundaries. Without spelling it out, by the use of this one reference cited without further comment Hodder is saying: 'Look, what I'm saying here isn't just a postprocessual party line. An important and prestigious figure from a different group has said much the same thing'.

Hodder creates other theoretical and socio-political alliances, and positions his ideas very carefully with respect to widely held sentiments in archaeological theory. If you are sceptical of the naivetés of the New Archaeology, then follow me. If you are committed to the idea of a distinctive European archaeology, then reject positivism, accept subjectivity, embrace history – in short, accept in broad terms my theoretical position. Acceptance will not cost you much in terms of abandoned theories – in many ways, it's what you have been doing all along, before New Archaeology came around.

Hodder is careful to couple this archaeological argument with a description of what is at stake politically. He 'wraps' his chapter with references to the writings of Gustav Kossina, the German archaeologist whose ideas lent support to Fascist notions of Aryan supremacy. If academe and politics is linked in this way, then Hodder's appeal to a European academic middle class full of liberal and internationalist sentiments feeling embattled in an age of nationalism is clear. If you are a 'good European', both in your archaeology and in your cultural and political sentiments, you should be doing postprocessual archaeology.

Renfrew and Bahn also try to occupy a middle ground between extremes that are portrayed as unbalanced and unreasonable. Look at the context of Renfrew and Bahn's comments. Their assessment is placed within a narrative of the development of archaeological thought. This narrative is strongly progressive in character, starting with the origins of archaeology and moving through great discoveries and individual archaeologists. The final development in theory, marking an advance on what has gone before, in this narrative is cognitive-processual archaeology. As a result, theory is portrayed as centring on a new consensus, 'willingly learning from any suitable developments in "postprocessual" archaeology' [who defines the criteria for what is or is not suitable?], though 'it does not accept the "revolutionary" rejection of the positive achievements of the New Archaeology' [who decides which claims are or are not revolutionary?]

Renfrew and Bahn make a masterly stroke in choosing where to place these statements: their comments are placed within a first year textbook. It is an excellent textbook as these things go, and has been very popular. This puts them in a position to build some very powerful and wide-ranging alliances. The most obvious of these alliances is a generation of new students in archaeology. Some of these students will go on in time to be a new generation of archaeologists; others, having taken one introductory course, will go on to be intellectual, cultural and political leaders in British and North American society. At the same time, placement within a first years textbook places the above statements in a 'black box'. Students on an introductory course tend to accept what they read as fact, or at least as an authoritative statement from 'experts'. They have five other courses to master, and not much time before the exam. In short, the vast majority of readers will be disinclined to take the time and effort to prise open the 'black box' and see what is inside. They could do so by turning to the Further Reading section. There, they find that the existence of this new 'mainstream' school of cognitive-processual archaeology is supported by five references, only one of which has a publication date in the 1990s (in other words, after the main impact of postprocessual ideas). Conversely, the student finds that the references in Renfrew and Bahn's reading list to support what they see as a 1970s reaction to the New Archaeology actually dates to the 1980s. Such a carefree switching of dates, if applied to the niceties of prehistoric chronology, would have us still believing in the diffusion of megaliths.

At the same time, their comments being placed in a 'mere' introductory text, Renfrew and Bahn do not have to give detailed academic documentation of this new consensus of cognitive- processual archaeology. This is useful for them, as in my view such a consensus does not exist. The term 'cognitive-processual' is little more than a linguistic ploy to capture the middle ground while minimizing the influence of other approaches.

The second masterstroke Renfrew and Bahn make is to acknowledge the existence of a diversity of viewpoints. Renfrew and Bahn rise above the petty theoretical fray, and instead make authoritative comments about it. And what a surprise it is for the reader when their impartial comments on where they think theory is going happily coincide with their own current research interests and viewpoints!

Who, of these four contrasting approaches to the description of archaeological theory, is the most 'honest'? In one sense, Binford, who is the only writer to give any hint that he feels theoretical currents are moving away from him. Who is the most successful?

Renfrew and Bahn, who manage simultaneously to acknowledge and marginalize other points of view, to erase their own roles as protagonists and appear as impartial commentators.

Well, I have to say that there is more than a whiff of hypocrisy about this. In the first place, Renfrew has pointed out that the very term 'postprocessual' is arrogant in assuming that it replaces something that has gone before and that is now redundant; I'd add that it is a one-word piece of rhetoric.

Second, it seems to me that your book does precisely what you attacked Renfrew and Bahn and the others for doing. It masquerades as an authoritative statement when it's actually a personal view.

Well, I didn't 'attack' Renfrew and Bahn; I tried to explore the way those texts situated themselves in a way that maximized their alliances and minimized those of their opponents. We all do this, of course, and this book is no exception.

This book also presents archaeological theory as a narrative. My conscious intent was to make links between theory, practice and intellectual context clearer by this method, for example between postprocessual archaeology and thinking within social theory as a whole in the 1980s. But of course such a narrative does present postprocessual archaeology as 'the final word' just as Renfrew and Bahn do for cognitive-processual archaeology. I enlisted a chain of allies for this view: shifts in theory in the human sciences as a whole, what was and is going on in the world outside archaeology. Some lines of thought are treated but marginalized in this analysis by being placed in final chapters (for example, feminist theory and the archaeology of gender has been a profound influence on postprocessual archaeology, but appears here in terms of the ordering of chapters to have been influenced by it). However, it is time to state a personal view.

Archaeology remains appallingly unaware of its own theoretical underpinnings; much if not most archaeological practice is quite uninformed about recent theoretical debates. One of the most encouraging things in recent years has been signs that this is changing.

Theoretical debate itself is of a very low intellectual standard. Many recent theoretical surveys, particularly by senior figures in archaeology, appear to be quite unaware of the literature they cite in support, attack or caricature. The more senior the figure, the more prestigious the publishing house, the more banal and uninspiring the analysis often seems. A colleague recently told me with some pride that he had given an international seminar attacking a certain school of thought having read one book on the subject, albeit backed up with 'many conversations in pubs'. Would he even dare to write an undergraduate essay having read one book on the Late Woodland period or on Bronze Age Europe? This generally low standard of debate means that uninformed position statements, platitudes and 'straw people' abound with very little critical analysis on all sides of the debate. There is also an assumption that one's own position has been intellectually victorious to the extent that scholars working in other traditions are mere intellectual dinosaurs or intellectual poseurs rather than serious archaeologists with genuine concerns (figures 12.1 and 12.2).

One area where, I feel, consensus has emerged is that of epistemology. On the one hand, few would now subscribe to a narrowly positivist position, and most would agree that an appeal to 'testing' is far more complex and problematic than it appeared at first sight. The proliferation of studies on middle-range theory and taphonomy that I discussed in chapter 3 can clearly be seen in this light. Few also

Figure 12.1 Archaeological theory in 1988 (cartoon by Simon James).

Figure 12.2 Archaeological theory in 1998 (cartoon by Matthew Johnson).

would try to assert that our interpretations of the archaeological record are entirely free of social and political influence. On the other hand, I know of no archaeologist who would overtly declare him or herself a relativist; indeed, the charge of unqualified relativism is strenuously denied by all parties in theoretical debate. Relativism is a spectre that haunts archaeology and the social sciences generally; we are all afraid of it, though the beast seems to spend most of its time lurking in the shadows as an unidentified terror, almost never showing itself clearly. In this sense, as we concluded in the last chapter, *what is revealing about contemporary thinking is the universal fear of relativism* – like atheism in sixteenth-century Europe or communism in the 1950s, it has to be ritually denounced by all parties.

Such a consensus somewhere between narrow positivism and unbridled relativism finds itself allied to post-positivist philosophies of science such as 'realism' and 'weak social constructivism'.

I have two reactions to the debate over epistemology. First, there is a variance between theory and practice. What is striking is that an insistence on the epistemological primacy of the data does not necessarily go hand in hand with using those data. To clarify this point at the risk of personalizing the issue, Chris Tilley may be attacked by many as a closet relativist, but there are more 'data' worked through in close and critical detail in his two recent books than in the entire careers of some of his critics.

Second, at the risk of sounding flippant, debates over epistemology may be necessary but they are certainly boring. There are other issues in theory that I find much more interesting, including the nature of social change; questions of agency and social structure; the cultural context of archaeological practice; the archaeology of gender; the relationship between archaeological and literary theory; the emergence of social complexity and the current diversity of cultural evolutionary models.

One particularly striking aspect of recent debates is the way theoretical debate shifts back and forth across the Atlantic, and the way this has set up a series of dynamics between generations. For example, there is more interesting analysis within the framework of cultural evolution now in North America than there is in Britain. In part this is the result of the completeness of the sweep of postprocessual thinking within those parts of British archaeology departments that are attuned to theoretical debates. Many young scholars in Britain, rightly or wrongly, feel that processual archaeology has been an utterly dead tradition since the late 1970s, though they express different degrees of scepticism over the various alternatives. As a result, many sessions at the British TAG and resultant publications have a depressing feel of sameness to them. 'My God, you guys are doing normal science!' exclaimed a North American colleague at a recent TAG conference, having sat through three days of papers of very similar postprocessual theoretical orientation.

Conclusion

When I started thinking about how to write this book, I felt that archaeological theory had reached something of an impasse, a full stop. The process of researching it, in particular reading closely argued and interesting case studies from periods and on themes with which I was not immediately familiar, has restored my faith in the vitality of the intellectual state of archaeology. Yes, there is a great deal of low-quality theory out there, but there is also a great deal of exciting new work that utilizes a range of approaches. This new work is coming particularly from younger scholars who are moving beyond narrow theoretical affiliations. Most importantly, this new work combines data and theory – it works through theoretical insights with close and critical reference to archaeological material. And it does so from a wide variety of viewpoints, and with a welcome sense of eclecticism – that is, a willingness to draw widely on theory rather than stick to a given 'party line'.

I came to archaeology not quite as Roger Beefy, but as the 'dirt archaeologist' character who has been questioning things in this volume. All the practising archaeologists I had worked with before university were contemptuous of theory; in late 1970s Britain, rescue archaeology was at its peak, and there was too much digging to do to worry about linear movement zones and mutual causal deviation amplifying processes. The first year of my university course, which was strongly oriented towards a narrow view of cultural evolution and the New Archaeology, tended to confirm these suspicions. Grand evolutionary schema seemed boring and irrelevant to the particularities of archaeological practice. I'd read around history and historical sociology, and as Bruce Trigger also noted, the rejection of history seemed especially naive. Perhaps in retrospect this was a biased and partial reading of the literature; but it was the one I made at the time.

This view was reinforced through experiences of theory outside mainstream archaeology. My work on the 'English school' of landscape history and experience of historical theory drew me to an appreciation of how different disciplines really did have very different theoretical criteria and methodologies. In this sense, the insight that arguments are never evaluated in conditions of pure objectivity, but are always formulated and considered within a certain social milieu, was not a theoretical lesson but a practical one derived from talking and working with archaeologists, historians, architectural historians and geographers. Again, practical experience rather than theoretical demonstration has led me to see a fragmentation of method within the discipline as a whole; I see very little in common between the method and theory of, say, the archaeology of the American Southwest and that of the medieval European church. Both would consider the methods of the other as utterly unproductive; if a 'theorist' has any role in archaeology, it must surely be to translate – to show how both schools have their own validity, their own intellectual credentials, and why both should respect the other's traditions and take the time to talk to the other.

My main aim in writing this book was to persuade the reader of the excitement, importance and relevance of theory, and to encourage him or her to adopt a consciously critical attitude to the things she or he is taught by senior figures – 'experts' – about the theory and practice of the discipline. I want the student to prise open black boxes rather than leave them untouched. The rather naive hope behind this was that a diversity of approaches to the archaeological record is a good thing, as the interaction of different approaches tends to produce interesting and fruitful results, a more truthful and more stimulating account of the past; and more broadly, that the intrinsic value of liberal academic study lies in its development of a positive critical attitude to the self and to society and culture as a whole. I don't much care which 'ism' future generations of archaeologists find most appealing, except in so far as it enhances and fosters such critical attitudes. The moment an archaeological theory begins to sound like a recipe-book to be followed blindly is probably the moment at which it has outlived its usefulness.

What I do care about is the lack of serious critical thought that pervades much of the recent literature on all sides of the debate. Papers that end with the depressingly banal conclusion that 'there is something to be said for both sides' or that 'we should look for a middle ground' should be banned – not because a middle ground is in itself a bad thing, but because the search for such a middle ground all too often becomes an easy replacement for the hard work of serious yet sympathetic critique of one's own and others' theoretical positions.

As I once heard someone say in a dusty bar somewhere in West Texas, 'there ain't nothin' in the middle of the road 'cept white lines and dead armadillos'. And the odd archaeological theorist.

Selective Glossary

Sir, I have found you an argument; but I am not obliged to find you an understanding.

Dr Johnson, to a tedious interrogator; Boswell, June 1784

Many of the terms discussed below have led to confusion since they mean different things to different people. Terms like 'class', 'culture', 'evolution', 'process', 'type' and 'power' can appear quite simple but very often tend to mystify since they are used by the author in one sense and read in quite another. A good example is the term 'theory' itself (see below). Part of the problem with such terms is that they vary their meaning according to context or disciplinary background. For example, 'cultural materialism' has entirely different, almost diametrically opposed meanings in the respective fields of cultural anthropology and literary theory.

I have only listed terms here that appear in the text but that deserve further amplification. I started out with the aim of compiling a full glossary of all the specialized terms I have seen used in archaeological theory, but it became rapidly apparent that such an exercise would require a further book. Clarke's *Analytical Archaeology* (1972) has a good glossary of terms used in systems theory and related fields. Hodder et al. (1995) has a useful glossary. Further help with the human sciences generally may be sought in Johnson (1995), while Humm (1992) has a glossary on feminist thought. Lechte (1994) has brief discussions of contemporary thinkers. Raymond Williams's *Keywords* (2nd edition 1988) is a fascinating read. The appendix in Culler (1997) offers concise views of the main schools in literary theory.

If many terms are not here, those that are have considerably over-simplified definitions. The best way to appreciate the full meaning and context of many of the words examined here is to read the relevant chapter – terms can only be understood within the context of the intellectual movement(s) of which they form a part. Terms also change their meaning. Between my writing of these words and your reading of them, many of these terms will have subtly changed.

Agency The issue of how we think about intentional action and the resources needed to act, as in 'structuralism lacks a theory of agency' (in other words, structuralism can't explain why individuals act in a diversity of ways rather than blindly executing a preconceived pattern). Often paired with STRUCTURE.

Annales school A French school of historical thought, part of which stresses the interrelationship of different timescales (the *longue dureé* or long-term, the medium-term, and short-term events of *l'histoire evenementielle*). Annales historians also focus on the study of mentalities. See chapter 10.

Antiquarianism In this book, mere collection of ancient artefacts without relating these to past processes. The antiquarianism of sixteenth- to eighteenth-century Europe and America was more sophisticated than this and demands more complex treatment, however.

Behaviourism The proposition that we should focus exclusively on observable behaviours and refrain from referring to people's thoughts in our explanations of that behaviour.

Cognitive-processualism A school of thought that claims to combine a broad processual background with a recognition of the importance of looking at cognitive factors. 'An alternative to the materialist orientation of the functional-processual approach, it is concerned with (1) the integration of the cognitive and symbolic with other aspects of early societies; (2) the role of ideology as an active organizational force. It employs the theoretical approach of methodological individualism' (Renfrew and Bahn 1995).

Contradiction A term with Marxist connotations: see DIALECTIC.

Critical theory See chapter 6. A school of thought derived in part from Marxism, associated with Adorno, Habermas and Marcuse, and often referred to as the 'Frankfurt school'. Critical theorists aim to unmask the inner workings of a society which they suggest lie concealed from view by the mystifications of ideology.

Culture An archaeological culture is a repeatedly recurring assemblage of traits – pottery and house forms, burial practices – seen over a discrete time and space. It may or may not relate to a human culture. In the broader sense, a culture can be many things, including:

1 a body of shared ideas and beliefs (the normative view);
2 an 'extra-somatic' (outside the body) system adapted to the external environment (systemic view);
3 a structure or code analogous to language;
4 an attribute of civilized behaviour, as in 'every cultured person should have some knowledge of archaeology'.

Culture history A term usually used in America to refer to a traditional approach to the mapping of cultures and cultural influence.

Cybernetics The science of energy flow, often associated with systems theory.

Decentring Humanists see individuals as autonomous, coherent and authors of their own meaning: the poststructuralist 'decentring of the subject' deconstructs all these ideas.

Deconstruction A weapon from the armoury of poststructuralism. By showing that any word or sentence has many meanings and that those meanings themselves refer to a multiplicity of other meanings within language, any text, however apparently obvious or banal, can be 'deconstructed' or shown to have many meanings other than its apparent one. Deconstruction can be used in politically radical ways (to show for example how the word 'masculine' is both unstable and privileged) though it can also lead to a disabling and politically neutral relativism.

Diachronic Through time (as opposed to SYNCHRONIC).

Dialectic A complex term from Hegelian and Marxist thought. It refers to the contradiction or conflict of ideas or of groups within a wider framework. That framework collapses from within, resulting in the rise of new social or intellectual forms that in turn develop new contradictions. Thus, for example, Marx's account of feudalism is dialectical since it suggests that there were contradictions within the feudal system that brought the whole system crashing down, to be replaced by nascent capitalism and its own contradictions. A dialectical view of social change or of intellectual development can be contrasted with an evolutionary or progressive view.

Diffusion The spread of ideas between cultural groups.

Direct historical approach A North American term, referring to the project of delineating culture groups in prehistory by working from 'known' groups in ethnography and ethnohistory back into the protohistoric and prehistoric past.

Discourse A set of rules of how to write and think that is specific to particular disciplines or institutions: thus 'all the apparatus of empiricist discourse are mobilized in this article . . .'. A buzzword among archaeologists influenced by Foucault.

Empiricism The belief that the data will 'speak for themselves' without the benefit of intervening theories. Often used loosely as a term of abuse to indicate theoretical naiveté in general: 'Oh well, you'll call me an old empiricist I know, but I think we should just dig and not bother about theory'. Also used loosely, interchangeably and confusingly with POSITIVISM.

Epistemology How we know what we know, or the validity of knowledge claims. For example, the question 'can we ever really know what people were thinking in the Formative Period?' is an *epistemological* question.

Essentialism The belief that there are certain attitudes or emotions that are 'natural' or biologically endowed, either to humans in general or to a specific sex; much debated by feminists and others. Thus the statement 'in prehistory, men must have been more warlike as they lacked the mothering instinct' is an *essentialist* statement. Essentialist claims are often supported with reference to biological arguments (for example, that men's and women's brains are structured differently); essentialist statements therefore often have a basis in sociobiology or related schools of thought. Alternatively, they are derived from humanism.

Ethnocentrism Two meanings: the belief that one's own values and attitudes have held true in all times and places; and/or the belief that one's own culture is morally superior to others, not simply different.

Evolution A term historically derived from Darwin and Spencer. When used in archaeological writing, its meaning varies. It can involve some or all of:

1 The application of Darwinian principles of random mutation and natural selection to humans in the past. Some argue that the only valid unit of selection is the individual, while others view cultural practices or entire cultures as appropriate units.
2 The idea that human societies can be ranked on a scale of complexity, and that through time there has been a move from simple to complex. This can be linked with ideas of progress in human life.

Falsificationism The belief that while we can never 'prove' anything, science advances by coming up with hypotheses that it is possible to disprove or falsify.

Feminist archaeology The belief that gender roles are partially or completely socially constructed rather than endowed by biology, and that women in particular have suffered from oppression in Western society. This has the implication that (a) archaeologists need to examine gender roles and inequalities within the profession; (b) we need to be more critical about biases and assumptions made about ancient societies; and (c) we need to question the way academic knowledge has been constructed in, it is argued, a 'phallocentric' or male-dominated manner. Not all archaeologists interested in 'an archaeology of gender' call themselves feminists, and not all feminists would necessarily fully agree with point (c) above.

Formalism A school of economic theory that suggests we can extend Western ideas of economic rationality to non-Western societies.

Frankfurt School See CRITICAL THEORY.

Functionalism The belief that the different institutions and practices of a human group are interrelated in a manner analogous to that of a body, so that the form of one can be explained by its functional relationship to other elements.

Hermeneutics The study of how we give meanings to cultural products, or how we interpret human actions and their products (for example, written texts, social actions, works of art, or artefacts).

Heuristic To find out, to learn or to throw up fresh ideas, as in 'we didn't gain any grand theory from this simulation, we just did it for heuristic purposes – it threw up some new ideas and possible interpretations that we need to test out in the next research stage'.

Historicism Various meanings. Often used as a code-word for Marxism; alternatively, New Historicist literary theory is 'a critical movement insisting on the prime importance of historical context to the interpretation of texts of all kinds' (Hamilton 1996: 2).

Historiography Various meanings, including historical theory and the history of historical thought.

Humanism The belief that there is an essential 'human condition' regardless of historical circumstance.

Hypothesis A prediction about the relationship between variables, as in 'My hypothesis is that marginal environments and risk are positively correlated'.

Idealism Theoretical usage differs from commonplace usage. An idealist believes that thoughts are prior to actions, in other words that the mental world is more important than the material. In Collingwood's historical idealism, the central method of historical and archaeological interpretation is to rethink the thoughts of past peoples empathetically.

Ideology See chapter 6. A set of overt or implicit beliefs or views of the world. According to Marxists, ideology serves to legitimate or mask the 'real' state of social relations.

Inductivism The belief that archaeological research starts with observations from the data, building general statements from them (in contrast with the HDN model, in which data collection is hypothesis-driven).

Legitimation See IDEOLOGY.

Logocentrism For poststructuralists, logocentrism is the illusion fostered by positivist science that there is a concrete world beyond 'the text', to which the text refers, and that meanings can therefore be fixed in some final 'reality'. Poststructuralists argue that meanings are never fixed in this way and deny what they call 'the logocentric fallacy'.

Marxian This term is used in two different (and confusing) senses. Some American archaeologists use it to refer to academic insights from the work of Marx without their political connotations (which they describe as Marxist). On the other hand, some social theorists use Marxian to refer to Marx's work in a narrow sense, where for them Marxism refers to the broader tradition of thought inspired by Marx's work.

Materialism Various meanings. Literally, a materialist believes that the material, physical world should be given more significance than the ideal or mental world. Some Marxists use the terms 'Marxism' and 'materialism' interchangeably. It is also used as a code-word by some American archaeologists to indicate Marxism without its political connotations. For literary theorists, cultural materialism is the idea that culture and history are linked dialectically; it is sometimes seen as 'the British version of New Historicism', though it tends to be more openly committed to left-wing politics. Finally, materialism is used to describe an acquisitive mind-set that many archaeologists feel is bound up with the origins of capitalism, as in 'the increased comfort of homes in the sixteenth century reflects a new spirit of materialism'.

Methodology The techniques and methods used to collect and interpret archaeological data. Some feel methodology is part of theory; others insist that it be kept separate.

Methodological individualism The belief that societies are nothing more than collections of individuals, and that therefore we can only explain 'social' phenomomena through individual psychology.

Modernism Used loosely to refer to belief in Science, Truth and Progress.

Multiculturalism The celebration of diverse ethnic backgrounds.

Multilinear Of a model that suggests more than one possible course, for example of social evolution.

Nomothetic (also nomological) Generalizing, as in 'The New Archaeology had nomothetic aims'.

Normative The assumption that artefacts are expressions of cultural ideas or norms.

Paradigm A set of beliefs or assumptions that underpin the whole way of doing 'normal science'. The term was invented by Kuhn, who suggested that science was characterized by long periods of stability punctuated by revolutionary 'paradigm shifts', for example between Newtonian and Einsteinian physics. There is much debate about whether Kuhn's assessment is accurate, and if so whether the New Archaeology (or for that matter postprocessual archaeology) marked a true 'paradigm shift'.

Particularize To explain or understand something in terms of its peculiar qualities.

Phenomenology The study of human experience and consciousness in everyday life.

Polythetic With many features or criteria.

Postmodernism According to Lyotard, 'incredulity towards metanarratives'.

Processual A school of archaeological thought that stresses the idea of process, tends to generalize and adopts a broadly positivist approach. Processualism can be seen as a developed, more mature form of the New Archaeology.

Realism A philosophy of science 'between' positivism and constructivism. Realists maintain that there is a real external reality and have a commitment to causal explanation.

Relativism The belief that all possible accounts of the past are equally valid in their own terms, there being no neutral or objective way to judge between them. Also used in anthropology as the view that other cultures are simply different from our own, not 'better' or 'worse'.

Reductionism The belief that complex phenomena can be explained by reducing them to a set of often very simple variables: often linked to essentialist or sociobiological arguments. Often used as a term of abuse. Thus, 'To suggest that we can explain the presence of weapons in these graves simply by reference to Man's aggressive instinct is both reductionist and essentialist'.

Reification Taking an idea or cluster of ideas and treating it as a definite thing. Thus, 'the Neolithic', 'the Formative Period' and 'postprocessual archaeology' are all reifications. Usually used perjoratively, as in 'There is no such thing as a school of cognitive-processualism. It is a reification of a few disparate articles'.

Semiotics The study of signs.

Social constructivism Also known as social constructionism. The proposition that scientific knowledge is not a neutral body of data independent of cultural practices and values, but is actually created within society. In this view scientific data and practices are wholly social constructs (strong constructivism) or partly (weak constructivism). In practice, social constructivists are interested in laboratory practices and publication of information as processes to be studied sociologically rather than as purely 'scientific' debates in the narrow sense of the term.

Sociobiology The idea that cultural practices are biologically rather than socially constructed, based on the drive to reproduce genes.

Structure Enduring cultural or social relations. Sometimes used interchangeably with 'system' by functionalists, though for Marxists and structuralists the structure underlies the social system.

Structuralism The belief that culture is governed by rules analogous to those of language.

Structuration theory A term associated with Giddens to describe how social agents or individuals relate to social structures. Giddens suggests that actors are constrained by their social environments, but pursue active strategies; the clash of agency then produces change in social structures.

Substantivism A school of economic theory that holds that our ideas of economic 'rationality' are not applicable to other cultures.

Synchronic At one particular moment in time (as opposed to DIACHRONIC).

Systems Can be used in a variety of senses from the very general ('the social system that was the Roman Empire came under stress in the third century AD') to very particular. In its particular forms, systems theory is close to functionalist beliefs that cultures can be seen as bodies – themselves systems – composed of various subsystems. Change in one subsystem will thus react against other subsystems and either be 'dampened down' (negative feedback leading to homeostasis) or produce wider change (positive feedback leading to transformation such as systems collapse).

Teleology A narrative with a definite development towards a point; for example, a traditional Marxist account of history is *teleological* in that it suggests an inexorable progress towards communism.

Theory General definition in chapter 12. It has also been used specifically to refer to a particular kind of structural-Marxism formulated by Althusser and others; thus, E. P. Thompson's essay *The Poverty of Theory* was actually an attack on Althusserian Marxism rather than on theory as such.

Totalizing A scheme of thought is totalizing if it attempts to place a set of diverse experiences within one large scheme applicable to all times and places. For example, social evolutionary models can be argued to be totalizing in so far as they place all human societies within one stage or another of a grand evolutionary scheme. Usually used by opponents of such thinking as a term of critique.

Unilinear Following one course, as in social evolution.

Further Reading

General Points

When reading any scholarly book in archaeology, theory included, it's a good idea to take a look at its reviews in journals such as *Antiquity*, *American Antiquity*, *American Anthropologist*, *Current Anthropology* or the *Archaeological Journal*, plus the thematic 'period' journals (such as *Proceedings of the Prehistoric Society*; *Britannia*; *Medieval Archaeology*; *Post-Medieval Archaeology*; *World Archaeology*; *Historical Archaeology*). These often tell you more about the prejudices of the reviewers than they do about the book, but are a good way of isolating areas of contentious debate.

Journals with theory articles: *Antiquity* has been a good place for theory articles over the last decade or so. They are decidedly variable in quality, but they are relatively readable given the editorial insistence of reaching a wide audience. The *Journal of Theoretical Archaeology* is of decidedly variable quality. *American Antiquity*, *Journal of European Archaeology*, *Journal of Archaeological Research*, *Journal of Anthropological Archaeology* and *American Anthropologist* all have good theory articles if sometimes lost among the preponderance of empirical material. The *Journal of Archaeological Method and Theory* is of consistent quality, and the new *Journal of Material Culture* promises much.

You can complement reading with attendance at conferences. The main British theory 'talking-shop' is the Theoretical Archaeology Group conference (TAG), which is held every December at a different university each year. Many go to TAG simply to see old friends and drink some warm beer, but it is also a 'barometer' of what's the latest trend in theory today, at least in Britain. The majority of papers are given by research students or younger staff and organization is supposed to be 'bottom-up'. The fee is currently £20 or less, there is usually free floor-space for students and the unwaged, and everybody regardless of status pays their own way to come. Andrew Fleming and I explored the history of TAG and some of the tensions between its egalitarian ethic and the reality in Fleming and Johnson (1990).

There is also a Theoretical Roman Archaeology Conference held every second year in Britain, and a 'Nordic TAG' (Tusa and Kirkinen 1992;

Anderson et al. 1997). The German 'Theorie-Arbeitgemeinschaft' ('T-AG') has a newsletter, regular seminars and also organizes sessions in many of the larger German conferences (see Harke 1993).

RATS (Radical Archaeologists Talk Shop) is 'an informal group of left-leaning archaeologists' (James Delle, personal communication) rather than a theory group as such. It brings together archaeologists from the northeastern USA and beyond and usually meets annually somewhere in New England or New York.

Otherwise you have to pick and choose between sessions and papers at major conferences. In North America, the Society for American Archaeology and the American Anthropological Association (SAA and AAA) hold symposia with theoretical content.

The Arch-Theory email discussion group is run out of Lampeter, Wales. Debate varies in liveliness but in the past has been extremely interesting.

The reading list that follows is partial, and will be out of date between the time I write these words and you read them. It is confined to English-language publications, and is biased towards publications readily accessible on both sides of the Atlantic. I have first listed some introductory readings, and then given suggestions for further reading on a chapter-by-chapter basis. The aim of these references is not to provide a complete encyclopaedia on a particular theme; rather, they indicate the background to the arguments laid out in the text, and contain suggestions for further reading for the more advanced student.

Introductory Texts

There are no really good general introductory surveys of theory that I know of. The best place to start for a historical perspective is Trigger (1989b). Trigger's section on Soviet archaeology is already a bit dated, and the latest chapters already need updating, but he has a good sense of the balance between academic and wider influences in the development of archaeology.

Renfrew and Bahn (second edition 1996) and Thomas (1998) are excellent general introductions to archaeology with the merit of recognizing that theoretical concerns are integral to what we do. Both are over-simplified, however, particularly with regard to postprocessual archaeology. Otherwise, most introductions to archaeology tend to concentrate on field techniques.

Binford, L. R. (1983a) *In Pursuit of The Past.* This is well written, easy to read and gives a powerful, convincing account of his view of archaeology. Note that it was actually written by John Cherry and Robin Torrence from transcripts from Binford's lecture series in Britain and the Netherlands – Binford is a brilliant, charismatic lecturer.

Hodder, I. (1985) *Reading the Past.* Some students I know find this difficult, but I think it's pretty straightforward. It's a little dated now in its critiques of other forms of archaeology. The second edition is little altered from the first: see the review by Griffin (1991).

Preucel, R. and Hodder, I. (eds) (1996) *Contemporary Archaeology in Theory: A Reader.* A collection of 26 articles on most key aspects of archaeological theory. Very good for browsing. Some would argue that epistemology, testing and evolutionary and behavioural archaeology are inadequately represented.

Four lectures give a good flavour of the overall thrust of Americanist archaeological theory in the 1990s: Redman (1991), Trigger (1991), Brumfiel (1992) and Cowgill (1993). All are summarized in Watson (1995).

Preface: The Contradictions of Theory

Popular suspicion of 'intellectuals' is of course a precise inversion of intellectual fear and suspicion of the masses: see Carey (1992). For recent debates over 'theory' and 'political correctness' see debates in the *New York Review of Books*.

Chapter 1 Common Sense is Not Enough

The discussion of ley lines is drawn from Williamson and Bellamy (1983).

Flannery (1982) is a comic account of recent theoretical stereotypes that continues to be relevant in the late 1990s. Because most feel such debates are irrelevant, few 'atheoretical' writers have been moved to put defences of their position in print. Elton (1991) is a passionately written, lucid condemnation of 'theory' in history. Elton chaired the committee that drew up the first version of the National Curriculum in History for England, which is the main medium through which schoolchildren encounter archaeology.

An account of the difficulties of theory in another discipline, with which I find myself in general agreement, is Culler (1997) chapter 1. Many of Eagleton's (1991) opening comments on ideology are relevant also.

Chapter 2 The 'New Archaeology'

Of Peter Ackroyd's novels, *Hawksmoor* and *The House of Doctor Dee* are cult reading among archaeologists. Sir Thomas Browne's essay can be found in Robbins (1972).

Further reading on archaeology before the New Archaeology: Lyman et al. (1997a, 1997b) are introductions to Americanist 'culture history' and reprints of selected papers respectively. I have avoided going in to the historical development of New Archaeology in any depth; such project would involve looking at the anthropological/North American influences of White, Steward, Seltzer, Willey and Phillips on the one hand, and economic/British influences of Childe, Higgs and Jarman, Grahame Clark and David Clarke on the other. My thanks to Bob Preucel for clarifying this point.

Childe's view of culture is summarized in McNairn (1980: 46–74). It should be noted that Childe's thought changed markedly through his life – see his 1958 article. Grahame Clark's thought developed over time from a stress on the economic (for example, Clark 1952) to a celebration of a politically reactionary humanism (for example, Clark 1982).

Meltzer (1979) and Patterson (1986) are good introductions to the New Archaeology. Leone (1972) is a reader that includes most of the key early papers and gets across the diversity and excitement of early New Archaeology well. Binford's early papers reprinted in his *An Archaeological Perspective* (1972) are essential reading for anyone who wants to understand the underlying mood and origins of the New Archaeology. His introduction and connecting passages are also entertaining and lucid, in contrast to his more formal academic writing style.

Flannery's edited volume *The Early Mesoamerican Village* (1972) is an edited volume of case studies that over 25 years later should be read by specialists in all areas and periods. The case studies show New Archaeology in action, warts and all; Flannery links the sections with brilliant dialogues between the old-style Real Mesoamerican Archaeologist, the Skeptical Graduate Student and the Great Synthesisor. These dialogues not only set out the issues clearly, they give a real flavour of the 'revolution'.

Read some of the texts, particularly in anthropology, the New Archaeologists turned to. White's *The Science of Culture* (1949) is clearly written, and prefigures some of the processual stress on science and systems. The chapter on Akenaton is a brilliant demolition of the idea that individuals' actions are random, unpredictable or important in history. Much New Archaeology was anticipated by Walter Taylor in *A Study of Archeology* (1948); his emphasis on a 'conjunctive' approach is a forerunner of functional emphases.

Renfrew's *Before Civilisation* (1973a) is the most accessible book on the impact of New Archaeology in Europe. Renfrew shows how scientific advances dovetailed with changes in theoretical perspectives on monuments such as megaliths. Clarke's *Analytical Archaeology* (1978: the second edition revised by Bob Chapman) is a difficult but essential read. It is hard to overestimate the influence of this book. Clarke's (1973) article also had wide impact and sets the theoretical basis of New Archaeology alongside parallel developments in method and technique.

Megaliths: Renfrew (1973a) is a popular account. It's worth comparing Renfrew with more recent 'postprocessual' interpretations of megaliths – see, for example, Thomas (1999), Bradley (1993) and Tilley (1994).

Hawkes (1968) is a short and in my view misconceived but influential critique of New Archaeology from the perspective of British traditional archaeology.

Chapter 3 Archaeology as a Science

Frankenstein: Mary Shelley's novel has been interpreted as a feminist critique of the moral limits of (masculine) scientific rationality: see Gilbert and Gubar (1979: 213–47) and Mellor (1988).

Watson, LeBlanc and Redman (1984) is a pretty classic statement of archaeology-as-science; see chapter 1, and succeeding chapters for systems theory and ecology. The classic early example of 'testing' is Hill (1970), though the examples discussed here give a better idea of how the notion has developed in archaeology.

Positivism in the human sciences: Giddens (1974) is a useful introduction to Comte, Durkheim and others. Roscoe (1995) is a useful commentary on parallel issues in cultural anthropology. Bell (1994) takes a 'refutationist' approach though he is still positivist in the broad sense used here.

Humanist distrust of science is often based on the implicit premise that what makes us distinctively human (culture, art, religion) is precisely that which is ignored by science; therefore, uncritical use of science will move archaeology away from 'the proper study of mankind', that is 'man'. See C. Hawkes (1954) and J. Hawkes (1968).

Kuhn's philosophy of science is explored in a classic but long and difficult text (Kuhn 1962). For an introduction to the issues and a clearly written exploration of Kuhn's significance in the human sciences as a whole, see Fuller (1992). For Feyerabend, see (1988 and 1995). I could have led the reader away from positivism via the work of Hansen, Quine and Putnam also.

Gibbon (1989) is a comprehensive archaeological critique of positivism and a lucid view of a 'realist' position. Courbin (1988) argues, in detail, that there is no example of 'testing' in archaeology that can be shown to work in practice. Hill (1991) is a stout defence of hypothesis testing and the cumulative nature of knowledge (compare his views with others in the same volume). Alison Wylie's writings on epistemology are absolutely central. They make dense reading, but this is because they deal with difficult issues and refuse to descend into platitudes.

Social constructivism: Latour (1987), chapter 1, is a provocative and accessibly written introduction to the constructivist view of science and should be read not just as an account of social constructivism but as a guide to thinking critically about research in the natural and human sciences as a whole. See also Latour and Woolgar (1979), Knorr-Cetina and Mulkay (1983) and Lynch (1985). Pickering (1984) is a brilliant case study but difficult to follow if you don't have a scientific background. For a discussion of different varieties of constructivism including 'strong' and 'weak' versions see Sismondo (1993), the reply by Knorr-Cetina (1993) and the subsequent discussion in the same volume. Critics of social constructivism include Holton

(1993), Gross and Levit (1994) and most famously Lewis Wolpert (1992). Delanty (1997) tries to steer a 'middle course' between constructivism and realism, while rejecting positivism entirely.

Examples of social constructivism in archaeology are rarely laid out in explicitly constructivist terms: see Epperson (1996), Mirza and Dungworth (1995) and Pluciennik (1996) on race and DNA.

Chapter 4 Testing, Middle-range Theory and Ethnoarchaeology

The discussion on analogy here is necessarily brief. It owes much, first, to Orme's (1981) work stressing the large contribution ethnographic analogy has played in all archaeology however 'traditional' and, second, to Wylie's (1985) discussion, which demonstrates that there is no clear alternative to analogical thinking in interpretation.

The best place to start with Binford is his *In Pursuit of the Past* (1983a) before moving on to his more difficult writings, particularly *Bones* (1981b) and *Debating Archaeology* (1989). Binford's first essay on analogy was 1967; his 1980 article is also good. His Nunamiut work is discussed both in 1983a and more extensively in 1978. Also, see the Binford/Hodder debate in *Man* 23: 373–5. For the Mousterian debate, see Binford (1983b), chapters 4 and 5. An effective critique of Binford's conception of middle-range theory is Raab and Goodyear (1984); see also Kosso (1991).

Experimental archaeology: Whittaker (1994) on stone tools.

Ethnoarchaeological studies of crop processing include studies by Hillman and Jones in Zeist and Casparie (1984); also Hastorf (1988), Miksicek (1987). For transport costs and the 'Schlepp effect' see Perkins and Daly (1968).

Behavioural archaeology: Schiffer (1976, 1987, 1995), Skibo et al. (1995) and Gould and Schiffer (1981). For the Tucson Garbage Project, see Rathje et al. (1992) and references therein. Binford distances himself from behavioural archaeology (see Binford 1981a), though to the outside observer behavioural archaeology's stress on research into formation processes and Binford's middle-range research seem to be very similar.

Hodder's early work is in Hodder (1982a), though a more readable start to ethnoarchaeology is Hodder (1982b). He criticizes Binford's use of analogy in (1982b: 20–4).

Moore (1987) is important not just in its implications for ethnoarchaeology but in its use of feminist and textual theory in the interpretation of space. Other interdisciplinary studies of 'material culture in the present' include Miller (1985). There has been much recent interest in interdisciplinary studies of modern material culture: see for example Miller (1987, 1995).

Chapter 5 Culture as a System

Metaphors of culture: Toynbee's twelve-volume *A Study of History* was fashionable in his day for his delineation of organic rhythms of civilizations, though he is almost forgotten now. The view of societies as embodiments of Big Ideas goes back to the nineteenth-century philosopher Hegel and beyond (Hegel 1956).

For the intellectual sources of systems thinking, see the histories of the New Archaeology cited above.

Early systems thinking: Renfrew (1973a) is a good introduction; he discusses systems thinking in more depth in his 1972 and 1984 volumes. Chapters 2 and 3 of Clarke (1978), though few would now subscribe to Clarke's very formal delineation of systems. Flannery (1972, 1973a) are two classic early systemic studies. Earle and Erickson (1977) is a good collection of systemic approaches to exchange. Compare with Earle and Erickson (1982).

Hodges (1982) is a systemic approach to early medieval Europe. Hodges isn't always consistent in his theory.

Systems collapse: Tainter, J. (1990); Yoffee and Cowgill (1988). For the Classic Maya collapse in particular, see Sabloff (1990) as an introduction; Culbert (1973); Neiman (1997) takes a self-styled Darwinian evolutionary perspective; his arguments convince though I am not entirely clear what is specifically Darwinian about his theory. For a review of recent Maya literature see Fash (1994). See also Wilks (1985) for an interesting perspective on how archaeologists' changing explanations of the collapse reflect contemporary political and environmental concerns. For Chaco Canyon, Sebastian (1996) advances a 'sociopolitically based' model in opposition to the environmental explanations.

For critiques of systems theory, see Shanks and Tilley (1987). Habermas's critique is much broader than is indicated here, extending to the nature of ideology in late capitalist society (see Habermas 1970 and 1975; Bernstein 1985) and the nature of postmodernity; the best introduction to his thought is Pusey (1987). Giddens (1984) is another useful critique.

Heterarchy: Crumley (1979, 1987); Brumfiel (1992); Brumfiel and Fox (1994); Brumfiel and Earle (1987); Renfrew (1986); Ehrenreich *et al.* (1995). See also broader collections of papers that balance systemic approaches with emphasis on historical uniqueness: Scarry (1996); Flannery and Marcus (1983). Political economy: Earle (1997), Brumfiel and Earle (1987). Muller (1997) is a good case study.

World systems theory: the general inspiration is Wallerstein (1974). Applications to archaeology include Kohl (1987) and Kristiansen and Larsen (1987). World systems theory in Mesoamerica: Schortman and Urban (1994).

Chaos and complexity theory: Kohler (1993); Reisch (1991); Gerding and Ingemark (1997).

On 'freedom' and slavery, see Patterson (1982). I am grateful to Bob Preucel for drawing my attention to this point.

Chapter 6 Looking at Thoughts

Hawkes (1954) for his seven 'levels of inference' and the difficulty of looking at thoughts.

Binford's views on the inadmissibility of cognition as a factor in archaeological explanation are best expressed in his paper in *Man* (1986) and his brief Commentary in Renfrew and Shennan (1982).

'Cognitive-processual' archaeology: many of the key papers for both 'cognitive' and 'postprocessual' approaches are collated in Whitley (1998). Mithen's work (especially 1990 and 1997) is especially important. Mithen (1998) promises to be a key collection of papers, but was not published at the time of writing. Renfrew (1982) is an instructive read. Remember that this is an inaugural lecture at the University of Cambridge. Renfrew is addressing an audience of the 'great and the good' from all disciplines, and is in part making a powerful plea for the intellectual and political status of archaeology within the university. See also Renfrew (1993).

Flannery and Marcus (1993) sketches out an approach to cognitive archaeology that is largely independent of postprocessual concerns. Renfrew and Zubrow (1994) styles itself a collection of papers addressing cognition from a processual viewpoint, though in my view the intellectual affiliations of the various contributors are more diverse. Case studies include Flannery and Marcus (1976); Davidson and Noble (1996); Mellars and Gibson (1997). Brown (1997) is a review of a variety of approaches as applied to the Eastern Woodlands of North America.

An important area of recent work has been examination of cognition within the context of human evolution: see Mithen (1990, 1995 and 1996).

Structuralism: Bradbury (1987) is a brilliant parody. Tilley (1990) contains a series of studies of thinkers in the structuralist tradition in the human sciences and is a good introduction to the way these thinkers have informed post-processual literature. Conkey (1989) is a good summary of structuralist concerns, tied to the example of cave art. Other examples of structural analysis are discussed in other chapters, but examples include Glassie (1975), Deetz (1977), Washburn (1983). Bapty and Yates (1990) explore the implications of poststructuralism.

Marxism: Giddens (1979) is still a clear summary of the key points of classical Marxism. Bloch (1983) discusses parallel debates in anthropology. McGuire (1992) is a sophisticated discussion. There is no substitute for reading Marx himself; see McClellan (1977). Childe is the most famous Marxist archaeologist – he combined a materialist model close to traditional Marxism with a diffusionary element. See Childe (1958, 1979), his 'popular' books (1936, 1942) and discussions in McNairn (1980) and Trigger (1980).

Ideology: Eagleton (1991) reviews the concept in general terms. The writings of Mark Leone (1984, 1988, 1995, forthcoming) are the best examinations of ideology in archaeology; the work of the Archaeology in Annapolis project has done much to explore these issues in relation to 'public archaeology' (Leone *et al.* 1987; Potter 1994). See also Miller and Tilley (1984) and references for chapter 11.

Conclusion: Patrik (1985) characterizes different theoretical approaches in terms of different characterizations of what the archaeological record is.

Chapter 7 Postprocessual and Interpretative Archaeologies

Origins: Hodder (1985) explains something of the origins of postprocessual archaeology; Hodder et al. (1995) is an excellent overview of contemporary activity. Many of the key papers are reprinted in Whitley (1998). The dialogue between Iain Mackenzie and Mike Shanks (1994) and between John Barrett and E. A. Bartley (1994) is also accessible and useful in coming to grips with postprocessual ideas.

For problems of testing and simulation, see Hodder and Orton (1976); Hodder's ethnoarchaeological work can be found in Hodder (1982b). Watson's (1991) article pointed out to me the striking parallels between Binford and Hodder in their intellectual development.

Hodder (1998) is good not just on how to do postprocessual archaeology, but on theorized descriptions of what all archaeologists do in practice and how all those practices are underpinned by theory, 'interpretation at the trowel's edge'.

Shanks and Tilley (1987 and 1988) had a huge impact on publication. They are both difficult, but absolutely central to any understanding of postprocessual archaeology. *Social Theory* has a summary at the back. McGuire (1993) is not just an article about Marxism, but offers a useful survey of the relationship between different strands of postprocessual thought and their academic and social context.

Historical idealism: Collingwood's *Idea of History* (1946) is his definitive statement of historical idealism; his *Autobiography* (1939) is shorter, more readable, and makes the context of his thinking much clearer.

Agency: the current interest in agency is not confined to postprocessualism; just as cognition is attracting attention from processual thinking, so is 'the individual' however defined. The origins of concerns with agency are usually traced to Bourdieu (1977) and Giddens (1979, 1984; see Held and Thompson 1989 for useful critique and bibliography). I have always found the work of Erving Goffman (1959, 1971) far more useful and lucid and recommend it as an introduction to the issues surrounding structure and action. A different approach to agency and structure is taken from within the postprocessual tradition through the idea of practice (Barrett 1994).

The phenomenological tradition: Gosden (1994); Tilley (1994); Thomas (1999).

Critics of postprocessualism: many early critiques were responses to Hodder and Shanks and Tilley rather than to postprocessualism as such. These included Kristiansen (1988); Patterson (1990); Schiffer (1988); Wylie (1992a); Binford (1987); and papers in Yoffee and Sherratt (1993). Watson (1990, 1991) criticizes Shanks and Tilley from the angle of positivism. Earle and Preucel (1987) is a considered response, though already a bit dated. Klejn (1993a, b) does not seem to have read the literature; see the thoughtful response to Klejn by Murray (1995). The debate between Thomas and Mithen is revealing (Thomas 1988 and 1991; Mithen 1991). Englestad (1991) and Smith (1994) are critiques of postprocessualism from a feminist perspective. Knapp (1996) and Preucel (1995) offer up-to-date assessments.

For an idea of the variance between different postprocessual traditions, compare Bapty and Yates (1990) and Baker and Thomas (1990), two contrasting volumes that arose from the same conference.

Case studies: Johnson (1993, 1996) are my attempts to apply a postprocessual perspective to the archaeology of late medieval and early modern England, areas still dominated by 'traditional' rather than processual approaches. Tilley (1991, 1994) apply textual and phenomenological approaches respectively to data from prehistoric Europe. McGuire and Saitta (1996) approach the traditional question 'were 14th century Southwestern pueblos egalitarian or hierarchical?' and show how an approach stressing 'lived experience' can move beyond such either/or thinking (though they would not give their approach a specifically postprocessual label). See also the succeeding debate in *American Antiquity* 63: 2. Duke and Wilson (1995) looks at North American Plains archaeology.

Chapter 8 Archaeology and Gender

There is a plethora of books on feminism in general. Humm (1992) is an anthology that gets across the variety of perspectives; Harding's paper in that volume points to debates between different feminist philosophies of science. Stanton and Stewart (1995) is a useful discussion. McNay (1992) is a powerful anti-essentialist account of recent feminist concerns. I've avoided going through the topic of sexist language; for the basic arguments see Spender (1980). Moore (1988) explores the background issues in anthropology with clarity and is a useful synthesis of anthropological thought. See diLeonardo (1991), Harding (1990) and other papers in the same volume for feminist discussions of postmodernism.

Studies specific to archaeology: Gero and Conkey (1991) is a definitive collection of papers with a lucid introduction to the issues. Among the best papers are Hastorf, Gero, Wylie and Handsman. Gero and Conkey (1997) is a useful review of the recent literature with an invaluable bibliography. Hays-

Gilpin and Whitley (1998) is an excellent collection of significant reprinted articles. Wright (1996), Claassen (1992, 1994), Walde and Willows (1991), duCros and Smith (1993) and Balme and Beck (1995) are other edited collections.

History of women in archaeology: Diaz-Andreu and Sorenson (1998); Joyce (1994), Claassen (1994). Critique of archaeological practice: Gero (1985, 1991); Wylie (1993).

Archaeology of 'women': Ehrenberg (1989) weds a traditional archaeological format to a search for 'women'. A famous study is Gimbutas (1989, 1991); most feminists would distance themselves from Gimbutas's arguments; see Russell (1993) for a discussion of the underlying issues.

Sex and gender: Meskell (1999) argues that even 'sex' is culturally constructed.

'Processual' approaches to gender: Brumbach and Jarvenpa (1997) use 'a gender-resource mapping approach' in which gender is seen as a variable within a more general 'subsistence settlement model'. Again, Mobley-Tanaka (1997) develops a gendered view of pueblo architecture within a framework of 'social stress'.

Career issues: various articles in Reyman (1992) and du Cros and Smith (1995); Nelson et al. (1994); Wylie (1993); Gero (1985, 1988).

Case studies (many of these could be put under the 'postprocessual' subheading): Gibbs (1987); Gilchrist (1993); Hodge McCoid and McDermott (1996). Gender in historical archaeology: Wall (1994); Gilchrist (1993); Spector (1993); Yentsch (1991). Seifert (1991) is an excellent edited collection.

Women and human evolution: Hager (1997).

Published criticisms of feminist archaeology are hard to find. Anthony (1995) criticizes 'eco-feminist' approaches though most feminists would disavow these approaches in any case. Klejn (1993) simply rules such approaches out of court. Nicholas (1994) makes pertinent comments on the Goddess myth. Gero and Conkey (1997), writing from a feminist standpoint, make some critical comments, implying that much gender archaeology has failed to take the feminist critique sufficiently seriously.

Chapter 9 Archaeology and Evolution

The discussion of the origins of evolutionary thought owes much to Orme (1981).

Evolution in the human sciences as a whole: for an introduction to Darwin and discussion of recent Darwinian thought, the two major thinkers are Steven Jay Gould (1989, 1997) and Richard Dawkins (1989). Both write accessibly and have been extremely influential; Gould in particular has stressed the role of contingency and historical accident in evolution, and has played an indirect role in the 'softening' of many evolutionary models. Flew (1984) is a concise introduction. Fabian (1998) is an edited volume of accessible articles that gives a good idea of the very wide variation in contemporary evolutionary thought. Ridley (1997) is a good introductory 'reader'. For a critical approach see Midgley (1985) and Giddens (1984).

Evolution of social complexity: a good overview of recent Americanist work is provided by Wason (1994), Fash (1994), Kowalewski (1990), Kolb (1994) and Spencer (1997). Criticisms of social evolution and a refined approach attempting to define and measure 'inequality' and 'heterogeneity' in societies is outlined by McGuire (1983). The studies in Part IV of Preucel and Hodder (1996) give a good flavour of the diversity of approaches to socipolitical complexity.

Darwinian/Lamarckian models of biological evolution: Dunnell (1980, 1989); Rindos (1989). Teltser (1995) is a collection of papers dealing with methodological issues raised by selectionist approaches. Barton and Clark (1997) contains some good papers. In particular, Fraser Neiman is a lucid and enthusiastic proponent of such models (1997 and forthcoming). Other recent collections include Maschner (1996), O'Brien (1996), Arnold (1996).

Case studies: Arnold et al. (1997) versus Raab and Larson (1997): two contrasting views of the interpretation of the same set of environmental data. Larson et al. (1996): compare with McGuire and Saitta (1996), both parties working on similar material.

Sociobiology: there are very few examples of sociobiological explanation in archaeology that I know of. Falk (1997) is a study in human evolution with clear archaeological implications.

Risk: Halstead and O'Shea (1989); Gilman (forthcoming).

Optimal foraging theory: see Mithen for an individual-based approach to cultural ecology; also the debate between Mithen and Thomas (Thomas 1988, 1991; Mithen 1991). Mithen (1989) on ecological approaches to art; compare with other studies in the same volume.

Case studies: Larson and Michaelsen (1990) and Larson *et al.* (1996) see Anasazi cultural development as a response to population growth and climatic deterioration; see reply by Allison (1996) focusing on whether their chronology works. Contrast also with McGuire and Saitta in the same volume.

A variety of recent work balances 'social' and 'ecological' approaches in a consideration of environment; for example, Hastorf and Johanessen (1991) and Schortman and Urban (1992). Schiffer (1996) argues for a *rapprochement* between behavioural and evolutionary archaeology. See also studies in Crumley (1994).

Criticisms of cultural evolution in archaeology: Yoffee (1979); Trigger (1984, 1997); Shanks and Tilley (1987); Boone and Smith (forthcoming); Patterson (1995); McGuire (1992).

Chapter 10 Archaeology and History

Bentley (1997) offers a complete coverage of historical theory but is a very mixed collection of papers. Halsall (1997) is a good introduction to the issues but over-simplified in parts; it tends to equate historical archaeology with that of early medieval Europe. Elton (1991) and Evans (1997) are restatements of traditional views.

Annales school: Le Goff and Nora (1985) is a collection of varied papers, ranging from (early) work on climate, demography and quantitative methods to (later) studies of ideologies and mental structures. Braudel (1980) is a collection of his papers; see also Le Roy Laduire (1974, 1978). Annales archaeology: Knapp (1992) is the best collection of Annales-influenced papers, the best of which is Duke (1992), though Moreland's paper in this volume argues convincingly against the utility of Annales thinking for archaeology. See also Bintliff (1991).

The 'linguistic turn': Joyce (1995); Easthope (1993). The work of Hayden White (1987) and Dominic LaCapra (1987) has been central in the critique of history as a narrative: see Jenkins (1995, 1997). Hunt (1989) is a useful introduction to the New Cultural History.

'Processual' approaches to historical archaeology include South (1977a, 1977b), Binford (1977).

Deetz's work, particularly his application of structuralism to historical archaeology, has had a huge influence. His simply written yet theoretically sophisticated application of structuralism to historical archaeology, *In Small Things Forgotten* (1977), remains my favourite archaeology book. See also Deetz (1988) and Yentsch and Beaudry (1992).

The historical archaeology of capitalism is a huge and growing field. A few introductory references are Leone (1995 and forthcoming); Orser (1996); Johnson (1996); Delle (1998).

'Contact period' studies embody a wide range of approaches: compare Leonard (1993) with Turnbaugh (1993) in the same volume. Contrasts between colonial and indigenous interpretations are discussed in Anawalt (1996) and Crowell (1997).

Collections of case studies of historical archaeology informed by postprocessual ideas include Little and Shackel (1992), particularly the papers by Little and Purser; McGuire and Paynter (1991), especially the paper by Yentsch; Kepecs and Kolb (1997); and Tarlow and West (1998). Yentsch (1994) is a classic study of historical archaeology. Lightfoot et al. (1998) is a fascinating study of practices and identities. Gilchrist (1993) is a study of medieval nunneries. See also Wall (1994), Spector (1993).

Bodiam Castle: Coulson (1992), Taylor et al. (1990).

Chapter 11 Archaeology in a Postmodern World

The postmodern condition: Lyotard (1984). Lyotard, rarely among postmodern thinkers, writes in an accessible and elegant way. Rorty (1980, 1985) also writes accessibly. Harvey (1989) is a classic review and critique of postmodernism from a Marxist perspective. See also Featherstone (1991) and Hollinger (1994).

Postmodernism in other disciplines: Jencks (1977) (architecture), Gregory (1994) (geography), Jenkins (1995, 1997), White (1987) and Hunt (1989) (history).

Foucault has an undeserved reputation as a difficult writer. It's best to take him on his own terms; like many postmodernists, he frequently writes in a rhetorical rather than analytical style, and frequently uses extended metaphors (most famously that of archaeology itself). Again, Foucault refuses to be pinned down to a set of concrete causes or a cut-and-dried 'model'. Read some of his books on tangible issues such as *Madness and Civilisation* and *Discipline and Punish* before moving on to his more methodological works such as *An Archaeology of Knowledge* and *The Order of Things*.

Archaeology and politics: parts VII and VII of Preucel and Hodder (1996), especially Gero and Root and Trigger. Compare Trigger's essay here with his 1989 paper; see also Hinsley (1989). Eller (1997) is a concise and lucid general introduction to the issues around 'multiculturalism'. Bender (1998) is a passionate account of the politics of Stonehenge. Jones (1997) is a fascinating account of past interpretations of Chichen Itza. Ferguson (1996) is an up-to-date review of the literature on Native Americans and archaeology.

The Annapolis Project is an excellent case study in building a critical public awareness. See Leone et al. (1987) and Leone and Potter (1984); also Potter (1994). Ucko (1989) is entertaining, but should be read with critical caution.

Nationalism, for obvious reasons, is an increasing preoccupation with European archaeologists: Hamilakis and Yalouri (1996); Atkinson et al. (1996). Diaz-Andreu and Champion (1996) and Kohl and Fawcett (1996) are good collections of case studies, though see Hamilakis (1996) for an effective critique of the latter. Cooper et al. (1995) and Walsh (1992) discuss the theoretical basis of 'heritage management' and cultural identity in Britain. Nazi Germany: Arnold (1990) and Arnold and Hassmann (1995); Harke and Wolfram (1993); Jones et al. (1996).

African burial ground: Thomas (1998: 544–54) is a good short introduction. See also Epperson (1996 and forthcoming). On wider issues of African-American archaeology, see Ferguson (1992), Blakey (1995) and Singleton (1985, 1995, and references therein). On wider issues of the misuse of genetics, see Pluciennik (1996); Mirza and Dungworth (1995).

Identification of postprocessualism with relativism: various papers in Kohl and Fawcett (1996). Ask yourself: are they a fair reading of the relevant texts? And what alternative do they suggest? The 'new synthesis': Trigger (1989b); Wylie (1992b); Brumfiel (1996). Fotiadis (1994) is a restatement that this claimed objectivity is illusory. Davis (1992), Gosden (1992) and Saitta (1992) offer thoughtful discussion of related aspects of this debate. Lampeter Archaeology Workshop (1997) offer a critical response.

Chapter 12 Conclusion: Conflict and Consensus

The discussion of rhetoric is heavily influenced by Latour (1987).

Preucel (1991b) is an excellent collection to view the current diversity of thinking, though I disagree with Preucel's conclusion of common ground. Patrik's (1985) influential article argues for the coexistence of different schools of thought centred around different definitions of what constitutes the archaeological record.

Lamberg-Karlovsky (1989) is an excellent example of a personal view presented as a neutral, authoritative position statement, advocating pluralism on one page while ruling completely out of court approaches he does not like as 'self-indulgence' and 'twaddle'.

Addendum: Theory Outside the English-speaking World

I have confined this list to English-language publications.

'World theory': Schmidt and Patterson (1995); Ucko (1995). Africa: Hall (1996) has a comprehensive bibliography.

'Europe': Diaz-Andreu and Champion (1996); Hodder (1991 a, b); Klejn (1993); Kuna and Venclova (1995); Neustupny (1993). There is a themed section on Central European Archaeology in Transition in *Antiquity* 67: 121–56. Tusa and Kirkinen (1992); Helskog and Olsen (1995) for Scandinavia. Iberia: Diaz-Andreu (1993), Lillios (1995), Oyuela-Caycedo (1994).

Latin America: Patterson (1994); see the succeeding debate in *American Antiquity* 62: 2. McGuire (1993) gives a useful summary of Marxist traditions in Latin American archaeology. Funari (1997a, 1997b) on traditions in Brazil and South America.

Bibliography

Alcock, L. 1976. *Arthur's Britain: History and Archaeology, AD 367–634.* London, Penguin.

Allison, J.R. 1996. Comments on the impacts of changing variability and population growth on virgin Anasazi cultural development. *American Antiquity* 61(2): 414–18.

Anawalt, P.R. 1996. Aztec knotted and netted capes: colonial interpretations versus indigenous primary data. *Ancient Mesoamerica* 7: 187–206.

Anderson, A.-C., Campbell, F., Gillberg, A., Hansonn, J., Jensen, O.W., Karlsson, H. and Rolöw, M. (eds) 1997. *The Kaleidoscopical Past: Proceedings of the 5th Nordic TAG Meeting, Gothenburg 1997.* Gotarc Serie C: Arkeologiska Skrifter. Dept of Archaeology, University of Gothenburg.

Andren, A. 1998. *Between Artefacts and Texts: Historical Archaeology in Global Perspective.* New York, Plenum.

Anthony, D.W. 1996. Nazi and eco-feminist prehistories: ideology and empiricism in Indo-European archaeology. In Kohl and Fawcett (eds), 82–97.

Arnold, B. 1990. The past as propaganda: totalitarian archaeology in Nazi Germany. *Antiquity* 64: 464–78. Reprinted in Hodder and Preucel (eds), 549–69.

Arnold, B. and Gibson, D.B. (eds) 1995. *Celtic Chiefdom, Celtic State.* Cambridge, Cambridge University Press.

Arnold, B. and Hassmann, H. 1996. Archaeology in Nazi Germany: the legacy of the Faustian bargain. In Kohl and Fawcett (eds), 70–81.

Arnold, D.E. 1995. *Ceramic Theory and Cultural Process.* Cambridge, Cambridge University Press.

Arnold, J.E. (ed.) 1996. *Emergent Complexity: The Evolution of Intermediate Societies.* Archaeological Series 9. Ann Arbor, International Monographs in Prehistory.

Arnold, J.E., Colten, R.H. and Pletka, S. 1997. Contexts of cultural change in southern California. *American Antiquity* 62 (2): 300–18.

Atkinson, J.A., Banks, I. and O'Sullivan, J. 1996. *Nationalism and Archaeology: Scottish Archaeological Forum.* Glasgow, Cruithne Press.

Balme, J. and Beck, W. (eds) 1995. *Gendered Archaeology: The Second Australian Women in Archaeology Conference*. Research Papers in Archaeology and Natural History 26. Canberra, Australian National University.

Baker, F., Taylor, S. and Thomas, J. (eds) 1990. *Writing the Past in the Present*. Lampeter, St David's University College.

Bapty, I. and Yates, T. (eds) 1990. *Archaeology After Structuralism: Post-Structuralism and the Practice of Archaeology*. London, Routledge.

Barrett, J.C. 1994. *Fragments From Antiquity: An Archaeology of Social Life in Britain, 2900–1200 BC*. Oxford, Blackwell Publishers.

Barrett, J.C. and Bartley, E.A. 1994. A conversation in two acts. In Mackenzie (ed.), 152–61.

Barton, C.M. and Clark, G.A. (eds) 1997. *Rediscovering Darwin: Evolutionary Theory in Archaeological Explanation*. Papers of the American Anthropological Association 7. Arlington, American Anthropological Association.

Beck, L.A. (ed.) 1995. *Regional Approaches to Mortuary Analysis*. New York, Plenum Press.

Bell, J.A. 1994. *Reconstructing Prehistory: Scientific Method in Archaeology*. Philadelphia, Temple University Press.

Bender, B. 1998. *Stonehenge: Making Space*. Oxford, Berg.

Bentley, M. (ed.) 1997. *Companion to Historiography*. London, Routledge.

Bernstein, R.J. (ed.) 1985. *Philosophy and Modernity*. Oxford, Polity Press.

Bettinger, R.L. and Eerkens, J. 1997. Evolutionary implications of metrical variation in Great Basin projectile points. In Barton and Clark (eds), 177–91.

Binford, L.R. 1962. Archaeology as anthropology. *American Antiquity* 11: 198–200.

Binford, L.R. 1964. A consideration of archaeological research design. *American Antiquity* 29: 425–41.

Binford, L.R. 1967. Smudge pits and hide smoking: the use of analogy in archaeological reasoning. *American Antiquity* 32 (1): 1–12.

Binford, L.R. 1972. *An Archaeological Perspective*. New York, Seminar Press.

Binford, L.R. 1977. Historical archaeology: is it historical or archaeological? In Ferguson (ed.), 13–22. Reprinted in Binford 1983b, 169–78.

Binford, L.R. 1978. *Nunamiut Ethnoarchaeology*. New York, Academic Press.

Binford, L.R. 1980. Willow smoke and dog's tails: hunter-gatherer settlement systems and archaeological site formation. *American Antiquity* 45: 4–20. Reprinted in Hodder and Preucel (eds), 39–60.

Binford, L.R. 1981a. Behavioural archaeology and the Pompeii premise. *Journal of Anthropological Archaeology* 37 (3): 195–208.

Binford, L.R. 1981b. *Bones: Ancient Men and Modern Myths*. New York, Academic Press.

Binford, L.R. 1983a. *In Pursuit of the Past: Decoding the Archaeological Record*. London, Thames and Hudson.

Binford, L.R. 1983b. *Working at Archaeology.* New York, Academic Press.
Binford, L.R. 1987. Data, relativism and archaeological science. *Man* 22: 391–404.
Binford, L.R. 1989. *Debating Archaeology.* New York, Academic Press.
Bintliff, J. (ed.) 1991. *The Annales School and Archaeology.* Leicester, Leicester University Press.
Blakey, M.L. 1995. Race, nationalism, and the Afrocentric past. In *Making Alternative Histories: The Practice of Archaeology and History in Non-Western Settings.* Santa Fe, School of American Research, 213–28.
Blakey, M.L. 1998. Bioarchaeology of the African Burial Ground. In Thomas (ed.), 546–7.
Bloch, M. 1983. *Marxism and Anthropology.* Oxford, Clarendon Press.
Boone, J.L. and Smith, E.A. forthcoming. Is it evolution yet? A critique of evolutionary archaeology. *Current Anthropology.*
Bourdieu, P. 1977. *Outline of a Theory of Practice.* Cambridge, Cambridge University Press.
Bradbury, M. 1987. *Mensonge.* London, Andre Deutsch.
Bradley, R. 1993. *Altering the Earth: The Origins of Monuments in Britain and Continental Europe.* Edinburgh, Society of Antiquaries of Scotland.
Bradley, R. and Edmonds, M. 1993. *Interpreting the Axe Trade: Production and Exchange in Neolithic Britain.* Cambridge, Cambridge University Press.
Braudel, F. 1980. *On History.* London, Weidenfeld and Nicolson.
Brown, J.A. 1997. The archaeology of ancient religion in the Eastern Woodlands. *Annual Review of Anthropology* 26: 465–85.
Brumbach, H.J. and Jarvenpa, R. 1997. Ethnoarchaeology of subsistence space and gender: a subarctic Dene case. *American Antiquity* 62 (3): 414–36.
Brumfiel, E. and Earle, T.K. (eds) 1987. *Specialisation, Exchange and Complex Societies.* Cambridge, Cambridge University Press.
Brumfiel, E.M. 1992. Distinguished lecture in archaeology: breaking and entering the ecosystem – gender, class and faction steal the show. *American Anthropologist* 94: 551–67.
Brumfiel, E.M. 1996. The quality of tribute cloth: the place of evidence in archaeological argument. *American Antiquity* 61 (3), 453–62.
Brumfiel, E.M. and Fox, J.W. (eds) 1994. *Factional Competition and Political Development in the New World.* Cambridge, Cambridge University Press.
Burtt, F. 1987. 'Man the hunter': bias in children's archaeology books. *Archaeological Review from Cambridge* 6 (2): 157–74.
Carey, J. 1992. *The Intellectuals and the Masses: Pride and Prejudice among the Literary Intelligentsia, 1880–1939.* London, Faber.
Carr, C. and Neitzel, J.E. 1995. *Style, Society and Person: Archaeological and Ethnological Perspectives.* New York, Plenum.
Childe, V.G. 1929. *The Danube in Prehistory.* Oxford, Oxford University Press.
Childe, V.G. 1936. *Man Makes Himself.* London, Watts.

Childe, V.G. 1942. *What Happened in History.* Harmondsworth, Penguin.
Childe, V.G. 1958. Retrospect. *Antiquity* 32: 69–74.
Childe, V.G. 1979. Prehistory and Marxism. *Antiquity* 53, 93–5.
Christenson, A.L. (ed.) 1989. *Tracing Archaeology's Past: The Historiography of Archaeology.* Carbondale, Southern Illinois University Press.
Classen, C. (ed.) 1992. *Exploring Gender Through Archaeology.* Madison, Prehistory Press.
Claassen, C. (ed.) 1994. *Women in Archaeology.* Philadelphia, University of Pennslyvania Press.
Clark, J.G.D. 1952. *Prehistoric Europe: The Economic Basis.* London, Methuen.
Clark, J.G.D. 1982. *The Identity of Man as Seen by an Archaeologist.* London, Methuen.
Clarke, D. 1973. Archaeology: the loss of innocence. *Antiquity* 47: 6–18.
Clarke, D. 1978. *Analytical Archaeology.* Second revised edition 1978. London, Methuen.
Cobb, C.R. 1993. Archaeological approaches to the political economy of nonstratified societies. In Schiffer, M. (ed.) *Advances in Archaeological Method and Theory* 5. Tucson, University of Arizona Press, 43–100.
Cohen, G.A. 1978. *Karl Marx's Theory of History: A Defence.* Oxford, Clarendon Press.
Cohen, P.S. 1968. *Modern Social Theory.* London, Heinemann.
Collingwood, R.G. 1939. *An Autobiography.* Oxford, Oxford University Press.
Collingwood, R.G. 1946. *The Idea of History.* Oxford, Oxford University Press.
Conkey, M. 1989. The structural analysis of Palaeolithic cave art. In Lamberg-Karlovsky (ed.), 135–54.
Conkey, M. and Spector, J. 1984. Archaeology and the study of gender. In Schiffer, M. (ed.) *Advances in Archaeological Method and Theory* 7. New York, Academic Press, 1–38.
Cooper, M.A., Firth, A., Carman, J. and Wheatley, D. (eds) 1995. *Managing Archaeology.* London, Routledge.
Coulson, C. 1992. Some analysis of the castle of Bodiam, East Sussex. In Harper-Bill and Harvey (eds), 51–108.
Courbin, P. 1988. *What is Archaeology?* Chicago, Chicago University Press.
Cowgill, G. 1993. Distinguished lecture in archaeology: beyond criticising New Archaeology. *American Anthropologist* 95: 551–73.
Cooper, N. 1997. The gentry house in an age of transition. In Gaimster and Stamper (eds), 115–26.
Crowell, A.L. 1997. *Archaeology and the Capitalist World System: A Study From Russian America.* New York, Plenum.
du Cros, H. and Smith, L. (eds) 1993. *Women in Archaeology: A Feminist Critique.* Occasional Papers in Prehistory 23. Canberra, Australian National University.
Crumley, C.L. 1979. Three locational models: an epistemological assessment of anthropology and archaeology. In Schiffer, M.B. (ed.) *Advances in*

Archaeological Method and Theory 2. New York, Academic Press, 141–73.

Crumley, C.L. 1987. A dialectical critique of hierarchy. In Patterson and Galley (eds), 155–9.

Crumley, C.L. (ed.) 1994. *Historical Ecology, Cultural Knowledge and Changing Landscapes*. Santa Fe, School of American Research Press.

Culbert, T.P. (ed.) 1973. *The Classic Maya Collapse*. Albuquerque, University of New Mexico Press.

Culler, J. 1997. *Literary Theory: A Very Short Introduction*. Oxford, Oxford University Press.

Cumberpatch, C. and Hill, J.D. (eds) 1995. *Different Iron Ages: Studies on the Iron Age in Temperate Europe*. BAR International Series 602. Oxford, British Archaeological Reports.

Daniel, G.E. 1941. The dual nature of the megalithic colonisation of prehistoric Europe. *Proceedings of the Prehistoric Society* 7: 1–49.

Davidson, I. and Noble, W. 1996. *Human Evolution, Language, and Mind: A Psychological and Archaeological Enquiry*. Cambridge, Cambridge University Press.

Davis, W. 1992. The deconstruction of intentionality in archaeology. *Antiquity* 66: 334–47.

Dawkins, R. 1989. *The Selfish Gene*. Second edition. Oxford, Oxford University Press.

Deetz, J.F. 1972. Archaeology as a social science. In Leone, M. (ed.), 108–17.

Deetz, J.F. 1977. *In Small Things Forgotten: The Archaeology of Early American Life*. New York, Anchor.

Deetz, J.F. 1988. History and archaeological theory: Walter Taylor revisited. *American Antiquity* 55: 13–22.

Delanty, G. 1997. *Social Science: Beyond Constructivism and Realism*. Milton Keynes, Open University Press.

Delle, J. 1998. *An Archaeology of Social Space: Analysing Coffee Plantations in Jamaica's Blue Mountains*. New York, Plenum.

Demarest, A.A. 1989. Ideology and evolutionism in American archaeology: looking beyond the economic base. In Lamberg-Karlovsky (ed.), 89–102.

Derrida, J. 1988. Afterword: toward an ethic of discussion. In Graff, G. (ed), *Limited Inc*. Evanston, Northwestern University Press.

Diaz-Andreu, M. 1993. Theory and ideology in archaeology: Spanish archaeology under the Franco regime. *Antiquity* 67: 74–82.

Diaz-Andreu, M. and Champion, T. (eds) 1996. *Nationalism and Archaeology in Europe*. London, University College London Press.

Diaz-Andreu, M. and Sorenson, M.-L. (eds) 1998. *Excavating Women: A History of Women in European Archaeology*. London, Routledge.

diLeonardo, M. (ed.) 1991. *Gender at the Crossroads of Knowledge: Feminist Anthropology in the Postmodern Era*. Berkeley, University of California Press.

Duke, P. 1992. Braudel and North American archaeology. In Knapp (ed.), 99–111. Reprinted in Hodder and Preucel (eds) (1996), 240–57.

Duke, P. and Wilson, M.C. (eds) 1995. *Beyond Subsistence: Plains Archaeology and the Postprocessual Critique*. Tuscaloosa, University of Alabama Press.

Dunnell, R.C. 1980. Evolutionary theory and archaeology. In Schiffer, M. (ed.), *Advances in Archaeological Method and Theory* vol. 3. New York, Academic Press.

Dunnell, R.C. 1989. Aspects of the application of evolutionary theory in archaeology. In Lamberg-Karlovsky (ed.), 35–49.

Eagleton, T. 1991. *Ideology: An Introduction*. London, Verso.

Earle, T. (ed.) 1993. *Chiefdoms: Power, Economy and Ideology*. Cambridge, Cambridge University Press.

Earle, T. and Preucel, R.W. 1987. Processual archaeology and the radical critique. *Current Anthropology* 28 (4): 501–38.

Earle, T.K. 1997. *How Chiefs Come to Power: The Political Economy in Prehistory*. Stanford, Stanford University Press.

Earle, T.K. and Erickson, J.E. (eds) 1977. *Exchange Systems in Prehistory*. New York, Academic Press.

Earle, T.K. and Erickson, J.E. (eds) 1982. *Contexts for Prehistoric Exchange*. New York, Academic Press.

Easthope, A. 1993. Romancing the Stone: history-writing and rhetoric. *Social History* 18 (2): 235–49.

Ehrenberg, M. 1989. *Women in Prehistory*. London, British Museum.

Ehrenreich, R.M., Crumley, C.L. and Levy, J.E. (eds) 1995. *Heterarchy and the Analysis of Complex Societies*. Washington, American Anthropological Association.

Eller, J.D. 1997. Anti-anti-multiculturalism. *American Anthropologist* 99 (2): 249–58.

Elton, G.E. 1991. *Return to Essentials*. Cambridge, Cambridge University Press.

Embree, L. (ed.) 1992. *Metaarchaeology: Reflections by Archaeologists and Philosophers*. Boston, Kluwer Academic Publishing.

Englestad, E. 1991. Images of power and contradiction: feminist theory and post-processual archaeology. *Antiquity* 65: 502–14.

Epperson, T. 1996. The politics of 'race' and cultural identity at the African Burial Ground excavations, New York City. *World Archaeological Bulletin* 7: 108–17.

Epperson, T. forthcoming. The contested commons: archaeologies of race, repression and resistance in New York City. In Leone (ed.).

Evans, R.J. 1997. *In Defence of History*. London, Granta.

Everson, W.K. 1974. *Classics of the Horror Film*. Secaucus, Citadel Press.

Fabian, A.C. (ed.) 1998. *Evolution: Society, Science and the Universe*. Cambridge, Cambridge University Press.

Falk, D. 1997. Brain evolution in females: an answer to Mr Lovejoy. In Hays-Gilpin and Whitley (eds), 115–37.

Fash, W.L. 1994. Changing perspectives on Maya civilisation. *Annual Review of Anthropology* 23: 181–208.

Featherstone, M. 1991. *Consumer Culture and Postmodernism*. London, Sage.

Ferguson, L. (ed.) 1997. *Historical Archaeology and the Importance of Material Things*. Society for Historical Archaeology Special Publications 2.
Ferguson, L. 1992. *Uncommon Ground: Archaeology and Early African America, 1650–1800*. Washington: Smithsonian Institution.
Ferguson, T.J. 1996. Native Americans and the practice of archaeology. *Annual Review of Anthropology* 25: 63–80.
Feyerabend, P. 1988. *Against Method*. Second revised edition. London, Verso.
Feyerabend, P. 1995. *Killing Time: The Autobiography of Paul Feyerabend*. Chicago, University of Chicago Press.
Flannery, K.V. 1972. The cultural evolution of civilisations. *Annual Review of Ecology and Systematics* 3: 399–426.
Flannery, K.V. 1973a. The origins of agriculture. *Annual Review of Anthropology* 2: 271–310.
Flannery, K.V. 1973b. Archaeology with a capital S. In Redman (ed.), 47–58.
Flannery, K.V. (ed.) 1976. *The Early Mesoamerican Village*. New York, Academic Press.
Flannery, K.V. 1982. The Golden Marshalltown: a parable for the archaeology of the 1980s. *American Anthropologist* 84: 265–78.
Flannery, K.V. and Marcus, E.J. 1976. Formative Oaxaca and Zapotec cosmos. *American Scientist* 64 (4): 374–83.
Flannery, K.V. and Marcus, E.J. (eds) 1983. *The Cloud People: Divergent Evolution of the Zapotec and Mixtec Populations*. New York, Academic Press.
Flannery, K.V. and Marcus, E.J. 1993. Cognitive archaeology. *Cambridge Archaeological Journal* 3: 260–70. Reprinted in Preucel and Hodder (eds) (1996), 350–63.
Fleming, A. and Johnson, M.H. 1990. The Theoretical Archaeology Group (TAG): origins, retrospect, prospect. *Antiquity* 64: 303–7.
Flew, A. 1984. *Darwinian Evolution*. London, Palladin.
Fotiades, M. 1994. What is archaeology's 'mitigated objectivism' mitigated by? Comments on Wylie. *American Antiquity* 59, 545–55.
Foucault, M. 1977. *Discipline and Punish: The Birth of the Prison*. Harmondsworth, Penguin.
Foucault, M. 1980. *Power/Knowledge*. Brighton, Harvester Wheatsheaf.
Fuller, S. 1992. Being there with Thomas Kuhn: a parable for postmodern times. *History and Theory* 31 (3): 241–75.
Funari, P.P.A. 1997a. European archaeology and two Brazilian offspring: classical archaeology and art history. *Journal of European Archaeology* 5 (2): 137–48.
Funari, P.P.A. 1997b. Archaeology, history, and historical archaeology in South America. *International Journal of Historical Archaeology* 1 (3): 189–206.
Gaimster, D. and Stamper, P. (eds) 1997. *The Age of Transition: The Archaeology of English Culture 1400–1600*. Oxford, Oxbow.
Galison, P. and Stump, P. (eds) 1996. *The Disunity of Science*. Palo Alto, Stanford University Press.
Geertz, C. 1984. Anti anti-relativism. *American Anthropologist* 86: 263–78.

Gero, J. 1985. Socio-politics and the woman-at-home ideology. *American Antiquity* 50: 342–50.

Gerding, H. and Ingemark, D. 1997. Beyond Newtonian Thinking – towards a non-linear archaeology: applying chaos theory to archaeology. *Current Swedish Archaeology* 5, 49–64.

Gero, J. 1988. Gender bias in archaeology: here, then and now. In Rosser (ed.), 33–43.

Gero, J. 1991. Gender divisions of labour in the construction of archaeological knowledge. In Walde and Willows (eds), 96–102.

Gero, J. 1996. Archaeological practice and gendered encounters with field data. In Wright (ed.), 251–80.

Gero, J. and Conkey, M. (eds) 1991. *Engendering Archaeology: Women and Prehistory.* Oxford, Blackwell Publishers.

Gero, J. and Conkey, M. 1997. From programme to practice: gender and feminism in archaeology. *Annual Review of Anthropology* 26: 411–37.

Gibbon, G. 1989. *Explanation in Archaeology.* Oxford, Blackwell Publishers.

Gibbs, L. 1987. Identifying gender representation in the archaeological record: a contextual study. In Hodder (ed.), 79–89. Reprinted in Hays-Gilpin and Whitley (eds) (1998), 231–54.

Giddens, A. (ed.) 1974. *Positivism and Sociology.* London, Heinemann.

Giddens, A. 1979. *Capitalism and Modern Social Theory.* Cambridge, Cambridge University Press.

Giddens, A. 1984. *The Constitution of Society: Outline of the Theory of Structuration.* Cambridge, Polity Press.

Giddens, A. 1993. *The Giddens Reader.* Stanford, Stanford University Press.

Gilbert, S.M. and Gubar, S. 1979. *The Madwoman in the Attic: The Woman Writer and the 19th Century Literary Imagination.* New Haven, Conn., Yale University Press.

Gilchrist, R. 1991. Women's archaeology? Political feminism, gender theory and historical revision. *Antiquity* 65: 495–501.

Gilchrist, R. 1993. *Gender and Material Culture: An Archaeology of Religious Women.* London, Routledge.

Gilman, A. forthcoming. Risk, technology, and social change. *Annual Review of Anthropology* 28.

Gimbutas, M. 1989. *The Language of the Goddess.* San Francisco, Harper and Row.

Gimbutas, M. 1991. *The Civilisation of the Goddess: The World of Old Europe.* San Francisco, Harper and Row.

Glassie, H. 1975. *Folk Housing in Middle Virginia: A Structural Analysis of Historic Artefacts.* Knoxville, University of Tennessee Press.

Goffman, E. 1959. *The Presentation of Self in Everyday Life.* New York, Anchor.

Goffman, E. 1971. *Relations in Public: Microstudies of the Public Order.* Harmondsworth, Penguin.

Gosden, C. 1992. Endemic doubt: is what we write right? *Antiquity* 66: 803–8.

Gosden, C. 1994. *Social Being and Time*. Oxford, Blackwell Publishers.
Gould, R. (ed.) 1978. *Explorations in Ethnoarchaeology*. Albuquerque, University of New Mexico Press.
Gould, R. 1980. *Living Archaeology*. Cambridge, Cambridge University Press.
Gould, R. and Schiffer, M. (eds) 1981. *The Archaeology of Us*. New York, Academic Press.
Gould, S.J. 1989. *Wonderful Life: The Burgess Shale and the Nature of History*. New York, Norton.
Gould, S.J. 1997. *The Mismeasure of Man*. Second revised edition. Harmondsworth, Penguin.
Gregory, D. 1994. *Geographical Imaginations*. Oxford, Blackwell Publishers.
Griffin, W. 1991. Review of *Reading the Past* (second edition). *Archaeological Review from Cambridge* 10 (1): 124–8.
Gross, P.R. and Levit, N. 1994. *Higher Superstition: The Academic Left and its Quarrels with Science*. Baltimore, Johns Hopkins University Press.
Gwilt, A. 1996. Ageing structures and shifting ideologies. *Antiquity* 70: 699–702.
Habermas, J. 1970. *Towards a Rational Society: Student Protest, Science and Politics*. London, Heinemann.
Habermas, J. 1975. *Legitimation Crisis*. London, Heinemann.
Hager, L. (ed.) 1997. *Women in Human Evolution*. London, Routledge.
Hall, M. 1996. *Archaeology Africa*. London, James Currey.
Halsall, G. 1997. Archaeology and historiography. In Bentley, M. (ed.), 805–27.
Halstead, P. and O'Shea, J. (eds) 1989. *Bad Year Economics: Cultural Responses to Risk and Uncertainty*. Cambridge, Cambridge University Press.
Hamilakis, Y. 1996. Through the looking glass: nationalism, archaeology and the politics of identity. *Antiquity* 70: 975–8.
Hamilakis, Y. and Yalouri, E. 1996. Antiquities as symbolic capital in modern Greek society. *Antiquity* 70: 117–29.
Hamilton, P. 1996. *Historicism*. London, Routledge.
Harding, S. 1990. Feminism, science, and the anti-enlightenment critiques. In Nicholson (ed.), 83–106.
Harke, H. and Wolfram, S. 1993. The power of the past. *Current Anthropology* 34: 182–4.
Harper-Bill, C. and Harvey, R. (eds) 1992. *Medieval Knighthood IV: Papers from the Fifth Strawberry Hill Conference 1990*. Woodbridge, Boydell.
Harvey, D. 1989. *The Condition of Postmodernity: An Enquiry into the Origins of Cultural Change*. Oxford, Blackwell Publishers.
Hastorf, C.A. 1988. The use of palaeoethnobotanical data in prehistoric studies of crop production, processing, and consumption. In Hastorf and Popper (eds), 119–44.
Hastorf, C.A. 1992. *Agriculture and the Onset of Political Inequality before the Inka*. Cambridge, Cambridge University Press.

Hastorf, C.A. and Johanessen, S. 1991. Understanding changing people/plant relationships in the prehispanic Andes. In Preucel (ed.), 140–55. Reprinted in Hodder and Preucel (eds) (1996), 61–78.

Hastorf, C.A. and Popper, V.S. (eds) 1988. *Current Palaeoethnobotany: Analytical Methods and Cultural Interpretations of Archaeological Plant Remains*. Chicago, University of Chicago Press.

Hawkes, C. 1954. Archaeological theory and method: some suggestions from the Old World. *American Anthropologist* 56: 155–68.

Hawkes, J. 1968. The proper study of mankind. *Antiquity* 42: 255–62.

Hawkes, T. 1976. *Structuralism and Semiotics*. London, Methuen.

Hays-Gilpin, K. and Whitley, D.S. (eds) 1998. *Reader in Gender Archaeology*. London, Routledge.

Hegel, G.W.F. 1956. *The Philosophy of History*. New York, Dover.

Held, D. and Thompson, J.B. (eds) 1989. *Social Theory of Modern Societies: Anthony Giddens and His Critics*. Cambridge, Cambridge University Press.

Helskog, K. and Olsen, B. (eds) 1995. *Perceiving Rock Art: Social and Political Perspectives*. Oslo, Norvus Press.

Hill, J.D. and Cumberpatch, C.G. (eds) 1995. *Different Iron Ages: Studies on the Iron Age in Temperate Europe*. BAR International Series 602. Oxford, British Archaeological Reports.

Hill, J.N. 1970. *Broken K Pueblo: Prehistoric Social Organisation in the American Southwest*. Tucson, University of Arizona Press.

Hill, J.N. 1991. Archaeology and the accumulation of knowledge. In Preucel (ed.), 42–53.

Hillman, G. 1984. Interpretation of archaeological plant remains: the application of ethnographic plant models from Turkey. In Zeist and Casparie (eds), 1–42.

Hinsley, C.M. 1989. Revising and revisioning the history of archaeology: reflections on region and context. In Christenson (ed.), 79–96.

Hodder, I. 1982a. *The Present Past*. London, Batsford.

Hodder, I. 1982b. *Symbols in Action: Ethnoarchaeological Studies of Material Culture*. Cambridge, Cambridge University Press.

Hodder, I. 1985. Postprocessual archaeology. In Schiffer, M. (ed.), *Advances in Archaeological Method and Theory* 8. New York, Academic Press, 1–26.

Hodder, I. (ed.) 1987. *The Archaeology of Contextual Meanings*. Cambridge, Cambridge University Press.

Hodder, I. 1991a. *Archaeological Theory in Europe: The Last Thirty Years*. Oxford, Blackwell Publishers.

Hodder, I. (ed.) 1991b. *Archaeological Theory in Europe: The Last Three Decades*. London, Routledge.

Hodder, I. 1998. *The Archaeological Process: Towards a Reflexive Methodology*. Oxford, Blackwell Publishers.

Hodder, I. and Orton, C. 1976. *Spatial Analysis in Archaeology*. Cambridge, Cambridge University Press.

Hodder, I., Shanks, M., Alexandri, A., Buchli, V., Carman, J., Last, J. and Lucas, G. (eds) 1995. *Interpreting Archaeology: Finding Meaning in the Past*. London, Routledge.

Hodge McCoid, C. and McDermott, L.D. 1996. Towards decolonising gender: female vision in the Upper Palaeolithic. *American Anthropologist* 98 (2): 319–26.

Hodges, R. 1982. *Dark Age Economics*. London, Duckworth.

Hollinger, R. 1994. *Postmodernism and the Social Sciences*. London, Sage.

Holton, G. 1993. *Science and Anti-Science*. Cambridge, Harvard University Press.

Humm, M. (ed.) 1992. *Feminisms: A Reader*. London, Harvester.

Hunt, L. (ed.) 1989. *The New Cultural History*. Berkeley, University of California Press.

Jencks, C. 1977. *The Language of Postmodern Architecture*. New York, Pantheon.

Jenkins, K. 1995. *On 'What is History?': From Carr and Elton to Rorty and White*. London, Routledge.

Jenkins, K. (ed.) 1997. *The Postmodern History Reader*. London, Routledge.

Johnson, A.G. 1995. *The Blackwell Dictionary of Sociology: A User's Guide to Sociological Language*. Oxford, Blackwell Publishers.

Johnson, M.H. 1989. Conceptions of agency in archaeological interpretation. *Journal of Anthropological Archaeology* 8, 189–211.

Johnson, M.H. 1993. *Housing Culture*. London, University College London Press.

Johnson, M.H. 1996. *An Archaeology of Capitalism*. Oxford, Blackwell Publishers.

Jones, G. 1984. Interpretation of archaeological plant remains: ethnographic models from Greece. In Zeist and Casparie (eds), 43–62.

Jones, L. 1997. Conquests of the imagination: Maya-Mexican polarity and the story of Chichen Itza. *American Anthropologist* 99 (2): 275–90.

Jones, S., Graves-Brown, P. and Gamble, C.S. (eds) 1996. *Cultural Identity and Archaeology: The Construction of European Communities*. London, Routledge.

Joyce, P. 1995. The end of social history? *Social History* 20 (1): 73–85.

Joyce, R.A. 1994. Dorothy Hughes Popenhoe: Eve in an archaeological garden. In Claassen (ed.), 51–66. Reprinted in Preucel and Hodder (eds) (1996), 501–16.

Kelley, J.H. and Hanen, M.P. 1988. *Archaeology and the Methodology of Science*. Albuquerque, University of New Mexico Press.

Kepecs, S. and Kolb, M.J. (eds) 1997. New approaches to combining the archaeological and historical records. *Journal of Archaeological Method and Theory* 4.

Klejn, L.S. 1993. It's difficult to be a god. *Current Anthropology* 34: 508–11.

Klejn, L.S. 1993. To separate a centaur: on the relationship of archaeology and history in Soviet tradition. *Antiquity* 67: 339–48.

Knapp, B. (ed.) 1992. *Archaeology, Annales and Ethnohistory*. Cambridge, Cambridge University Press.

Knapp, B. 1996. Archaeology without gravity: postmodernism and the past. *Journal of Archaeological Method and Theory* 3: 127–58.

Knorr-Cetina, K.D. and Mulkay, M. 1983. *Science Observed: Perspectives on the Social Study of Science*. London, Sage.

Knorr-Cetina, K.D. 1993. Strong constructivism – from a sociologist's point of view: a personal addendum to Sismondo's paper. *Social Studies of Science* 23, 555–63.

Kohl, P. 1987. The use and abuse of world systems theory: the case of the pristine West Asian state. *Advances in Archaeological Method and Theory* 11: 1–35.

Kohl, P. and Fawcett, C. (eds) 1996. *Nationalism, Politics and the Practice of Archaeology*. Cambridge, Cambridge University Press.

Kohler, T.A. 1993. News from the Northern American southwest: prehistory on the edge of chaos. *Journal of Archaeological Research* 1 (4): 267–321.

Kolb, M.J. 1994. Monumentality and the rise of religious authority in pre-contact Hawai'i. *Current Anthropology* 45: 521–33.

Kosso, P. 1991. Method in archaeology: middle-range theory as hermeneutics. *American Antiquity* 56 (4): 621–7.

Kowalewski, S.A. 1990. The evolution of complexity in the Valley of Oaxaca. *Annual Review of Anthropology* 19: 39–260.

Kristiansen, K. 1988. The black and the red: Shanks and Tilley's programme for a radical archaeology. *Antiquity* 62: 473–82.

Kristiansen, K. and Larsen, M. (eds) 1987. *Centre and Periphery in the Ancient World*. Cambridge, Cambridge University Press.

Kroeber, A.L. 1948. *Anthropology*. London, Harrap.

Kuhn, T. 1962. *The Structure of Scientific Revolutions*. Chicago, University of Chicago Press.

Kuna, M. and Venclova, N. (eds) 1995. *Whither Archaeology? Papers in Honour of Evzen Neustupny*. Prague, Institute of Archaeology.

LaCapra, D. 1987. *History, Politics and the Novel*. Ithaca, Cornell University Press.

Lamberg-Karlovsky, C.C. (ed.) 1989. *Archaeological Thought in America*. Cambridge, Cambridge University Press.

Lampeter Archaeology Workshop 1997. Relativism, objectivity and the politics of the past. *Archaeological Dialogues* 2: 164–98.

Larson, D.O. and Michaelsen, J. 1990. Impacts of climatic variability and population growth on Virgin Branch Anasazi cultural developments. *American Antiquity* 55: 227–49.

Larson, D.O., Neff, H., Graybill, D.A., Michaelsen, J. and Ambos, E. 1996. Risk, climatic variability, and the study of southwestern prehistory: an evolutionary perspective. *American Antiquity* 61 (2): 217–41.

Latour, B. 1987. *Science in Action*. Milton Keynes, Open University Press.

Latour, B. and Woolgar, S. 1979. *Laboratory Life: The Social Construction of Scientific Facts*. London, Sage.

Le Goff, J. and Nora, P. 1985. *Constructing the Past: Essays in Historical Methodology*. Cambridge, Cambridge University Press.

Le Roy Ladurie, E. 1974. *The Peasants of Languedoc*. London, Scolar Press.

Le Roy Ladurie, E. 1978. *Montaillou: Cathars and Catholics in a French Village, 1294–1324*. London, Scolar Press.

Le Roy Ladurie, E. 1979. *The Territory of the Historian*. London, Harvester.

Lechte, J. 1994. *Fifty Key Contemporary Thinkers*. London, Routledge.

Leonard, R.D. 1993. The persistence of an explanatory dilemma in Contact Period studies. In Rogers and Wilson (eds), 31–42.

Leone, M.P. (ed.) 1972. *Contemporary Archaeology: A Guide to Theory and Contributions*. Carbondale, Southern Illinois University Press.

Leone, M.P. 1984. Interpreting ideology in historical archaeology: using the rules of perspective in the William Paca Garden in Annapolis, Maryland. In Miller and Tilley (eds), 25–36.

Leone, M.P. 1988. The Georgian order as the order of merchant capitalism in Annapolis, Maryland. In Leone and Potter (eds), 235–61.

Leone, M.P. 1995. An historical archaeology of capitalism. *American Anthropologist* 97 (2): 251–68.

Leone, M.P. (ed.) forthcoming. *The Historical Archaeology of Capitalism*. New York, Plenum.

Leone, M.P. and Potter, P. 1984. *Archaeological Annapolis: A Guide to Seeing and Understanding Three Centuries of Change*. Annapolis, Historic Annapolis Foundation. Reprinted in Preucel and Hodder (eds) (1996), 570–98.

Leone, M.P. and Potter, P. 1988. *The Recovery of Meaning: Historical Archaeology in the Eastern United States*. Washington, Smithsonian Institution.

Leone, M., Potter, P. and Shackel, P. 1987. Towards a critical archaeology. *Current Anthropology* 28: 283–302.

Lightfoot, K., Martinez, A. and Schiff, A.M. 1998. Daily practice and material culture in pluralistic social settings: an archaeological study of culture change and persistence from Fort Ross, California. *American Antiquity* 63 (2): 199–222.

Lillios, K.T. (ed.) 1995. *The Origins of Complex Societies in Late Prehistoric Iberia*. Archaeological Monographs 8. Ann Arbor, International Monographs in Prehistory.

Little, B. and Shackel, P. (eds) 1992. Meanings and uses of material culture. *Historical Archaeology* 26: 3.

Lyman, R.L., O'Brien, M.J. and Dunnell, R.C. 1997a. *The Rise and Fall of Culture History*. New York, Plenum.

Lyman, R.L., O'Brien, M.J. and Dunnell, R.C. (eds) 1997b. *Americanist Culture History: Fundamentals of Time, Space and Form*. New York, Plenum.

Lynch, M. 1985. *Art and Artifact in Laboratory Science: A Study of Shop Work and Shop Talk in a Research Laboratory*. London, Routledge.

Lyotard, J.-F. 1984. *The Postmodern Condition: A Report on Knowledge*. Manchester, Manchester University Press.

McClellan, D. (ed.) 1977. *Karl Marx: Selected Writings*. Oxford, Oxford University Press.

McGuire, R.H. 1983. Breaking down cultural complexity: inequality and heterogeneity. In Schiffer, M.B. (ed.) *Advances in Archaeological Method and Theory* 8. New York, Academic Press, 91–142.

McGuire, R.H. 1992. *A Marxist Archaeology*. San Diego, Academic Press.
McGuire, R. 1993. Archaeology and Marxism. In Schiffer, M. (ed.) *Archaeological Method and Theory* 5. Tucson, University of Arizona Press, 101–58.
McGuire, R.H. and Paynter, R. (eds) 1991. *The Archaeology of Inequality*. Oxford, Blackwell Publishers.
McGuire, R.H. and Saitta, D.J. 1996. Although they have petty captains, they obey them badly: the dialectics of Prehispanic Western pueblo social organisation. *American Antiquity* 61: 197–216.
Mackenzie, I. (ed.) 1994. *Archaeological Theory: Progress or Posture?* Aldershot, Avebury.
Mackenzie, I. and Shanks, M. 1994. Archaeology: theories, themes and experience. In Mackenzie (ed.), 19–40.
McNairn, B. 1980. *The Method and Theory of V. Gordon Childe*. Edinburgh, Edinburgh University Press.
McNay, L. 1992. *Foucault and Feminism: Power, Gender and the Self*. Oxford, Polity Press.
Maschner, H.D.G. 1996. *Darwinian Archaeologies*. New York, Plenum Press.
Mellars, P. and Gibson, K. (eds) 1997. *Modelling the Early Human Mind*. Cambridge, Cambridge University Press.
Mellor, A.K. 1988. *Mary Shelley: Her Life, Her Fiction, Her Monsters*. London, Routledge.
Meltzer, D. 1979. Paradigms and the nature of change in American archaeology. *American Antiquity* 44: 644–57.
Meskell, L. 1999. *Archaeologies of Social Life: Age, Sex, Class, etc. in Ancient Egypt*. Oxford: Blackwell Publishers.
Midgley, M. 1985. *Evolution as a Religion: Strange Hopes and Stranger Fears*. London, Methuen.
Miksicek, C.H. 1987. Formation processes of the archaeobotanical record. *Advances in Archaeological Method and Theory* 10: 211–47.
Miller, D. 1985. *Artefacts as Categories*. Cambridge, Cambridge University Press.
Miller, D. 1987. *Material Culture and Mass Consumption*. Oxford, Blackwell Publishers.
Miller, D. (ed.) 1995. *Acknowledging Consumption: A Review of New Studies*. London, Routledge.
Miller, D. and Tilley, C. (eds) 1984. *Ideology, Power and Prehistory*. Cambridge, Cambridge University Press.
Mirza, M.N. and Dungworth, D.B. 1995. The potential misuse of genetic analyses and the social construction of 'race' and 'ethnicity'. *Oxford Journal of Archaeology* 14(3): 345–54.
Mitchell, P. 1981. *The Open Book of the Prehistoric World*. London, Hodder and Stoughton.
Mithen, S. 1989. Ecological interpretations of Palaeolithic art. *Proceedings of the Prehistoric Society* 57, 103–14. Reprinted in Preucel and Hodder (eds) (1996), 79–96.
Mithen, S. 1990. *Thoughtful Foragers: A Study of Prehistoric Decision Making*. Cambridge, Cambridge University Press.

Mithen, S. 1991. 'A cybernetic wasteland'? Rationality, emotion and Mesolithic foraging. *Proceedings of the Prehistoric Society* 57(2): 9–14.

Mithen, S. 1995. Palaeolithic archaeology and the evolution of mind. *Journal of Anthropological Research* 3 (4): 305–22.

Mithen, S. 1996. The early prehistory of human social behaviour: issues of archaeological inference and cognitive evolution. *Proceedings of the British Academy* 88, 145–77.

Mithen, S. 1997. *The Prehistory of the Mind: The Cognitive Origins of Art, Religion and Science*. London, Thames and Hudson.

Mithen, S. (ed.) 1998. *Creativity in Human Evolution and Prehistory.* London, Routledge.

Mobley-Tanaka, J.L. 1997. Gender and ritual space during the pithouse to pueblo transition: subterranean mealing rooms in the North American Southwest. *American Antiquity* 62 (3): 437–48.

Moore, H.L. 1987. *Space, Text and Gender.* Cambridge, Cambridge University Press.

Moore, H.L. 1988. *Feminism and Anthropology.* Oxford, Polity Press.

Muller, J. 1997. *Mississippian Political Economy.* New York, Plenum.

Murray, T. 1995. On Klejn's agenda for theoretical archaeology. *Current Anthropology* 36: 290–2.

Neiman, F.D. 1997. Conspicuous consumption as wasteful advertising: a Darwinian perspective on spatial patterns in Classic Maya terminal monument dates. In Barton and Clark (eds), 267–90.

Neiman, F.D. forthcoming. What is evolutionary archaeology? *Annual Review of Anthropology* 28.

Nelson, M.C., Nelson, S.M. and Wylie, A. (eds) 1994. *Equity Issues for Women in Archaeology.* Archaeological Papers No.5. Washington, American Anthropological Association.

Neustupny, E. 1993. *Archaeological Method.* Cambridge, Cambridge University Press.

Nicholas, G.P. 1994. On the Goddess Myth and methodology. *Current Anthropology* 35: 448–9.

Nicholson, L.J. (ed.) 1990. *Feminism/Postmodernism.* London, Routledge.

O'Brien, M.J. (ed.) 1996. *Evolutionary Archaeology: Theory and Application.* Salt Lake City, University of Utah Press.

Orme, B. 1981. *Anthropology for Archaeologists: An Introduction.* Ithaca, Cornell University Press.

Orser, C. 1996. *An Historical Archaeology of the Modern World.* New York, Plenum.

Oyuela-Caycedo, A. (ed.) 1994. *History of Latin American Archaeology.* Aldershot, Avebury.

Patrik, L.E. 1985. Is there an archaeological record? In Schiffer, M.B. (ed.) *Advances in Archaeological Method and Theory* 8. New York, Academic Press, 27–62.

Patterson, O. 1982. *Slavery and Social Death: A Comparative Study.* Cambridge, Harvard University Press.

Patterson, T.C. 1986. The last sixty years: towards a social history of Americanist archaeology. *American Anthropologist* 88: 7–26.

Patterson, T.C. 1990. Some theoretical tensions within and between the processual and the postprocessual archaeologies. *Journal of Anthropological Archaeology* 9 (2): 189–200.

Patterson, T.C. 1994. Social archaeology in Latin America: an appreciation. *American Antiquity* 59: 531–7.

Patterson, T.C. 1995. *Towards a Social History of Archaeology in the United States*. Fort Worth, Harcourt Brace.

Patterson, T.C. and Galley, C.W. (eds) 1987. *Power Relations and State Formation*. Washington, American Anthropological Association.

Perkins, D. and Daly, P. 1968. A hunter's village in neolithic Turkey. *Scientific American* 219: 96–106.

Pickering, A. 1984. *Constructing Quarks: A Sociological History of Particle Physics*. Edinburgh, Edinburgh University Press.

Piggott, S. 1968. *Ancient Europe*. Edinburgh, Edinburgh University Press.

Platt, C. 1981. *The Parish Churches of Medieval England*. London, Secker and Warburg.

Pluciennik, M. 1996. Genetics, archaeology and the wider world. *Antiquity* 70, 13–14.

Potter, P. 1994. *Public Archaeology in Annapolis: A Critical Approach to History in Maryland's Ancient City*. Washington, Smithsonian Institution.

Preucel, R.W. 1991a. The philosophy of archaeology. In Preucel (ed.), 17–29.

Preucel, R.W. (ed.) 1991b. *Processual and Postprocessual Archaeologies: Multiple Ways of Knowing the Past*. Southern Illinois University at Carbondale Occasional Paper No. 10. Carbondale, Southern Illinois University Press.

Preucel, R.W. 1995. The postprocessual condition. *Journal of Archaeological Research* 3 (2): 147–75.

Preucel, R. and Hodder, I. (eds) 1996. *Contemporary Archaeology in Theory: A Reader*. Oxford, Blackwell Publishers.

Pusey, M. 1987. *Jürgen Habermas*. London, Tavistock.

Raab, L.M. and Goodyear, A.C. 1984. Middle-range theory in archaeology: a critical review of origins and applications. *American Antiquity* 49 (2): 255–68.

Raab, L.M. and Larson, D.O. 1997. Medieval climatic anomaly and punctuated cultural evolution in coastal southern California. *American Antiquity* 62 (2): 319–36.

Rathje, W.L., Hughes, W.W., Wilson, D.C., Tani, M.K., Archer, G.H., Hunt, R.G. and Jones, T.W. 1992. The archaeology of contemporary landfills. *American Antiquity* 57 (3): 437–47.

Redman, C. (ed.) 1973. *Research and Theory in Current Archaeology*. New York, Wiley.

Redman, C.L. 1978. *The Rise of Civilisation: From Early Farmers to Urban Society in the Ancient Near East*. San Francisco, Freeman.

Redman, C.L. 1991. Distinguished lecture in archaeology: in defence of the seventies. *American Anthropologist* 93: 295–307.

Reisch, G.A. 1991. Chaos, history, and narrative. *History and Theory* 30 (1): 1–20.

Renfrew, A.C. 1973a. *Before Civilisation: The Radiocarbon Revolution and Prehistoric Europe*. Harmondsworth, Penguin.

Renfrew, A.C. (ed.) 1973b. *The Explanation of Culture Change*. London, Duckworth.

Renfrew, A.C. 1982. *Towards an Archaeology of the Mind: An Inaugural Lecture Delivered Before the University of Cambridge on 30 November 1982*. Cambridge, Cambridge University Press.

Renfrew, A.C. 1984. *Approaches to Social Archaeology*. Edinburgh, Edinburgh University Press.

Renfrew, A.C. (ed.) 1986. *Peer Polity Interaction and Socio-Political Change*. Cambridge, Cambridge University Press.

Renfrew, A.C. 1993. Cognitive archaeology: some thoughts on the archaeology of thought. *Cambridge Archaeological Journal* 3 (2): 248–50.

Renfrew, A.C. and Bahn, P. 1996. *Archaeology: Theories, Methods and Practice*. Second revised edition. London, Thames and Hudson.

Renfrew, A.C. and Cooke, K. (eds) 1979. *Transformations: Mathematical Approaches to Culture Change*. London, Academic Press.

Renfrew, A.C. and Shennan, A. (eds) 1982. *Ranking, Resource and Exchange*. Cambridge, Cambridge University Press.

Renfrew, A.C. and Zubrow, E. 1994. *The Ancient Mind: Elements of Cognitive Archaeology*. Cambridge, Cambridge University Press.

Reyman, J. (ed.) 1992. *Rediscovering Our Past: Essays on the History of American Archaeology*. Aldershot, Avebury.

Ridley, M. (ed.) 1997. *Evolution: An Oxford Reader*. Oxford, Oxford University Press.

Rindos, D. 1989. Undirected variation and the Darwinian explanation of cultural change. *Archaeological Method and Theory* 1, 1–45.

Robbins, R. (ed.) 1972. *Sir Thomas Browne: Religio Medici, Hydriotaphia, and the Garden of Cyrus*. Oxford, Oxford University Press.

Rogers, J.D. and Wilson, S.M. (eds) 1993. *Ethnohistory and Archaeology: Approaches to Postcontact Change in the Americas*. New York, Plenum.

Rorty, R. 1980. *Philosophy and the Mirror of Nature*. Princeton, Princeton University Press.

Rorty, R. 1985. Habermas and Lyotard on postmodernity. In Bernstein, R.J. (ed.), 161–75.

Rorty, R. 1989. *Contingency, Irony and Solidarity*. Oxford, Blackwell Publishers.

Roscoe, P.B. 1995. The perils of 'positivism' in cultural anthropology. *American Anthropologist* 97 (3): 492–504.

Rosser, S.V. (ed.) 1988. *Feminism within the Science and Health Care Professions: Overcoming Resistance*. New York, Pergamon.

Russell, P. 1993. The Palaeolithic mother-goddess: fact or fiction? In du Cros and Smith (eds), 93–7. Reprinted in Hays-Gilpin and Whitley (eds) (1998), 261–8.

Sabloff, J. 1990. *New Archaeology and the Ancient Maya*. New York, Scientific American.

Sahlins, M. 1995. *How 'Natives' Think: About Captain Cook, For Example*. Chicago, University of Chicago Press.

Saitta, D. 1992. Radical archaeology and middle-range theory. *Antiquity* 66: 886–97.

Saunders, A.D. 1977. Introduction to five castle excavations. *Archaeological Journal* 134: 1–10.

Scarry, J.F. (ed.) 1996. *Political Structure and Change in the Prehistoric Southeastern United States*. Gainesville, University of Florida Press.

Schiffer, M. 1976. *Behavioural Archaeology*. New York, Academic Press.

Schiffer, M.B. 1987. *Formation Processes of the Archaeological Record*. Albuquerque, University of New Mexico Press.

Schiffer, M.B. 1988. The structure of archaeological theory. *American Antiquity* 53 (3): 461–85.

Schiffer, M.B. 1995. *Behavioral Archaeology: First Principles*. Salt Lake City, University of Utah Press.

Schiffer, M.B. 1996. Some relationships between behavioural and evolutionary archaeologies. *American Antiquity* 61: 643–62.

Schmidt, P.R. and Patterson, T.C. (eds) 1995. *Making Alternative Histories: The Practice of Archaeology and History in Non-Western Settings*. Santa Fe, School of American Research Press.

Schortman, E.M. and Urban, P.A. (eds) 1992. *Resources, Power, and Regional Interaction*. New York, Plenum.

Schortman, E.M. and Urban, P.A. 1994. Living on the edge: core/periphery relations in ancient southeastern Mesoamerica. *Current Anthropology* 35: 401–13.

Sebastian, L. 1996. *The Chaco Anasazi: Sociopolitical Evolution in the Prehistoric Southwest*. Cambridge, Cambridge University Press.

Seifert, D. (ed.) 1991. Gender in historical archaeology. *Historical Archaeology* 25 (4): 1–155.

Shalin, D.N. 1992. Critical theory and the pragmatist challenge. *American Journal of Sociology* 98 (2): 237–79.

Shanks, M. 1992. *Experiencing the Past*. London, Routledge.

Shanks, M. and Tilley, C. 1987. *Social Theory and Archaeology*. Oxford, Polity Press.

Shanks, M. and Tilley, C. 1992. *Re-Constructing Archaeology: Theory and Practice*. Second edition. London, Routledge.

Shanks, M. and Tilley, C. 1996. The craft of archaeology. *American Antiquity* 61 (1): 75–88.

Singleton, T. (ed.) 1985. *The Archaeology of Slavery and Plantation Life*. Orlando, Academic Press.

Singleton, T. 1995. The archaeology of slavery in North America. *Annual Review of Anthropology* 24: 119–40.

Sismondo, S. 1993. Some social constructivisms. *Social Studies of Science* 23: 515–53.

Skibo, J.M., Walker, W.H. and Neilsen, A.E. 1995. *Expanding Archaeology*. Salt Lake City, University of Utah Press.

Smith, L. 1994. Heritage management as postprocessual archaeology. *Antiquity* 88, 300–9.

Sorenson, M.L.S. 1992. Gender archaeology and Scandinavian Bronze Age studies. *Norwegian Archaeological Review* 25 (1): 31–49.

South, S. 1997a. *Method and Theory in Historical Archaeology*. New York, Academic Press.

South, S. (ed.) 1977b. *Research Strategies in Historical Archaeology*. New York, Academic Press.

Spector, J. 1993. *What This Awl Means: Feminist Archaeology at a Wahpeton Dakota Village*. St Paul, Minnesota Historical Society Press.

Spencer, C.S. 1997. Evolutionary approaches in archaeology. *Journal of Archaeological Research* 5: 209–64.

Spender, D. 1980. *Man Made Language*. London, Routledge.

Stanton, D. and Stewart, A. (eds) 1995. *Feminisms in the Academy*. Ann Arbor, University of Michigan Press.

Steward, J. 1955. *Theory of Culture Change: The Methodology of Multilinear Evolution*. Chicago, University of Illinois Press.

Steward, J. 1977. *Evolution and Ecology*. Chicago, University of Illinois Press.

Tainter, J. 1990. *The Collapse of Complex Societies*. Cambridge, Cambridge University Press.

Tarlow, S. and West, S. (eds) 1998. *The Familiar Past? Archaeologies of Late Historic Britain*. London, Routledge.

Taylor, C.C., Everson, P. and Wilson-North, R. 1990. Bodiam Castle, Sussex. *Medieval Archaeology* 34: 155–7.

Taylor, W. 1948. *A Study of Archaeology. Memoirs of the American Anthropological Association* 69.

Teltser, P.A. 1995. *Evolutionary Archaeology: Methodological Issues*. Tucson, University of Arizona Press.

Thomas, D.H. 1998. *Archaeology*. Third edition. Orlando, Harcourt Brace.

Thomas, J. 1988. Neolithic explanations revisited: the Mesolithic–Neolithic transition in Britain and south Scandinavia. *Proceedings of the Prehistoric Society* 54: 59–66.

Thomas, J. 1991. A reply to Steven Mithen. *Proceedings of the Prehistoric Society* 57 (2): 15–20.

Thomas, J. 1999. *Time, Culture and Identity: An Interpretative Archaeology*. London, Routledge.

Tilley, C. (ed.) 1990. *Reading Material Culture*. Oxford, Blackwell Publishers.

Tilley, C. 1991. *Material Culture and Text: The Art of Ambiguity*. London, Routledge.

Tilley, C. 1994. *A Phenomenology of Landscape*. London, Routledge.

Trigger, B.G. 1980a. *Gordon Childe: Revolutions in Archaeology*. London, Thames and Hudson.

Trigger, B.G. 1980b. Archaeology and the image of the American Indian. *American Antiquity* 45: 662–76.

Trigger, B.G. 1984. Archaeology at the crossroads: what's new? *Annual Review of Anthropology* 13: 275–300.

Trigger, B.G. 1989a. Hyperrelativism, responsibility and the social sciences. *Canadian Review of Sociology and Anthropology* 26: 776–91.

Trigger, B.G. 1989b. *A History of Archaeological Thought*. Cambridge, Cambridge University Press.

Trigger, B.G. 1991. Distinguished lecture in archaeology: constraint and freedom – a new synthesis for archaeological explanation. *American Anthropologist* 93: 551–69.

Trigger, B.G. 1993. Marxism in contemporary Western archaeology. In Schiffer, M. (ed.) *Advances in Archaeological Method and Theory* 5. Tucson, University of Arizona Press, 159–200.

Trigger, B.G. 1995a. Expanding middle-range theory. *Antiquity* 69: 449–58.

Trigger, B.G. 1995b. Romanticism, nationalism, and archaeology. In Kohl and Fawcett (eds), 263–79.

Trigger, B.G. 1997. *Sociocultural Evolution*. Oxford, Blackwell Publishers.

Tringham, R. 1991. Households with faces: the challenge of gender in prehistoric architectural remains. In Conkey and Gero (eds), 93–131.

Turnbaugh, W.A. 1993. Assessing the significance of European goods in 17th century Naragansett society. In Rogers and Wilson (eds), 133–57.

Tusa, N. and Kirkinen, T. (eds) 1992. *Nordic TAG: The Archaeologist and His/Her Reality. Report from the 4th Nordic TAG Conference*. Helsinki, University of Helsinki.

Ucko, P. 1989. *Academic Freedom and Apartheid*. London, Duckworth.

Ucko, P. (ed.) 1995. *Theory in Archaeology: A World Perspective*. London, Routledge.

Unstead, R.J. 1953. *Looking at History 1: From Cavemen to Vikings*. London, Black.

Walde, D. and Willows, N.D. (eds) 1991. *The Archaeology of Gender. Proceedings of the 22nd Annual Chacmool Conference*. Calgary, University of Calgary Press.

Wall, D.Z. 1994. *The Archaeology of Gender: Separating the Spheres in Urban America*. New York, Plenum.

Wallerstein, I. 1974. *The Modern World-System*. New York, Academic Press.

Walsh, K. 1992. *The Representation of the Past: Museums and Heritage in the Postmodern World*. London, Routledge.

Washburn, D.K. (ed.) 1983. *Structure and Cognition in Art*. Cambridge, Cambridge University Press.

Wason, P.K. 1994. *The Archaeology of Rank*. Cambridge, Cambridge University Press.

Watson, P.J. 1991. A parochial primer: the new dissonance as seen from the midcontinental United States. In Preucel (ed.), 265–76.

Watson, P.J. 1995. Archaeology, anthropology and the culture concept. *American Anthropologist* 97 (4): 683–94.

Watson, P.J., LeBlanc, S.A. and Redman, C.L.R. 1984. *Archaeological Explanation: The Scientific Method in Archaeology*. New York, Columbia.

Watson, R.A. 1990. Ozymandias, king of kings: post-processual radical archaeology as critique. *American Antiquity* 41: 410–15.
Watson, R.A. 1991. What the New Archaeology has accomplished. *Current Anthropology* 32: 275–91.
White, H. 1987. *The Content of the Form: Narrative Discourse and Historical Representation*. Baltimore, Johns Hopkins University Press.
White, L. 1949. *The Science of Culture: A Study of Man and Civilisation*. New York, Farar, Stroux and Giroux.
Whitley, D.S. (ed.) 1998. *Reader in Archaeological Theory: Post-Processual and Cognitive Approaches*. London, Routledge.
Whittaker, J.C. 1994. *Flintknapping: Making and Understanding Stone Tools*. Austin, University of Texas Press.
Wilks, R.R. 1985. The ancient Maya and the political present. *Journal of Anthropological Research* 41 (3): 307–26.
Williams, R. 1988. *Keywords: A Vocabulary of Culture and Society*. London, Fontana.
Williamson, T. and Bellamy, E. 1983. *Ley Lines in Question*. London, Heinemann.
Wolpert, L. 1992. *The Unnatural Nature of Science*. London, Faber.
Wright, R. (ed.) 1996. *Gender and Archaeology*. Philadelphia, University of Pennsylvania Press.
Wylie, A. 1985. The reaction against analogy. *Advances in Archaeological Method and Theory* 8: 63–111.
Wylie, A. 1992a. On scepticism, philosophy, and archaeological science. *Current Anthropology* 33: 209–13.
Wylie, A. 1992b. The interplay of evidential constraints and political interests: recent archaeological research on gender. *American Antiquity* 57: 15–35. Reprinted in Preucel and Hodder (eds), 431–59.
Wylie, A. 1992c. On 'heavily decomposing red herrings': scientific method in archaeology and the ladening of evidence with theory. In Embree (ed.) (1992), 269–88.
Wylie, A. 1993a. A proliferation of new archaeologies: 'Beyond Objectivism and Relativism'. In Yoffee and Sherratt (eds), 20–6.
Wylie, A. 1993b. Workplace issues for women in archaeology: the chilly climate. In du Cros and Smith (eds), 245–60.
Wylie, A. 1996. The constitution of archaeological evidence: gender politics and science. In Galison and Stump (eds), 311–43.
Yentsch, A. 1991. The symbolic divisions of pottery: sex-related attributes of English and Anglo-American household pots. In McGuire and Paynter (eds), 192–230. Reprinted in Preucel and Hodder (eds) (1996), 315–48.
Yentsch, A.E. 1994. *A Chesapeake Family and Their Slaves*. Cambridge, Cambridge University Press.
Yentsch, A.E. and Beaudry, M.C. (eds) 1992. *The Art and Mystery of Historical Archaeology: Essays in Honour of James Deetz*. Boca Raton, CRC Press.
Yoffee, N. 1979. The decline and rise of Mesopotamian civilisation: an ethnoarchaeological perspective on the evolution of social complexity. *American Antiquity* 44: 5–35.

Yoffee, N. and Cowgill, G.L. (eds) 1988. *The Collapse of Ancient States and Civilisations*. Tucson, University of Arizona Press.

Yoffee, N. and Sherratt, A. (eds) 1993. *Archaeological Theory: Who Sets The Agenda*? Cambridge, Cambridge University Press.

Zeist, W.V. and Casparie, W.A. (eds) 1984. *Plants and Ancient Man: Studies in Palaeoethnobotany*. Rotterdam, Balkema.

Index